COMPUTER ETHICS

ANALYZING INFORMATION TECHNOLOGY

Deborah G. Johnson

University of Virginia
with contributions from

Keith W. Miller
University of Illinois–Springfield

Prentice Hall
Upper Saddle River, New Jersey
Columbus, Ohio

Library of Congress Cataloging-in-Publication Data

Johnson, Deborah G.
 Computer ethics: analyzing information technology/Deborah G. Johnson with Keith W. Miller.
 —4th ed.
  p. cm.
 Includes bibliographical references and index.
 ISBN-13: 978-0-13-111241-4 (alk. paper)
 ISBN-10: 0-13-111241-4 (alk. paper)
 1. Electronic data processing—Moral and ethical aspects. I. Miller, Keith, II. Title.
 QA76.9.M65J64 2008
 303.48′34–dc22

2008040152

Editor in Chief: Dickson Musslewhite
Editorial Assistant: Nart Varoqua
Senior Editor: Dave Repetto
Editorial Assistant: Pat Walsh
Editorial Project Manager: Sarah Holle
Director of Marketing: Brandy Dawson
Marketing Manager: Lindsey Prudhomme
Production Manager: Wanda Rockwell
Creative Director: Jayne Conte
Cover Design: Margaret Kenselaar
Cover Illustration: Guy Crittenden/Stock Illustration Source, Inc.
Full-Service Project Management/Composition: Nitin Agarwal, Aptara®, Inc.
Printer/Binder: R. R. Donnelley

Pearson Education Ltd., London
Pearson Education Singapore, Pte. Ltd
Pearson Education Canada, Inc.
Pearson Education–Japan
Pearson Education Australia PTY, Limited

Pearson Education North Asia, Ltd., Hong Kong
Pearson Educación de Mexico, S.A. de C.V.
Pearson Education Malaysia, Pte. Ltd.
Pearson Education Upper Saddle River, New Jersey

Prentice Hall
is an imprint of

www.pearsonhighered.com

10 9 8 7 6 5 4 3 2 1
ISBN-13: 978-0-13-111241-4
ISBN-10: 0-13-111241-4

CONTENTS

PREFACE

When I first began thinking and writing about computer ethics, I often found myself taking on the role of someone who counters hype. At the time, there seemed to be a good deal of hype about how computers were going to revolutionize the world. Of course, there were some thoughtful treatments of the potential of computers to transform the world as we know it and some intriguing and deep accounts of the social changes that seemed to be underway. My job—so it seemed—was to sort out the hype from the serious analyses. One of my strategies was to identify and emphasize that which remained the same—aspects of society that were unaffected or being reinforced and solidified. As I reflect back on that time and what has happened since, it does seem that some pretty dramatic changes have occurred. And the challenge of sorting out the significant changes from those that are superficial is all the more daunting. Changes of many different kinds have occurred and these changes have been influenced by many factors, only one of which is the development and widespread use of computers, information technology, and the Internet. As argued in Chapter 1, we should be careful not to think that the forces of change have been in only one direction. Computers and information technology have shaped the world of today but social, political, economic, and cultural conditions have also shaped the development of computers, information technology, and the Internet. This edition of *Computer Ethics* attempts to take into account the complex, multidirectional relationship between technology and society.

Computers and information technology are now so fundamental to the information societies that many of us live in, that the exercise of trying to identify a domain of life in which information technology does *not* play a role is both enlightening and challenging. We tried with this new edition to rethink the field of computer ethics so as to capture the powerful role that computers and information technology now play in so many aspects of everyday life. However, because the field is now so broad, tough choices had to be made, choices about what to include and what to leave out. In the end, we developed a structure that, we believe, serves as a framework for addressing an array of issues, some of which we have addressed extensively, others we have treated in a cursory fashion, and yet others we have not even mentioned.

The 4th edition contains several important new features. Perhaps most importantly, this edition includes the voice of Keith Miller. Keith and I met when he first began teaching a course on computer ethics over twenty years ago. As one of the first computer scientists to take on the responsibilities of such a course, Keith is a pioneer and veteran of the field. He brought his knowledge and experience to each chapter of the book. Working together was an enormous boon for this edition. Whether we agreed or disagreed on a particular issue—and we did disagree—we worked through the presentation of material together. At times it seemed that Keith was protecting the interests of computer science students and teachers, and I was concerned about accessibility to the less technically sophisticated readers. We believe we have achieved a good balance.

As we began working on this edition, we were confronted with a complicated question about terminology. Although the field continues to be called "computer ethics," the attention of computer ethicists has expanded to include a much broader range of technologies more often now referred to as information technology. We debated whether to consider our focus to be that of information and communication technologies and use the acronym ITC, or computers and information technology and use CIT; we tried other alternatives as well. In the end we came to a complicated decision. Because Chapter 1 focuses on the field and its goals, methods, and mission, we stayed with the term "computer ethics" for that chapter. After Chapter 1 and throughout the rest of the book, we use the phrase "information technology" or the acronym "IT." Finally, we added a new subtitle to the title of the book to reflect the broader scope of the book and the field.

This edition includes a new theoretical approach. We have incorporated concepts and insights from the field of science and technology studies (STS). STS theories frame technology as sociotechnical systems and this, in turn, brings the connection between ethics and technology into sharper perspective. The new approach is explained in Chapter 1.

As in earlier editions, all but one of the chapters begin with a set of scenarios designed to draw readers into the chapter topic. The scenarios present the issues in what we hope is an engaging and practical form. The scenarios illustrate the significance of the broader, more abstract matters addressed in the chapter. With a few exceptions, the scenarios are new and many of them are real cases. In our selection of scenario topics we have been mindful of the experiences of college-age students.

For those familiar with the 3rd edition, an explanation of the new organization may be helpful. As in the 3rd edition, there are separate chapters on ethical concepts and theories, privacy, property rights, and professional ethics. As before, the introductory chapter discusses the scope of the field. However, in this edition we have moved somewhat away from theorizing about the uniqueness of computer ethical issues and have, instead, framed the issues as part of a broader enterprise of understanding the connections between ethics and technology. As mentioned above, the introductory chapter also introduces important new ideas from STS. Chapters 3 and 6 represent a significant reorganization of material. Each of these chapters combines material from the 3rd edition with entirely new material. The overarching theme in Chapter 3 is that information societies are constituted with, and configured around, information technology, and this means that ethical issues have distinctive characteristics. The overarching theme of Chapter 6 is what we call "digital order." The chapter focuses on several different issues that affect activities on the Internet. Order, we emphasize, is created by law, markets, social norms, and architecture. The chapter on professional ethics has been moved to the end of the book. Computer science students may well want to read this chapter early on, but it no longer serves as the motivation for subsequent chapters.

As the book goes to press, we have plans for a website to supplement the material presented in the book. The website will include additional scenarios, podcast discussions, links to other sites, and more. It should be available and easy to find by the time the book is published.

Deborah G. Johnson
June 16, 2008

ACKNOWLEDGMENTS

I am particularly grateful to the University of Virginia's School of Engineering and Applied Sciences for granting me a sesqui leave for the spring semester of 2008. Were it not for this leave, I would not have been able to complete this edition.

During the leave I served as a fellow in residence at two locations of the Erasmus Mundus Master of Applied Ethics program. I spent three weeks in the Department of Philosophy at the Norwegian University of Science and Technology in Trondheim, Norway and three weeks in Linköping University's Centre for Applied Ethics in Linköping, Sweden. During this time I had the opportunity to present drafts of several of the chapters in student seminars, faculty seminars, and public lectures. It is difficult to overstate the value of the honest and helpful responses that I received in both places. And, it was not just the helpfulness of the comments, it was also the warmth and enthusiasm of those whom I met.

I would also like to thank the following reviewers for their helpful suggestions: Karine Barzilai-Nahon, of the University of Washington, Seattle, WA; Xiang Chen, of California Lutheran University, Thousand Oaks, CA; Demetria Enis-Cole, of the University of North Texas, Denton, TX; Peter Madsen, of Carnegie Mellon University, Pittsburgh, PA; and Day W. Radebaugh, of Wichita State University, Wichita, KS.

ABOUT THE AUTHORS

Deborah G. Johnson is the Anne Shirley Carter Olsson Professor of Applied Ethics and Chair of the Department of Science, Technology, and Society at the University of Virginia. Johnson has devoted her career to understanding the connections between ethics and technology. She received the John Barwise prize from the American Philosophical Association in 2004, the Sterling Olmsted Award from the Liberal Education Division of the American Society for Engineering Education in 2001, and the ACM SIGCAS Making A Difference Award in 2000.

Keith W. Miller (Contributor) is a Professor of Computer Science at the University of Illinois at Springfield. His work in software engineering and computer ethics provide complementary perspectives to questions that challenge computer professionals. He is the editor in chief of IEEE Technology and Society, and helped develop the Software Engineering Code of Ethics and Professional Practice. He was named a University of Illinois Scholar in 2000–2003 and received the ACM SIGCAS Outstanding Service Award in 2006.

CHAPTER 1

Introduction to Sociotechnical Computer Ethics

CHAPTER OUTLINE

SCENARIOS

Scenario 1.1 A Virtual Rape

Background:

The following incident took place in the early 1990s and was described by Julian Dibbell in 1993. LambdaMOO is a multiuser designed (MUD) object-oriented program, a complex database maintained inside Xerox Corporation in Palo Alto, California, and open to public access via the Internet. Today there are many more games of this kind with significantly enhanced capabilities. Nevertheless, LambdaMOO remains an intriguing exemplar of the complicated conceptual and ethical issues that arise around computers and information technology.

Case

It happened in the living room in LambdaMOO. The program allows users to create and design the interaction space; a user can create a character with any number of attributes and can build spaces and objects. As users interact with one another as the characters that they have created, they see streams of text, both dialogue and stage descriptions.

One night Bungle entered LambdaMOO and used a subprogram, Voodoo doll, to take control of other characters. Using the Voodoo doll subprogram, Bungle took control of legba and Starspinner, and had the two engage in sadistic actions, with one eating pubic hair and sodomizing the other. Legba and Starspinner were helpless throughout the entire incident. The episode ended when another character, Zippy, used a subprogram to freeze Bungle's commands.

This virtual rape caused enormous ripples across the community of LambdaMOOers. One of the victims, legba, wanted Bungle to be "toaded"—that is, to have his account removed from LambdaMOO. Opinion was divided over what should be done to Bungle. On the evening of the third day after the incident, the users gathered in LambdaMOO to discuss Bungle's fate. There were four arguments: (1) The techno libertarians argued that rape in cyberspace was a technical inevitability, and that a solution would be to use defensive software tools to filter out the offender's words. (2) The legalists argued that Bungle could not legitimately be "toaded" because the MOO had no explicit rules at all; they proposed the establishment of rules and virtual institutions to exercise the control required. (3) The third group believed that only the programmers, or wizards as they are known in MOO, have the power to implement rules. (4) The anarchists, on the other hand, wanted to see the matter resolved without the establishment of social control. There was no agreement between these groups. To Bungle, who joined midway through the conference, the incident was simply a sequence of events in virtual reality that had no consequences for his real life existence.

After weighing the arguments, one of the programmers, the Wizard JoeFeedback, decided to "toad" Bungle and banish him from the MOO. As a result of this incident, the database system was redesigned so that the programmers could make changes based on an action or a petition of the majority of the LambdaMOO community. Eight months and 11 ballots later, widespread participation produced a system of checks and capabilities to guard against the type of violence that had occurred. As for Bungle, he is believed to be reincarnated as the character, Dr Jest.

Did Bungle (or the person controlling Bungle) do anything wrong? Who is responsible for what happened? Should anyone suffer "real-world" consequences?

[Revised from a scenario written for *Computer Ethics 3rd Edition* by Marc Quek Pang, based on J. Dibbell, "A Rape in Cyberspace" *Village Voice* (December 21, 1993), pp. 36–42]

Scenario 1.2 Surprises About Social Networking

Background

Facebook has been wildly popular from its beginning. Although generally identified as a "social networking" site, in recent years users have been surprised by a series of incidents and practices suggesting that the site is much more. A few years ago the company decided to change the architecture of the site so that any time a user added a friend to his or her list of friends, all of the user's friends were alerted to the change. Users didn't like the change and complained so much that Facebook changed the architecture of the site, making the new feature an option but not the default option. A second incident occurred when Facebook introduced a new feature that would generate advertising revenue for the company. The new schema, called Beacon, automated notification of a Facebook member's friends when the member made an online purchase. This advertised the product that the member bought, but it also generated some surprises. One of the stories told in the media was that of a man who was planning to surprise his wife with a ring. The man's plans were ruined when everyone in the man's network was notified of the purchase before the man had a chance to give the ring to his wife. Again users protested and Facebook dismantled Beacon. The third surprise is not associated with any single event. Facebook members have gradually—through a series of incidents—become aware that the site is being used by recruiters and law enforcement agencies to gather information for nonsocial networking purposes. For example, employers search Facebook for information on potential employees, and law enforcement agencies search for information and evidence related to crimes. They look for photos as well as communication related to social events before and after they occur.

Are there any ethical issues here? Did Facebook do anything wrong? Are employers and law enforcement agencies doing anything wrong when they use the site for their purposes?

Hypothetical Situation

Ashley joined Facebook many years ago and now has a site with much information and many pictures from her activities. Shawn, who works for a big company, has also been on Facebook for some years. He was recently employed by a big company in their human resources office. Shawn's job is to interview applicants for jobs; once an applicant has made it through the interview process, Shawn solicits references in writing as well as by phone. Recently Shawn's unit has been brainstorming about better ways to find out about applicants and in a meeting that Shawn didn't attend, the unit decided it would be a good idea to check out applicants on their websites. Shawn is asked to follow up on Ashley who made it through the interview with flying colors; Ashley was highly rated by the interviewers who believe she would be ideal for the job for which she is applying. Shawn easily finds Ashley on Facebook and reports to the interviewers that Ashley appears to party often, and that many of the pictures show her drinking. Fearing that Ashley might not take her job seriously enough, the company decides not to offer the job to Ashley. Ashley is surprised when, weeks later, she discovers that someone else has gotten the job.

Is there anything wrong here?

Scenario 1.3 RFID and Caring for the Elderly

Background

Radio-frequency identification (RFID) is a technology that uses small, passive devices as chips that can be detected from a short distance away from the tag. Some RFID chips are sufficiently small so that the circuitry can be painted directly on an object such as an item of clothing. RFID chips are often used in inventory control. "Computer chips" used to track family pets are RFID chips. A high-profile application of RFID chips is drive-through toll collections and public transportation cards. For almost a decade, a controversial application has been RFID chips placed under people's skin for identification purposes. (Wikipedia, http://en.wikipedia.org/wiki/RFID (accessed January 7, 2007).)

Hypothetical Situation

Kathy Pascal is the legal guardian of her elderly mother, Ada. Ada is in the late stages of Alzheimer's disease, and lives at Golden Oaks, a comfortable nursing home near Kathy's home. Ellen Eiffel, an administrator from Golden Oaks, has contacted Kathy about the possibility of placing an RFID tag under Ada's skin. The tag would be the size of a grain of rice, and Golden Oaks has sensors in many places on their grounds. These sensors record the location of all patients who have an RFID tag whenever they are near a sensor. Ms. Eiffel explains that the RFID tag would help Golden Oaks ensure Ada's safety if and when she started to wander off; it would also help in double checking medical records each time Ada received medicines or therapy. The administrator emphasizes that using the RFID tag would allow Golden Oaks to ensure Ada's safety without confining her to her room. Kathy is sad that her mother requires this kind of marking, but she also sees the advantages as her mother loses more and more of her mental capacity.

What should Kathy do?

INTRODUCTION: WHY COMPUTER ETHICS?

These scenarios illustrate the complex and fascinating character of the ethical and social issues that arise around computers and information technology.[1] Together the scenarios suggest a broad range of issues: Scenario 1.1 presents us with a form of behavior that didn't exist before computers and, thus, requires some analysis just to figure out whether there is any wrongdoing and who did it. Scenario 1.2 raises questions about privacy, uses and abuses of technology, and the obligations of companies to inform their customers about changes in the operation of the business. Scenario 1.3 raises more personal, although no less complicated, issues about how to treat someone who is not capable of making her own decisions, especially when the decision involves a new technology that may affect the kind of care the person will receive. The scenarios suggest that living in a world constituted in part by computers may involve distinctive and especially challenging ethical issues.

The scenarios point to a future that will be powerfully shaped by computers and information technology, assuming that is, that computers and information technology (IT) continue to develop at the speed and with the success it has in the past. If we have any hope of steering the development of future technologies in a direction that is good for humanity, that hope lies in understanding the social and ethical implications of our choices about IT. This book is devoted to just that. The ideas discussed here are intended to provide insight into the social and ethical implications of computers. Those insights should help us think more deeply about the future development of IT.

Although the three scenarios illustrate the range and complexity of ethical issues surrounding IT, some might argue that it is not exactly the technology that poses the ethical challenges but rather the uses of the technology, that is, the humans and human behavior around the technology. In the past, it was common to hear people say that technology is neutral—value neutral—and, therefore, ethics doesn't have anything directly to do with technology. As the old adage goes, "guns don't kill people, people kill people." The field of computer ethics developed when statements of this kind were still quite common and, as a result, much of the literature in the field struggles with questions of the following kind: Why do computers raise ethical issues? What is the connection between ethics and IT? Computer ethicists have struggled with the question of whether IT creates new ethical issues—issues that never existed before—or new versions of old ethical issues, issues that persist over centuries but take on new dimensions as the world changes.

At first glance, it seems that IT creates situations in which common or prevailing moral rules and principles don't seem to apply nor seem helpful in figuring out what one should do. For example, in Scenario 1.1, it takes some analysis just to identify what behavior or whose behavior, if any, could be considered unethical. Because Bungle is a virtual figure, how can it be his behavior? Is it the behavior of the person controlling Bungle? Should we even distinguish the behavior of Bungle from the

---

[1]Although the focus of this book is broadly on ethics and computers and information technology, because the field of study has traditionally been referred to as "computer ethics," we use "computers" and "computer ethics" in this chapter. In subsequent chapters, we shift to using "information technology" and "IT."

behavior of the person controlling Bungle? Either way, what exactly was the wrongdoing? Was it Bungle's rape of legba and Starspinner? Was it the use of a subprogram to control the behavior of other characters? What moral norms or principles were violated? The prohibition on rape is clear and powerful, but in this case no flesh-and-blood person was raped. Rather, a flesh-and-blood person manipulated a virtual (should we say "fictitious"?) character to enact a text-based rape of another virtual character in front of a community of observers who had no expectation that they would witness such behavior.

The other two scenarios also raise challenging questions. Did Facebook violate the privacy of its members when it introduced changes to the architecture of Facebook? Was this unethical, or simply bad business? Have Facebook members been misled into thinking the site is more private than it is? Has Facebook misled users by offering membership for free when, in fact, Facebook is a for-profit company that must find a way of making money from the site? Are recruiters and law enforcement agencies abusing the site when they use it for other than social networking purposes? As for the nursing home case, although children with elderly parents have often had to make difficult decisions with regard to parents who become incapable of making their own decisions, is the decision about implantation of an RFID chip somehow different than other such decisions? Are such implants dehumanizing and demeaning? Or are the chips the means to a compassionate end?

We will consider these questions in due course but for now, we have to step back and ask a set of larger questions about questions ("meta-questions") regarding the field of computer ethics. Scholars in this field have spent a lot of time trying to understand whether and how ethical issues surrounding IT are distinctive. They have asked whether the issues are so different that new moral theories are needed, or whether traditional theories might be extended to apply. As well, they have considered whether a new kind of methodology is needed for the field. We shall refer to this cluster of issues as the "why computer ethics?" question. The cluster includes: Why does IT create ethical issues? Do we need a special field of study for IT ethics? Why isn't this just applied ethics, plain and simple? In other words, why say that the ethical issues described in Scenarios 1.1–1.3 are computer or IT ethical issues, and not just ethical issues, period? What is the best way to understand and resolve ethical issues that involve IT?

The "why computer ethics?" question is complex. Part of the puzzle has to do with technology in general, because technologies other than computers have also posed complex ethical issues. Consider, for example, all of the concern that was expressed about the power of the atomic bomb during World War II. Should such a powerful tool be created, let alone used? What would it mean for world politics? Or consider, more recently, the public debates about nanotechnology, cloning, stem cell research, and mind-alternating pharmacology. All of these technologies have stirred fear and apprehension as well as fascination and hope. In each case, the literature expressing concern about the new technology has suggested that humanity has acquired a new capacity that takes us into new ethical territory. Part of the "why computer ethics?" question, thus, has to do with technology in general. Why do new technologies give rise to ethical issues? What exactly is the connection between ethics (be it moral theory or moral behavior) and technology?

The other part of the "why computer ethics?" puzzle has to do specifically with IT and whether there is something special about this set of technologies that gives rise to a distinctive kind of ethical issue. On the surface, IT seems to create many more ethical issues than other kinds of technology such as automobiles, electricity, and bridges. Perhaps there is something in particular about IT that disrupts and challenges prevailing moral norms and principles. We will return to this question in a moment.

The "why computer ethics?" question is what we might characterize as a metaquestion, a question about how we are asking our questions. The "why computer ethics?" question calls upon us to step back from engagement with the issues and reflect on our engagement. It asks us to reflect on what we are looking for, and on what we do when we analyze computer ethical issues. On the one hand, this kind of reflection is ideally done after one has some familiarity with the field and some experience analyzing computer ethical issues. For this reason, it would be best to wait until the end of the book to consider the question. On the other hand, an answer to the "why computer ethics?" question also provides a framework for identifying and understanding the issues. As well, an answer to the question points in the direction of an appropriate methodology to use in analyzing computer ethical issues. Hence, we need at least a preliminary answer to the question before we jump into the substance of the topic.

In the next sections, we will provide a preliminary answer to the "why computer ethics?" question, set the scene for subsequent chapters, and suggest a methodology for analyzing computer ethics issues. The answer we will propose recommends that we keep an eye on the connection between ethics and technology in general as the backdrop—the framework—in which computer ethics issues can best be understood.

THE STANDARD ACCOUNT

New Possibilities, a Vacuum of Policies, Conceptual Muddles

A survey of the literature in the field of computer ethics suggests that there is now something like a consensus answer to the "why computer ethics?" question. Computer ethicists seem to accept the general parameters of an account that James Moor provided in a 1985 article entitled, "What is Computer Ethics?" We will refer to this account as the standard account. According to Moor, computers create new possibilities, new opportunities for human action. All three of the scenarios at the beginning of this chapter illustrate this idea. Virtual environments like LambdaMOO didn't and couldn't exist before IT, not, at least, before the Internet had been created. The invention of Facebook created new possibilities for keeping in touch with friends no matter how far away they are or how long ago you last saw each other. Similarly, new possibilities for tracking and monitoring the movements of individuals were created with the invention of RFID. Of course, IT doesn't just create new possibilities for individuals acting alone; new forms of collective and collaborative action are made possible as well. Interest groups on any topic imaginable can form online and take action collectively; companies can operate globally with a relatively high degree of control and speed of action because of the Internet. Families can stay in close communication (maintaining strong bonds) while members are living in geographically distant places.

According to the standard account, these *new possibilities* give rise to ethical questions. Should we pursue the new possibility? How should we pursue it? Who will gain if the possibility is realized? Who will lose? Will pursuit of the new possibility affect fundamental human values? Computer ethicists have risen to the challenge of these new possibilities by taking up tough questions. Is data mining morally acceptable? Should software be proprietary? Are Internet domain names being distributed fairly? Who should be liable for inaccurate or slanderous information that appears in electronic forums? What should we do about child pornography on the Web? Some of these questions have been resolved (or, at least, concern has waned); some have been addressed by law; others continue to be controversial. New questions continue to arise as new possibilities are created. What will Second Life[2] mean? Should we build robots to take care of the elderly as the Japanese are doing? Should we delegate health decisions to artificially intelligent robot doctors? Should we insert intelligence chips in our brains?

That the new possibilities give rise to ethical questions seems to make sense, although we can press further. Why do ethical questions arise from new possibilities? Of course, part of the answer is simply that the new possibilities are "new." But part of the answer is also that new possibilities are not always or necessarily good (or purely good). They can affect different individuals differently. They can be disruptive and threatening to the status quo. The potential for good and ill often comes in a tangled package. Good consequences come along with negative consequences, trade-offs have to be made, and the technology has to be modified in response to political, social, and cultural conditions.

For example, virtual reality systems have enormous potential for good. Aside from the rich, entertainment value of gaming, virtual systems used for scientific modeling and simulation help in understanding the world and in training. But virtual systems could also lead, some fear, to a world in which individuals escape into fantasy worlds and have difficulty dealing with the "real world" of flesh and blood people. Similarly, a world in which RFID is used to monitor and track those who are hospitalized could mean a world in which the elderly are much better cared for than they are now, or it could mean the elderly have less and less human contact and nurses and doctors become deskilled and lose first-hand knowledge of illness and aging.

Thus, according to the standard account of computer ethics, the field's raison de trios (reason for being) is to evaluate the new possibilities from an ethical perspective. To be sure, the implications of adoption and use of a particular technology can and should be examined from a variety of perspectives, including economics and politics, but the ethical perspective is especially important because it is normative. When it comes to economics and politics, the point is often to describe and predict the likely consequences of adopting a new technology. This informs but does not address whether the new technology *should* be adopted. Ethical analysis considers the should-question and how a new possibility fits (or doesn't fit) moral values, notions, and practices.

---

[2]Created in 2003, Second Life is a popular 3-D virtual world site in which users interact through avatars. Because of the advanced capabilities of the site, users sometimes strongly identify with their avatars and become intensely involved in their virtual lives.

Moor (1985) describes the task of computer ethics as that of filling policy vacuums. According to Moor, when computers create new possibilities, there is a vacuum of policies. The new possibilities take us into uncharted territory, situations in which it is unclear what is at issue or which moral norms are relevant. Moor's notion of a policy vacuum captures the uncertainty that often surrounds the invention and adoption of new technologies. Here an example from the early days of computer technology illustrates Moor's point. When the first computers were installed, individuals began storing files on them, but there were no institutional or legal policies with regard to access and use. From our perspective today, it may seem obvious that most computer files should be treated as personal or private property, but the status of computer files was initially unclear (in part because the first computers were large mainframes located in buildings and owned by companies, agencies, and universities). Thus, when remote access became possible and hackers began roaming around and trying to get access, the moral and legal status of the files on mainframe computers was unclear. Whether or not hackers were committing crimes was unclear. Were they stealing? Perhaps, but the files that hackers accessed (and copied) were not removed. Were they trespassing? Hackers who gained access were nowhere near the physical location where the files were stored. As already indicated, at the time there were no laws explicitly addressing access to computer files. In Moor's terms, there was a policy vacuum with regard to the status of acts involving access to computer files. A new possibility had been created and there was a policy vacuum.

On Moor's account, the task of computer ethics is to fill policy vacuums, and he acknowledges that the task is far from easy. Filling the policy vacuum involves sorting out what Moor refers to as conceptual muddles. To illustrate a conceptual muddle, consider another case from the early days of computing, computer software. When computer software was first created, the challenge was to figure out how best to conceptualize it. The problem had to do with fitting computer software to prevailing intellectual property law; copyright and patent seemed the best possibilities. Copyright law specifies that abstract ideas cannot be copyrighted, only expressions of ideas. Typically this means expressing an idea in a written language. Patent law also prohibits ownership of abstract ideas, as well as laws of nature, and mathematical algorithms. Because abstract ideas are the building blocks of science and technology, giving an individual ownership has the potential to significantly dampen progress in the technological arts and sciences. New inventors would have to get permission from a private owner to use one of the building blocks. When it came to software it wasn't clear whether a copyright on a computer program would be granting ownership of an expression of an idea or the building blocks of the electronic world. In patent law the issue was even trickier because patent law specifies that abstract ideas, laws of nature, and mental steps cannot be owned. Although enormously large and complex, software can be thought of as a series of mental steps. That is, in principle a person can go through the steps in a program and mentally do what the program specifies. If someone were granted ownership of mental steps, then they could legally prohibit others from going through those steps in their minds. This would interfere with freedom of thought.

The question of whether to grant copyright or patents for computer programs was, then, deeply linked to the conceptualization of computer programs. That is, the policy vacuum couldn't be filled without a conceptualization of software. Could software be characterized as an expression of ideas? an application of abstract ideas? Could it be understood as something other than mental steps or mathematical algorithms? Or did a whole new set of laws have to be created specifically for computer software? If so, what should the new laws look like? Again, the conceptual muddle had to be sorted out in order to fill the policy vacuum.

In summary, then, according to the standard account of computer ethics: (1) ethical issues arise around IT because IT creates new possibilities for human action and there is a vacuum of policies with regard to the new possibilities, (2) the task of computer ethics is to evaluate the new possibilities and fill the policy vacuums, and (3) a significant component of this task is addressing conceptual muddles.

An Update to the Standard Account

The standard account has been extremely useful in moving the field of computer ethics forward for the last two decades. Nevertheless, over these years, a number of factors have changed. IT has changed and so have computer ethicists, at least in the sense that they have acquired a good deal of experience in analyzing IT ethical issues. At the same time, a new field of study has developed, science and technology studies (STS). This new field has provided insights into the relationship between technology and society, insights that are relevant to understanding how ethical notions and practices shape, and are shaped by, technology. These factors suggest that it is time for an update to the standard account.

To begin the update, notice that much of what has been said about IT ethics seems to apply quite readily to ethical issues involving other new technologies. Other new technologies also create new possibilities for human action, and the new possibilities lead to ethical questions about whether and how to pursue the possibilities. Should I donate my organs for transplantation? Should employers be allowed to use urine or blood tests to determine whether employees are using drugs? Should our food supply be genetically modified? Each of these questions arose when a new technology was developed, and the new possibility created an option for human action that hadn't existed before. Because of features of the new technology, prevailing moral norms or rules either didn't apply, or didn't apply neatly to the new possibility. For example, having a supervisor watch employees as they worked on an assembly line of a manufacturing plant was a standard part of such work, but when urine and blood tests for illegal drugs were developed and adopted by employers, it wasn't clear whether this was an extension of acceptable workplace watching practices or an inappropriately intrusive step into the private lives of individuals. Although there was a huge body of law relating to employer and employee rights, the applicability of the law to urine and blood testing was unclear. Is it comparable to watching employees at home? Is it like asking about an employee's race, sexual preference, or political beliefs? Is drug testing comparable to watching an employee work? So, there was a policy vacuum and a conceptual muddle. The point is that the standard account can be used to explain ethical issues arising around new technologies in general, and is not specific to IT ethics.

Moor's account is, then, an account of "new technology ethics"; something more is needed to make it an account of computer ethics. Of course, its broad applicability is not a reason to reject the account. It seems to be an accurate account of new technology ethics; we just have to keep in mind that it is not specific to IT.

Another, perhaps more subtle problem with the standard account is that the emphasis on "newness" may skew the kind of analysis that is done. The focus of attention is on one, and only one, stage in the lifecycle of technology, the stage in which it is first introduced. This directs attention away from, and largely blinds us to, other stages, especially the ongoing role of IT in constituting the social and moral world. IT is an ongoing part of the world we live in. Indeed, it is challenging to identify a domain of life in which IT doesn't play a role.

The focus on newness suggests that computer ethics issues arise when the technology is first introduced; the issues get resolved when the policy vacuums are filled and the conceptual muddles sorted out, and that is that. The reality is quite different. For one thing, policy vacuums sometimes go unfilled or they get filled, but in ways that perpetuate continuous struggle or tension over the policy. Sometimes policy vacuums are resolved with bad policies, policies with negative or undesirable consequences. In any of these cases, ethical analysis can have an important role in critiquing policies that have already formed, pointing to their misfit with notions of justice or responsibility or good consequences. Moreover, even when a policy issue gets resolved and gets resolved well, because IT constitutes the social and moral world, it is still important to draw attention to the role of IT in shaping moral practices.

The emphasis on newness in the standard account leads to other related problems. Because IT is no longer new, many who take up IT ethical issues (indeed, many readers of this book) will not have experienced a world without computers. Yes, novel applications, tools, and systems continue to be developed, but they are developed in a context in which people are already familiar with the technology. The technology already has meaning and users already have well-developed expectations. In other words, people already have conceptual models of the technology and how it works; they have knowledge that informs how they approach and use new applications. Also, there are already policies regulating the use of computer technology, policies that are extended to new applications and systems when they are introduced. Hence, it no longer seems appropriate to frame computer ethics as a field focused exclusively on the newness or novelty of IT.

Yet another reason for shifting away from the focus on newness is to avoid a presumption that seems to accompany it. When we focus on IT when it is new, we tend to think of the technology as arriving intact and being plopped into society where it is taken up and has an impact. This suggests that the technology came out of nowhere, or that it was developed in isolation from society and then "introduced." Many believe that technology is developed in protected environments such as laboratories, garages, and universities, as if the inventors or designers were following out some logic of nature. But this is an incomplete account; technologies are always developed in a social world. Laboratories, universities, and even garages are embedded in an existing culture, complete with systems of support, real-world constraints, and socially shaped ideas. What a product or tool looks like—the features it includes, what it makes possible—has everything to do with the social context *in* which it was created and the context *for* which it was created.

IT systems are designed to do certain tasks, to fit into particular environments, or fit the needs or desires of particular users. The process by which they are designed—who is involved, who has a say, who is funding the project—powerfully shapes the particular features a technology comes to have, and who it serves or doesn't serve. The invention and design context is filled with legal requirements, economic incentives, cultural attitudes, and consumers with particular profiles. Moreover, after a technology is first created, it is often modified either by users who find "work-arounds," or by developers who see that their product is being rejected, or by others who see something in it of value but see an alternative way to develop the general idea. Post-it notes were born when a failed glue found a new use. More often than not, successful technologies have gone through a long period of development with many missteps and unexpected turns along the way.

Inventors live and work in particular places and at particular periods in history, and this has significant effects on the range of possibilities open to them. The garage where Steve Jobs and Steve Wozniak assembled the first Apple computers was near Hewlett-Packard in Palo Alto where Wozniak had worked and Jobs had attended some lectures. The garage had electricity, and Wozniak had been trained as an electronic engineer. The new computers they designed used the existing technologies of a mouse and on-screen icons. When the two made their first batch of computers, a nearby computer hobby store bought them. Apple computers were products not only of the unique talents and skills of Jobs and Wozniak; they were also the products of the circumstances and possibilities that were available at that time and place.

The focus on newness can, then, blind us to the fact that the technologies we have today are not the only possible, or the best possible, technologies. Under different conditions and with different design and innovation contexts, we could have different technologies. When the possibility of different sorts of technology is pushed out of sight, IT ethicists miss an important opportunity for ethics to play a role in the design of IT systems. [Note: Several IT ethicists have not been blinded in this way, and have seized the opportunity to both focus on issues in the design of IT systems and be involved themselves in the design. Helen Nissenbaum, for example, helped to design a program called TrackMeNot that helps protect users' privacy when they use Google to search the Web. She and others have developed an approach to IT ethics that is referred to as *value sensitive design*.]

So, the standard account does not provide an account of distinctively "computer" or "IT" ethical issues; it gives an account of how new technologies, in general, involve ethical issues. Because IT is relatively new, and new applications continue to evolve, IT falls under the account. In putting the emphasis on newness, the standard account tends to push out of sight other stages in the lifecycle of technologies. Before adoption and use is the design stage, and here computer ethics can play a role in identifying ethical issues in both design processes and design features. After design and introduction, IT continues to contribute to the configuration of social arrangements, social practices, and social institutions. IT is part of, and shapes, many domains of life including government, education, politics, business, identity, and relationships. As well, the lifecycle of IT includes manufacturing, marketing, distribution, and disposal. The lens of ethics should be brought to bear on all of these stages in the lifecycle of IT.

The central focus of the rest of this book will be on the role of IT in constituting the social and moral world. For this purpose, it will be helpful to adopt what we will refer to as the sociotechnical systems perspective.

THE SOCIOTECHNICAL SYSTEMS PERSPECTIVE

In the last thirty years, a rich literature focused on the relationships among science, technology, and society has developed. The literature is part of a new field of study with undergraduate majors and graduate programs, several journals, and professional societies. The field is called "STS," referring either to "science and technology studies" or "science, technology, and society." We will develop a foundation for IT ethics using STS insights, concepts, and theories. For this, a brief review of the major claims of STS is essential.

STS literature is diverse, complex, and richly textured, so the description to follow is necessarily a simplification. To provide a quick overview of the core ideas in STS, we can think of STS as identifying three mistakes that should be avoided in thinking about technology. Parallel to each of the three mistakes is a recommendation as to how we should think about technology and society.

Reject Technological Determinism/Think Coshaping

STS cautions against adoption of a view referred to as "technological determinism." Although multiple definitions and forms of technological determinism have been articulated, technological determinism fundamentally consists of two claims: (1) technology develops independently from society, and (2) when a technology is taken up and used in a society, it determines the character of that society.

The first claim of technological determinism usually involves thinking that technological development follows scientific discoveries or follows a logic of its own, with one invention building on the next. Technological determinists may even think that technological development has a kind of natural evolution with each development building on previous developments. This view of how technology develops goes hand-in-hand with the belief, mentioned earlier, that inventors and engineers work in isolation. They work, it is supposed, in laboratories in which all that matters is manipulating the processes and materials of nature. Technological development is understood to be an independent activity, separate from social forces.

STS scholars reject this claim. They argue that scientific and technological development is far from isolated and does not follow a predetermined or "natural" order of development. The character and direction of technological development are influenced by a wide range of social factors including: the decisions a government agency makes to fund certain kinds of research; social incidents such as a war or terrorist attack that spark interest and effort to produce particular kinds of devices (e.g., for security); market forces that feed development in some areas and bring others to a halt; the legal environment, which may constrain innovation in certain areas and facilitate it in others; and cultural sensibilities that lead to objectionable meanings associated with certain technologies and desirable meanings for others.

Consider, for example, the enormous investment that the U.S. government (through its National Science Foundation) has made in the development of nanotechnology. The NSF receives far more requests for funding than it can grant, so making investments in nanotechnology means that the NSF will not make investments elsewhere. Consider how regulatory standards for automobile safety and standards for fuel efficiency have influenced the design of automobiles. And consider the debates over stem cell research and the requirement that researchers obtain the informed consent of subjects on whom they experiment. These are all elements that have shaped the technologies that are currently in use.

To be sure, nature has to be taken into account in technological development. Nature cannot be made to do just anything that humans want it to do. Nevertheless, nature does not entirely determine the technologies we get. Social factors steer engineers in certain directions and influence the design of technological devices and systems. Thus, the first tenet of technological determinism—that technology develops in isolation and according to its own logic—should be rejected outright.

According to the second tenet of technological determinism, when technologies are adopted by societies or particular social groups, the adoption brings about—determines—social arrangements and patterns of social behavior. In other words, when a society adopts a particular technology, it adopts a form of life, patterns of behavior. Perhaps the most famous statement of this was historian Lynn White's claim (1962) that from the invention of the stirrup came feudal society. He was suggesting that the adoption of the stirrup changed the nature of warfare and slowly but surely led to a society in which serfs were dominated by aristocrats. In IT ethics, a parallel type of claim is made about the Internet and democracy. Certain writers have suggested that when countries adopt the Internet, it is just a matter of time before democracy will reign; once, that is, individuals in any society have access to the Internet and all the information it makes available, those individuals will want democracy and democratic social institutions. This is an expression of technological determinism in the sense that it implies that a technology will determine the political structure of a country.

Although STS scholars reject outright the first claim of technological determinism, their response to the second claim is more complicated. The problem is that when we say that technology determines society, we are forgetting that the technology has been socially shaped; social factors and forces have influenced the development and design of the technology. As already discussed, STS studies show that the technologies we have today are products of highly complex and contingent social processes. Thus, the problem with claiming that technology determines society is that "determines" is too strong a term. Social factors affect the design, use, and meaning of a technology, and in this respect society can push back and reconfigure a technology, making it into something its designers never intended. Consider here how Facebook users pushed back and pressured the company to change the architecture back to what it was. The point is that although technology shapes society, it does not determine it.

Technology develops through a back-and-forth process that involves what is technologically possible and how society responds to the possibilities, pursuing some possibilities, rejecting others, and not even noticing others. So, technological determinism is not wrong insofar as it recognizes technology as a powerful force in shaping society; it is wrong to characterize this as "determining" society. Society and technology shape each other.

In effect, the STS counter to each tenet of technological determinism is the same; society influences technology. Recognition of the societal influences on the development of technology leads to an outright rejection of the first claim of technological determinism (that technology is developed in isolation) and a modification to, or weakening of, the second tenet (that technology determines society). The positive recommendation emerging out of this critique of technological determinism is that we acknowledge that technology and society cocreate (coshape; coconstitute) one another. The mantra of STS scholars is that technology shapes and is shaped by society, that society shapes and is shaped by technology.

In the previous section, in critiquing the standard account, we mentioned that the account seemed to frame computer technology as developed, and then "introduced" as if it came in some sort of predetermined form and was simply discovered. Framing the development of technology in this way commits the mistake of technological determinism. It suggests that users have only one choice: either reject or accept the technology as delivered. Nothing could be farther from the truth; IT is developed to fit into particular environments; users are often able to shape the technology by customizing settings, demanding changes from developers, and choosing between alternative products, and so on. Users also shape computer technology through the meaning they associate with it and through the behavior with which they engage the technology.

Reject Technology as Material Objects/Think Sociotechnical Systems

The second major insight that STS theory provides involves the rejection of another presumption that people often make about technology. They think and speak as if "technology" refers to physical objects or artifacts. According to STS scholars, this is at best misleading, and at worst constitutes a false conception of technology. To be sure, artifacts (human-made material objects) are components of technology, but artifacts have no meaning or significance or even usefulness unless they are embedded in social practices and social activities. This can be seen in a number of different ways. First, technologies do not come into being out of nowhere; they are created by intentional human activity and, as already described, shaped by social forces. This is true whether we think about a simple artifact created by a single individual fashioning natural materials (say, a person carving a stone into an arrowhead), or we think about an extremely complex artifact such as a mass-produced computer that requires elaborate social organization. Producing a computer involves the organization of people and things into manufacturing plants, mining of materials, assembly lines, distribution systems, as well as the invention of computer languages, education and training of individuals with a variety of expertise, and more. In other words, technology is a *social product*.

However, technology is not just the outcome of social activity, it is also socially constituted (it *is* social). The artifactual component of technology (the physical object) can function only as part of a social system. The mere existence of an artifact doesn't do anything. Consider, for example, a workplace monitoring system adopted by a corporation for use by those who supervise employees working on computers. The system is a social product in the sense that it took many people, organized in various ways and working intentionally, to develop the system. However, the system doesn't work once the code is written. The company making the system will have had to figure out how to legally "own" the system (via patent or copyright or trade secrecy) before they make it available. Documentation will have to be written. The system will have to be advertised or marketed, and it will have to be distributed. If customers buy the system, users have to be trained; users have to learn how to adapt the system to their particular needs (kind of work being done, number of employees, kind of output desired); and users have to learn how to interpret and use the data produced by the system. The customer may have to write a new policy regarding the system; they may have to inform workers and obtain their consent. In short, in order for the workplace monitoring system to work, the software has to be embedded in a set of social practices. The thing we call a "workplace monitoring system" consists not just of software but the combination of software and human arrangements and social practices; these all work together to make a functional system.

It is misleading, then, to think of technology as merely artifacts or of IT systems as merely software. STS theorists recommend that we think of technology as sociotechnical systems (Hughes, 1994). A frequent series of TV commercials for a cell phone company in the United States features a horde of technicians, operators, and other personnel who follow around customers of that company. That "horde" is a lighthearted illustration of exactly this STS concept: A cell phone is not just the artifact that you put to your ear, talk into, and listen for. A cell phone is the combination of the artifact and a network of people arranged in various ways to produce a complex of results.

Recognition that technology is not just artifacts, but rather artifacts embedded in social practices and infused with social meaning, is essential to understanding the connection between ethics and IT. Traditionally, ethics has been understood to be almost exclusively about human behavior and human action. Ethicists have not traditionally focused on technology, perhaps, because they believed that technology was simply material objects dropped into the world ready-made. Because material objects were thought simply to be products of nature, they were seen as neutral, and there seemed to be no point to ethical reflection about them. This is precisely the danger of thinking about technology as material objects. It pushes out of sight the fact that people and artifacts are intertwined, that people are influenced by artifacts, and that artifacts are shaped by humans. For ethicists to fail to see the role of technology in morality is to fail to see a powerful force shaping the moral questions confronting human beings. For engineers, inventors, and computer experts not to see the social practices that constitute technological systems they develop is to be blind to the significance and implications of what they are doing.

So, STS scholars reject the idea that technology is material objects, and entreat us always to think of technology as sociotechnical systems (combinations of things and people). As already indicated, this doesn't mean that artifacts are unimportant; they are enormously important. The material world powerfully shapes what people can and cannot do. However, we will be misled if we look only at artifacts. In fact, it could be argued that it is impossible to understand a technology by looking at the artifact alone. This would be like trying to understand the chess piece called "the rook" without knowing anything about the game of chess (the rules of the game, the goal, or other chess pieces). Yes, you can describe the shape and dimensions and the material of which the chess piece is made, but you cannot fully understand what a rook "is" without reference to the game of chess. It is the same for a workplace monitoring device, a word processor, or a data-mining tool: You cannot understand what they are merely by focusing on the code.

Reject Technology as Neutral/Think Technology Infused with Values

The third mistake identified in the STS literature is to think that technology is value neutral. Perhaps the most influential work on this topic is Langdon Winner's 1986 piece, "Do artifacts have politics?" Winner draws attention to the relationship between technology and systems of power and authority, arguing that particular technologies cannot exist or function without particular kinds of social arrangements. He argues that adoption of a particular technology means adoption of a particular social order. His example is that of nuclear power: Nuclear power necessitates a complex, hierarchical system of decision making; the production and distribution of nuclear power is achieved by social arrangements in which decisions are coordinated and someone is in charge. Experts of various kinds make decisions at various nodes in the organization. Contrast this with windmills that operate with a decentralized form of authority; each individual who has a windmill can decide how to operate the windmill and what to do with the power that is produced. Similarly, transportation by train requires a centralized system of organization, whereas bicycling is decentralized.

In explaining this relationship between technologies and patterns of authority and decision making (which may seem quite deterministic), Winner provides a powerful example of how an artifact can enforce social biases and privilege individual agendas. He describes how Robert Moses intentionally designed the bridges of Long Island, New York (built in the 1930s) to be at a height that would not allow public buses to go under the underpasses. This constrained bus routes and prevented poor people (largely African Americans) living in the city from getting to the beaches. In the 1930s poor people didn't have cars, so the only way they could reach the beaches during the heat of the summer was by public transportation. This account of Moses's intentions has been challenged, but whether or not it was consciously intended by Moses, the account illustrates that the height of bridges can constrain access to certain areas and thus can reinforce a race and class system.

The story is intriguing because it illustrates how a material object can be value-laden. One is tempted to say that social hierarchy was embedded in the materiality of the bridges. Of course, it isn't the physical structures alone that produced the social arrangement. It was the combination of the bridge's size and height, the size of other physical objects (buses of a particular size, the location of the beaches in relation to the city), and a set of social practices including the practice of going to public beaches, thinking of people in racial categories, and much more. The combination constituted a race-biased arrangement. Still, all of these parts constitute the soicotechnical system of which the physical bridge is a part, and that system was infused with social and moral values.

Winner can be interpreted as slipping into the mistake of technological determinism. He seems to be suggesting that a technology—the bridges of Long Island—determined the social order. Hence, it is important to remember here that the problem with technological determinism is not that it is wrong about technology "shaping" or "influencing" social arrangements; technology does shape and influence social behavior. Technological determinism goes too far in claiming that the technology determines the social arrangements. Here we see that the social arrangement was produced by the combination of the height of the bridges, the size of buses, preexisting social arrangements, and ideas about race and social hierarchy; a change in any one of these elements might have changed the result.

SOCIOTECHNICAL COMPUTER ETHICS

The three STS recommendations provide the foundation for what we will call "sociotechnical computer ethics." The payoff of using this approach will become clearer as we move from issue to issue and chapter to chapter, but we can demonstrate some of its value here if we return to the scenarios at the beginning of this chapter. The "Virtual Rape" case will be taken up in Chapter 3 but a closer look at the Facebook and RFID cases will get us started. Our analysis will be limited because we have not yet explored ethical concepts and theories. We will use Facebook to illustrate the STS recommendations and the RFID case to demonstrate how the sociotechnical perspective helps in ethical decision making.

The story of Facebook's development goes right to the heart of the first STS theme in the sense that Facebook was not the "next logical development in the natural evolution of IT"; Facebook didn't come out of nowhere. It was created by Mark Zuckerberg while he was at Harvard and thought it would be fun to create something that would support social interactions among students. Whether he was conscious of his knowledge or not, Zuckerberg used his understanding of patterns of interaction among college students; he designed a system that would fit into that world; he intentionally designed a system that would enhance and extend prevailing patterns of interaction. As the system began to be used, it affected social relations by facilitating students in finding out about one another and interacting more frequently via the system. Among other things, Facebook allows individuals to communicate asynchronously, with different people than they might otherwise and, of course, independent of where they are located. In these respects, Facebook shapes the nature of friendship. However, it would be an overstatement to say that Facebook "determines" social relationships. Facebook shapes, and is shaped by, the nature of relationships.

Perhaps the second STS lesson—not to think of technology as material objects—doesn't even need emphasizing to Facebook users because they think of the site not just as a material object or piece of software, but as a "social" networking site. They are aware that what makes Facebook work is not just lines of code, but users putting up content, browsing, and communicating with one another. The surprises described in Scenario 1.2 reinforced this idea because they made users painfully aware of the human actors involved in making the system work. Systems operators and administrators had made decisions to change the architecture of the system, and later they decided to change the architecture back to its original form. So, users were confronted with the fact that the system is not simply lines of code; it is partly lines of code, but the lines of code are written and maintained by programmers who take direction from administrators who respond to a variety of stakeholders, including users. Facebook is a sociotechnical system with many human and nonhuman components.

As a social networking site, Facebook is far from neutral. It is designed to facilitate social networking. Once again, the surprises to the users illustrate this point. Users didn't want a system that would send out information to their friends every time they made a change in their list of friends. Although the system makes individuals quite transparent to their friends, the Beacon schema bumped up against many users' desire from some sort of privacy about shopping. These incidents show that users' values and preferences were in tension with Facebook's values. The Facebook company wants a system that makes money; users want a system that makes some, but not other, information available to their friends. Changes in the architecture change the values embedded in the system.

Facebook illustrates the three STS themes and recommendations. Still, you might ask, how do these STS recommendations help us when it comes to ethical issues? That is, how does the sociotechnical systems perspective help in the analysis of IT ethical issues? The short answer is that the perspective gives us a fuller, more accurate, and richer understanding of situations in which moral questions and dilemmas arise. We can illustrate this by focusing on Scenario 1.3 in which an individual must make a decision about whether to have an RFID device implanted in her mother.

The first step is to keep in mind that RFID is a sociotechnical system, not simply a material object. Those who developed the chips to be implanted in patients saw a real-world context and a set of practices that might be improved by the use of the chips. So they designed the chips for use in the hospital context. In the design process, the developers had to pay considerable attention to how things are done in hospitals—who does what when; they had to take into account the interests of various stakeholders including, and especially, the hospital and patients. The developers had to think about what might go wrong and what their liability would be if something did go wrong. They would have had to think through how the device could be inserted, by whom, and under what conditions; how data on patients could be displayed; where the displays would be located; who would monitor the displays; who would need to be trained; and so on. All of this is to say that the RFID device at issue is a social product and a sociotechnical system. It is created by people with interests and targeted for other people organized in a particular setting. The system is a combination of material chips together with social practices involving implantation of the tag, display of the data produced by the tag, interpretation of the data, and responses to the data.

When installed at a facility, the RFID chip system becomes a component shaping the hospital environment. Patients may move about more freely because the device will inform staff as to their medical condition and whereabouts, staff will be trained to read and interpret displays, staff may be assigned more patients, and the physical architecture of hospitals may change because patients can move about more. Perhaps the most important lesson in this for Kathy Pascal in Scenario 1.3 is that her decision doesn't involve just insertion of a chip into her mother; it involves her mother being enmeshed in a complex sociotechnical system with many components.

Although Kathy should ask about the materials used in the chip and whether there are risks to implantation of those materials, she should also ask about how the chip will be implanted, how data will be received, and how decisions will be made using the data. She will want to compare the treatment her mother is likely to get with or without the chip system. Although her mother may be freer to move about, does this mean she will have less contact with people during her day? Is the science behind the detection devices (that will monitor her mother's medications) reliable? And so on.

Yes, the sociotechnical systems perspective seems to generate more questions than someone without the perspective would have thought to ask. Although this may seem a burden, it is unavoidable that better decisions involve taking into account more factors. Yet the sociotechnical system perspective doesn't just expand the range of factors to be taken into account; it helps in identifying or articulating particular kinds of concerns, and reveals new opportunities for resolution or intervention. For example, suppose Kathy is already concerned about the chip being demeaning and disrespectful of whatever autonomy her mother has. To figure out whether the chip will have this effect or not, if Kathy focuses on the chip alone, she will get nowhere. On the other hand, once she recognizes the chip as part of a larger system, she is led to gather information about the whole system and this may help her evaluate whether the system is demeaning or not. It depends on how her mother is treated during the surgical implantation, how the data is used by hospital staff, whether implantation means less human interaction with hospital personnel, and so on.

It may be that Kathy cannot do anything about the composition of the system; that is, her decision may be a matter of simply saying "yes" or "no" to the implant. But that yes/no decision can be made more wisely after the sociotechnical systems perspective reveals a range of options for hospital administrators and the systems developers. For example, if they find the device is being rejected because patients (or their loved ones) find it demeaning, they may be able to identify different nodes in the system where changes might be made. It may not be the chip itself that has to be changed or abandoned but rather a change in the implantation procedure, in the user interface, or in the training of hospital staff. Changes in one of these nodes will change the nature of the system and may alter perceptions or attitudes toward the system.

In summary, the sociotechnical systems perspective provides a richer account of situations in which ethical decisions are made, one that may help in articulating moral concerns as well as revealing additional avenues for addressing ethical questions and issues.

MICRO- AND MACRO-LEVEL ANALYSIS

One final distinction will set the scene for the next chapter. In ethics, a distinction is often made between macro- and micro-level analysis. Micro-level analysis focuses on individuals, their choices, and their behavior. In the scenario just discussed, Kathy Pascal is faced with a decision, a personal decision, and in this respect the scenario raises a micro-level question. What should Kathy do? What are her responsibilities? What factors should she take into account? By contrast, macro issues are generally focused on groups or organizations or even countries, and they are generally concerned with policies, rules, or systems. What should the hospital's policies and procedures be with respect to RFID devices? What privacy policies should the United States or the European Union adopt? Should employers monitor employee e-mail? Should software be proprietary?

This distinction is important as we identify, articulate, and answer ethical questions. However, the relationship between the two levels of analysis is complex. Issues at one level of analysis impact issues at another level. For example, in the Facebook scenario, we described Facebook at the macro level (that is, we described the Facebook company changing its policies) and then described a hypothetical situation that posed a micro ethical issue: What should Shawn do with information he finds on Facebook? Sometimes micro-level questions are answered by referring to a rule established at the macro level. For example, if we focus on an individual who breaks into a computer system and gains unauthorized access and ask the micro-level question whether the individual did anything wrong, we may answer that question simply by referring to a macro-level rule or law. The following sentence is an example of the interaction of micro and macro ethical analysis: "The hacker was wrong to gain unauthorized access because it is illegal."

Because the sociotechnical perspective frames technology as a system, it seems to draw more attention to macro-level issues. However, as we saw in our analysis of Kathy's situation, macro analysis enhances micro-level analysis. Thus, the sociotechnical systems perspective is compatible with, and useful to, both levels of analysis.

RETURN TO THE "WHY COMPUTER ETHICS?" QUESTION

We can now re-ask the "why computer ethics?" question: Why is a book (or course or field of study) focused on computer ethics needed? As was noted at the start, there are two questions here: Why a book on technology and ethics? Why a book specifically on computers or IT and ethics? Both questions can now be answered.

Technology is a part of human activity. It makes a difference in the way we live and act, it shapes the moral issues we confront and the courses of action (the options) that are available to us, and it affects the decisions we make, individually and collectively. The better we understand technology and how it shapes and is shaped by morality, the better our choices and decisions are likely to be. That is the answer to the first question. The second question arises because all technologies are not the same. Different technologies affect human activity and forms of life differently. The field of computer ethics focuses specifically on the role of IT in constituting the moral world. General studies of technology and ethics inform IT ethics, and IT ethics informs the broader study of technology and ethics. So the two work together.

Yet another question at the beginning of the chapter can now be addressed. What, we asked, is the relationship between "ethics" and "IT ethics"? Why isn't IT ethics just ethics? The sociotechnical systems perspective reveals that all social activities and practices are, in part at least, shaped by technology, so whether ethicists have recognized it or not, technology has, effectively, always played a role in moral practices and moral thought. Moral philosophy is focused on human action and social arrangements, and technology has always been intertwined with both. In this respect IT ethics is part of ethics, but in IT ethics we highlight and pay special attention to the role of IT as one of many elements that come into play in moral practices, decisions, and outcomes. Thus, it seems best to say that IT ethics is a subfield of ethics.

This particular subfield of ethics happens to be a lively scholarly area at the moment. Philosophers, computer scientists, sociologists, lawyers, and others are debating many issues surrounding IT and IT ethics. This book cannot adequately discuss all of the issues currently of interest in the literature. For example, a recent and intensely debated theory called "Information Ethics" insists that all information objects, including humans, should be afforded ethical respect because all information should be protected from entropy. If embraced, this theory would have broad-ranging implications for IT ethics. However, in this book, we will focus on more established ethical theories. [For those who want to follow the "information ethics" stream of analysis, L. Floridi's "Information ethics: On the philosophical foundation of computer ethics" *Ethics and Information Technology* 1: 37–56, 1999, is a good starting place.]

Conclusion

According to the standard account, ethical issues arise around IT because IT creates new possibilities for human action, and there is a vacuum of policies with regard to the new possibilities. The task of computer ethics is, then, to evaluate the new possibilities and fill the policy vacuums. A significant component of this task is addressing conceptual muddles. The standard account has been shown here not to be wrong but insufficient because it does not provide an account of distinctively "IT" ethical issues. It provides an account of how new technologies, in general, create ethical issues, and because IT is relatively new and new applications continue to evolve, IT falls under the account. The emphasis on newness was shown to be problematic for other reasons, as well. In particular, it puts the focus on IT when it is new and first introduced, and, thus, skews attention away from the ongoing role of the technology in structuring our moral conditions. Moreover, the standard account can blind us to the importance of the design of computer systems and, hence, to opportunities to change the moral conditions in various environments by changing the technology.

Drawing on insights from the field of STS, we have proposed an alternative account of IT ethics that we refer to as "sociotechnical IT ethics." Although sociotechnical IT ethics goes a long way toward supplementing the standard account and avoiding its pitfalls, the sociotechnical approach does not, by any means, make the task of IT ethics easy. The sociotechnical perspective emphasizes that the social and technological elements are interwoven, and it tells us that we are misleading ourselves if we think we can entirely disentangle these elements. This should make our conclusions more realistic and better informed, but it will also require more nuanced and sophisticated analysis.

Sociotechnical IT ethics has never, to our knowledge, been explicitly attempted on the scale of a book. In the chapters that follow we show that IT applications are sociotechnical systems, that is, combinations of software, hardware, and social practices, and that these combinations help to constitute the world in which human beings—individually and collectively—act. Viewing these systems as sociotechnical systems provides the foundation for richer analyses and more options for addressing ethical issues in IT.

Study Questions

1. What is encompassed in the question "why computer ethics?" In other words, what more specific questions are included in the broad question?
2. Give a concise summary of Moor's standard account of computer ethics.
3. What is a policy vacuum? Give an example, and explain it using the standard account.
4. What is a conceptual muddle, and how do they get in the way of filling policy vacuums? Illustrate with an example.
5. What is wrong with the standard account of computer ethics? Identify at least two criticisms, and explain.
6. What are the two tenets of the view referred to as "technological determinism"? What is the STS critique of each tenet?
7. What is wrong with thinking of technology as merely material objects?
8. What is a sociotechnical system?
9. Choose a familiar technology and describe its values.
10. What is the difference between micro-level ethical issues and macro-level ethical issues? Give an example of each.
11. Why is the study of ethics and technology needed? Why is the study of ethics, and IT in particular, needed?

CHAPTER 2

Ethics and Information Technology

INTRODUCTION: "DOING" ETHICS

In Chapter 1, we asked and answered the "why computer ethics?" question. Even though much of our attention there was on technology in general and not specifically on computers and IT, we can think of Chapter 1 as addressing the "computer" part of computer ethics. This chapter will address the "ethics" part.

The meaning of the term "ethics" is not easy to specify, and yet much of the controversy and skepticism about ethics seems to arise from ill-conceived notions of ethics. For example, some think of ethics as a set of rules that are universally binding on all people at all times; as such, they presume that moral rules must be derived from some sort of transcendental or higher authority, such as God or human nature or reason. Using this conception of ethics, it is easy to become skeptical when most attempts to identify the universally binding rules fail. Yet there are a variety of alternative approaches to ethics, approaches that have little to do with universal rules. Some emphasize right and wrong actions, others emphasize good and bad consequences, yet others emphasize virtue or justice. Moreover, a distinction should be made between theoretical and practical ethics. Theoretical ethics focuses on giving an account of morality, what it is, and how its claims are justified. Practical ethics draws on theoretical ethics, but is grounded in social practices and aims to understand, illuminate, and develop strategies for practical decision making.

The approach taken here is practical. Ethics is understood here to refer to a way of looking at human conditions and interactions using a set of concepts and theories that are distinctively normative. Ethics is a normative lens through which to view human arrangements, choices, and actions. [The meaning of the term "normative" will be explained further in a moment.]

We live in a world that requires making choices and acting. Our deliberations about how to act and what to choose often involve moral notions (right and wrong, loyalty, duty, justice, responsibility), ethical principles (do no harm, tell the truth, keep your promises), and ideas about what makes for a full and meaningful life (concern for others, community, friendship). In this book, we use analytical methods to illuminate the ethical aspects of situations and the ethical implications of deciding one way or another, or adopting one policy or another. In this way, we are framing computer ethics as a form of practical ethics. Although we draw on theoretical ethics, our primary interest is the ethical analysis of real situations, situations in which IT plays a role. As already mentioned, theoretical ethics is concerned with explaining the very idea of morality and with understanding the foundation of moral claims, typically universal moral claims. Our more modest goal here is to provide analysis that informs (although does not necessarily dictate) decision and action. The framework, concepts, and theories discussed here are intended to help readers think through situations that arise in the real world and reflect on what a better world would look like.

Sometimes the lens of ethics brings to light an aspect of a situation that seems to trump all other aspects. For example, suppose you are contemplating lying about a product that you are selling—say the product is a toy and you know that the paint on the toy contains a dangerous amount of lead. Here it would seem that no matter how you look at the situation—from the economic, legal, or cultural perspective—lying about the product seems wrong. Here ethics "trumps" all other aspects of the situation. Although this sometimes happens, not all situations are so clear. Often the ethical implications are intertwined with other dimensions of life—legal, economic, religious, political. Thus, the definition of ethics we will use here does not presuppose a priority to ethics. It does, nevertheless, presume that deliberation and action are better when the ethical aspects of a situation are taken into account.

The concepts and theories explained in this chapter come from a long history of philosophical thought. Philosophers have developed theories that explain the idea of morality, and have argued for various systems of ethical decision making. As with all fields, however, the state of understanding continues to change, with current ideas being contested, new ones offered, and the body of knowledge growing. This chapter scratches only the surface of a complex, heterogeneous, evolving body of knowledge. Although this chapter provides a quick sketch of ethical concepts and theories, our aim is to jump-start a dialogue on ethics that readers will continue in academic courses and throughout their lives, in their personal reflection, and in ongoing conversation with others.

Descriptive/Normative

The study of ethics is normative. When individuals or groups make decisions and act, the more they know about the state of the world, the better. However, having an accurate description of states of affairs in the world is only part of what is involved in acting wisely. Decisions and actions are aimed at the future. They are normative in the sense that they can go one way or another, and one chooses a direction when one acts. When one acts, one says, in effect, "this is what I want to happen" or "telling the truth will be better than lying" or "buying this television will make me happy" or "voting for Smith is more likely to lead to improvements in the city." These statements are all normative; they implicitly have to do with what is good/bad or better/worse or worthy/unworthy. So, although it is true that the more one understands the world in which one acts, the better decisions are likely to be, no matter how accurate one's understanding of the world, one ultimately has to make choices, and choices involve much more than the way the world is. Ethics has to do with steering one's life, making intentional choices, and contributing to the future. If you want to avoid doing harm and contribute to the improvement of human conditions, it is essential that you think about what constitutes a better condition, what makes for a better, more just, more peaceful, and more fulfilling world. In this respect, ethics is about ends. Moral actions, rules, principles, or guidelines are all aimed at achieving ends.

The distinction between descriptive and normative claims is important here although it is, by no means, simple. *Descriptive* statements are statements that *describe* a state of affairs in the world. For example: "The car is in the driveway"; "Georgia is south of Tennessee"; "XX percent of Chinese citizens have Internet access in their homes"; "XX percentage of traffic on the Web is to pornographic websites." These are all *empirical* claims in the sense that they can be verified or proven false by looking and seeing. Observations can be made, surveys can be administered, and individuals can be asked, although this isn't always easy to do. Consider the difficulties of verifying the following claim: "All societies consider some domain of life private, although which domain(s) of life is considered private varies a good deal from society to society." Verifying this claim would involve not only examining all societies, it would involve clarification as to what it means for a society to consider an area of life private. Nevertheless, the claim is descriptive; it is a claim about conditions in the world, conditions that can be examined to see whether the claim is accurate.

By contrast, normative claims are prescriptive and evaluative. Keeping with the above example, someone might claim: "Every society *should* keep some domains of life private." This is not an empirical claim; it cannot be verified by examining societies. The claim makes a recommendation and although empirical evidence might be brought in to support the claim, ultimately what *is* the case and what *ought to be* the case are different matters.

Social scientists gather empirical data and report their findings on a wide range of topics including moral attitudes and behavior. For example, psychologists and sociologists might identify the processes by which children develop moral concepts and sensibilities. Or they might measure how individuals value and prioritize various goods such as friendship, privacy, and autonomy. When anthropologists study a culture, they describe complex moral rules in the culture they observe. They are describing lived and observed moral systems. Similarly, historians may trace the development of a particular moral notion in an historical period. These historical and social scientific studies are descriptive; they examine morality as an empirical phenomenon. They do not, however, tell us what is right and wrong. They don't tell us what people *should* do, only what people, in fact, do. On the other hand, normative analysis deals with prescriptive and evaluative claims.

Earlier we said that the approach taken here is aimed at a kind of analysis that would be helpful in decision making and acting. That is precisely what normative analysis does. It is concerned with evaluating and critiquing states of affairs in search of ways to think about what was wrong or what would be better, a better state of affairs, better social arrangements, a better way to treat one another, ultimately to inform action. Ethical analysis is directed at human ends and goals—how we should treat one another, what constitutes justice and fairness, what we owe one another in virtue of being human, and when we should restrain our personal interests and desires. Making decisions, choosing, and setting policies are all intrinsically normative endeavors.

Normative claims cannot be supported simply by pointing to the facts about what individuals do or say or believe. Likewise, descriptive issues cannot be resolved by claims about what ought to be or what is just and fair. For example, although it is descriptively accurate to say that throughout human history some individuals have intentionally killed others, you probably wouldn't infer from this that it is okay for individuals to kill others when they choose (a normative claim). On the other hand, it is not uncommon to hear individuals justify the downloading of proprietary music on grounds that it is commonly done (even though it is illegal). Here there is what seems to be an invalid inference from a descriptive claim—"it is commonly done"—to a normative claim—"it's okay for me to do it." When we reflect on the reasoning here, it is difficult to see how the *descriptive* claim justifies the *normative* claim. The fact that individuals often engage in illegal behavior doesn't seem to tell us anything about whether the behavior is right or wrong.

On the other hand, the two kinds of claims often can be productively played off one another. Empirical information may be helpful in identifying ways of thinking about a normative issue. For example, exploring why individuals believe that downloading music is okay may provide some ideas that help to identify normative arguments or the moral principles at issue. Moreover, normative beliefs often influence which and what kind of empirical data we collect. For example, social scientists seek information about the degree to which citizens of various countries are using the Internet because they believe (normatively) that the spread of the Internet is an extremely important social phenomenon (that it is important for economic development, the spread of democracy, etc.).

Thus, although the goal in this book is to generate normative insights and analysis, we will use descriptive claims and evidence when it is helpful to do so. We will never, however, use a descriptive claim as the primary justification for a normative claim.

The Dialectic Method

How, you might now ask, does one "do" ethics? When it comes to describing moral beliefs and practices, we examine what people think and do, and gather and reflect on empirical information. However, facts and descriptions are not enough. Normative analysis generally involves identifying a principle or value, exploring what the principle or value implies, and making a case for a position. In practical ethics, this means connecting the principle or value to a particular situation, and considering arguments for various courses of action or decisions with regard to the situation. For example, in the virtual rape case described in Chapter 1, we might begin by trying to identify the behavior in question and link it to a moral concept. Rape is wrong but did Bungle or the person behind Bungle commit rape? If not, then what was the wrong? Can we think of the behavior as a violation of an implicit community standard? If so, then we would have to explain why community standards are so important. Or we might link the behavior to the harm associated with exposing individuals to sex and violence without warning them. If neither of these strategies work, then we have to find another way to characterize the behavior that connects it to a moral norm or principle.

Once a value or principle has been identified, ethical analysis proceeds with what is often referred to as a dialectic process. Here it is important to note that consistency and coherence are important tools for analysis. Using the dialectic method, normative claims are formulated into arguments. An argument is simply a claim and a set of reasons that justify the claim. Once arguments are formulated, they can be examined for their coherence, plausibility, and consistency, as well as for their fit with ordinary experience and relevant empirical information.

To understand the dialectic method, consider your own experience with discussions of ethical issues. You have probably witnessed, if not participated in, heated debates about euthanasia, abortion, affirmative action, and the distribution of wealth. Or consider discussions about downloading proprietary music, government surveillance of e-mail, or using robots to take care of the elderly. Often when individuals are asked to explain why they think a type of behavior or a policy is wrong, they have difficulty articulating their reasons. The first step in the dialectic process is to move from unreflective beliefs and gut feelings to claims that are connected to a value or principle that others are likely to accept. Unexamined claims can be the starting place for ethical analysis, but they are only starting places. Using the dialectic method, the reasons the individual has for making a claim have to be "put on the table." Why, we have to ask, would anyone claim that censorship is wrong, that downloading music isn't stealing, or that relying on robots to make decisions is dehumanizing?

If reasons for a moral belief cannot be put forward, then there can be no dialogue. More importantly, if an individual cannot give reasons for his or her moral beliefs or opinions, then it would seem there is nothing to recommend them. If I don't understand why you believe what you do, I have no "reason" to believe what you believe.

Discussions of ethical issues that stay at the level of statements of belief without reasons tend to end quickly with statements like "everyone is entitled to his or her own opinion." There is little point in talking about ethics in this way, except perhaps to see where others stand. The dialectic method proceeds by insisting that we each give reasons for our moral beliefs so that the reasons can be examined and critically evaluated.

The critical evaluation is often done in the context of trying to convince someone to reject a position, or to adopt another position, but it can also be done simply to explore a claim. When you critically evaluate the argument supporting a claim, you come to understand the claim more fully. A critical examination of the underpinnings of moral beliefs sometimes leads to a change in belief, but it may also simply lead to stronger and better-understood beliefs.

In the dialectic method, not only must you give reasons for your claims, you are also expected to be consistent from one argument or topic to the next. For example, instead of having separate, isolated views on abortion and capital punishment, the dialectic would lead you to recognize that both your views on abortion and your views on capital punishment rest on a claim about the value of human life and what abrogates it. If the claims appear to be inconsistent, then you should either change one of the claims or provide an account of how the two seemingly disparate positions are, in fact, consistent. In addition to moving from claims to reasons and arguments, and from one formulation of an argument to another, better formulation, the dialectic also moves back and forth from cases to principles or theory.

To illustrate the dialectic method, consider first a case that does not involve IT. Suppose you start out by making the claim that euthanasia is wrong. You articulate a principle as the reason for this claim. Say, for example, the principle is that human life has the highest value and, therefore, human life should never be intentionally ended. You might then test this principle by seeing how it applies in a variety of euthanasia cases. For example, is it wrong to use euthanasia when the person is conscious but in extreme pain? When the person is unconscious and severally brain damaged? When the person is terminally ill? When the person is young or elderly? Because your principle concerns the value of human life, it has implications beyond the issue of euthanasia. You might also test it by applying it to completely different types of cases. Is the intentional taking of human life wrong when it is done in a war situation? Is intentional killing wrong when it comes to capital punishment? Given your position on these cases, you may want to qualify the principle or hold to the principle and change your mind about the cases. For example, after seeing how the principle applies in various cases, you may want to qualify it so that you now assert that one should never intentionally take a human life *except* in self-defense or *except* when taking a life will save another life. Or you might reformulate the principle so that it specifies that the value of human life has to do with its quality. When the quality of life is significantly and permanently diminished, although it is still not permissible to intentionally kill, it is morally permissible to let a person die.

Whether the dialogue is inside your head (your own personal reflection), or a discussion with others, as it progresses, it leads to a more and more precise specification of the claim and its defense. The process clarifies what is at issue, and what the possible positions are. It moves from somewhat inchoate ideas to better and better arguments, and more defensible and better-articulated positions. Nevertheless, the dialectic does not always lead to a final and absolute conclusion. Nor will the dialogue necessarily lead to unanimous agreement among the discussants. Good dialecticians are always open to further discussion with the idea that even if you don't change your mind, every discussion is an opportunity to learn more, see another connection or aspect, and to hear another perspective.

We can illustrate the dialectic method further with a situation involving IT. Consider the following case described in a recent law journal article:

> On September 7, 2005, a former Delta Air Lines flight attendant filed a federal sexual discrimination lawsuit claiming that she was suspended and later fired because of material she posted on her personal blog. Ellen Simonetti was laid off after her "Queen of the Sky" blog showed a picture of her in her Delta uniform. The blog, a moderately fictionalized account of life in the air, never named Delta as her employer, but one photo did show a pin indicating she worked for the airline. Delta's decision to terminate her was based on "inappropriate photographs" of plaintiff in her uniform on the website. Ms. Simonetti claims that she was not aware of any company anti-blogging policy. According to a BBC News source, "there is guidance which suggests the company uniform cannot be used without approval from management, but use in personal pictures on websites is unclear."
>
> [T. Watson and E. Piro, "Bloggers beware: a cautionary tale of blogging and the doctrine of at-will employment" *Hofstra Labor & Employment Law Journal*, Winter, 2007]

In this case, the first step of linking the situation to a moral concept or theory may seem easy. What is at issue here is freedom of expression and censorship. The company (Delta) seems to want to prevent one of its employees from speaking freely (posting information); hence, it seems to be a case of interfering with freedom of expression. The company wants to censor its employee's blog. Once the case is linked to a concept, we have to explore the fit and see whether the concept can be used to illuminate, or even decide, the case. Is it a cut-and-dried case of an employer interfering with an employee's right to freedom of expression? Following this path, we would want to explore further the defense of freedom of expression. Do individuals have a right to freedom of expression? Why? Such a right might be defended by referring to legal rights. In the United States, this argument might be framed around the First Amendment. However, an argument might also be made that freedom of expression is a natural or human or moral right. Arguments have to be formulated and examined. Whatever way one goes on rights, the question that will come up is, "is the right absolute, or are there situations in which restrictions on free speech are justified?" One commonly noted case is that no one is allowed to yell "fire" in a crowded place. And, there are other domains in which free speech is restricted. Hate speech is a case in point.

One way or another, the dialectic is likely to move in the direction of employer–employee rights because employers do have the right to require their employees to sign agreements to keep trade secrets confidential, and they have the right to protect their reputation. Moreover, in U.S. law, employer–employee relationships are covered by what is called the "doctrine of at-will employment," which means that employers can fire employees with little cause. By moving the dialogue in this direction, the case is reframed as one that raises questions about the boundaries of employer–employee rights and obligations. In the law article from which the case is taken, the authors note that blogs are a new phenomenon so there are no legal precedents, but they seem skeptical that employee-bloggers will be protected from being fired for what they post on their blogs.

The dialogue can go in any number of directions, and our cursory look at euthanasia and blogging merely suggests how moral concepts and principles come into play and are then used to understand a situation and develop arguments.

As mentioned earlier, the dialectic method does not always lead to a definitive conclusion about what should be done or what precisely was wrong, but it almost always leads to better understanding. Thus, it is important to keep in mind at the onset that understanding can be improved and progress made, even when one has not reached absolute conclusions. Through the dialectic we learn which arguments are weaker and stronger, and why. We come to better understand the ideas that underpin our moral beliefs. We develop deeper and more consistent beliefs, and come to understand how moral ideas are interrelated and interdependent. The dialectic and the analysis show us what is at stake, help us to understand the values and interests relevant to various actors, and often help us to identify alternative forms of action or decision making.

When it comes to practical ethics, there seems no reason to believe that there is, or has to be, a single right answer to an ethical problem. Whitbeck (1998) argues that ethical problems are better understood on the model of design problems. When you give a design problem to multiple teams of engineers specifying the design requirements, you generally get different designs from each team. Even when you specify the features you want all designs to meet, engineers will creatively balance various factors against one another. Suppose you ask teams to design a car seat that meets regulatory requirements for safety, weighs no more than a specified amount, and costs no more than a certain amount to manufacture. Each team will come up with a different design, that is, using different materials, having a different shape, and with differing accessories. If we understand ethical decision making on the design model, there is no reason to believe that there is only one right way to act when one finds oneself in an ethical dilemma. On the other hand, it is important to note that thinking of ethical problems on the model of design problems does not lead to a free-for-all or anything-goes in ethics. As Whitbeck explains:

> Although no unique correct solution may exist, nonetheless, some possible responses are clearly unacceptable—there are wrong answers even if there is no unique right answer—and some solutions are better than others.

So it is with ethical issues. We may rule out some solutions to an ethical dilemma as utterly unacceptable. We may find a range of possible courses of action with varying advantages and disadvantages. We may not be able to identify a single action that is "the" right one or "the" morally obligatory one, and yet we can still conclude that we must do something. The dialectic process helps to sort out what actions are entirely unacceptable, and distinguish possible courses of action with various advantages and disadvantages.

As you will see in a moment, a familiarity with traditional moral concepts and theories will help in linking situations to moral concepts and theories and formulating reasons and arguments. Ethical theories provide frameworks in which arguments can be cast. Moreover, ethical theories provide common ground for discussion. They establish a common vocabulary and frameworks within which, or against which, ideas can be articulated. However, before introducing these concepts and theories, it will be helpful to further illustrate the dialectic method while exploring a notion that may come into play as you begin to think about and discuss ethical issues.

"Ethics Is Relative"

Many discussions of ethics begin with someone putting on the table the idea that "ethics is relative." Ethical beliefs depend, they claim, on what country you live in, where you were born, your age, or your personality. Claims of this type are also sometimes used to end debates about delicate issues such as abortion or euthanasia. That is, someone may conclude the discussion by saying: "everyone is entitled to his or her own opinion" or "I guess right and wrong depend on where you are sitting." Although seemingly simple, when subjected to the scrutiny of the dialectic method, claims of this kind turn out to be quite complex and perhaps confused. Hence, the "ethics is relative" claim is a good starting place to further illustrate the dialectic method.

To better understand what someone might have in mind when he or she claims that "ethics is relative," we can begin by using the descriptive–normative distinction drawn earlier. Is "ethics is relative" a descriptive or normative claim? What sort of justification might be given in each case? If "ethics is relative" is taken to be a descriptive claim, that is, a claim about what people think and do, then we can reformulate it into the following, more specific, claim: "ethical beliefs, rules, and practices vary from culture to culture and from time to time." Indeed, if this is what "ethics is relative" means, a good deal of evidence can be put forward to support it. Typically, three kinds of evidence are put forward in support:

1. At any given time (including the present), there is a great deal of variation in what particular individuals and groups consider right and wrong. For example, it is considered immoral for women to appear in public without their faces covered in some societies; what some consider to be bribery is common practice in certain places, an ordinary part of doing business; and polygamy is permissible in some cultures.

2. Moral norms vary over time so that what was considered wrong at one time, in a given society, may be considered right at another time. Slavery is a good example, as well as prohibitions on sex before marriage, and the use of physical force to punish children. The moral status of such practices has changed over time.

3. Moral beliefs seem to be largely influenced by when, where, how, and by whom one is raised. If I had been born in certain parts of the world, I might believe that it is wrong for a woman to appear in public without her face covered. Yet because I was raised in the United States in the twentieth century, by parents who had Western ideas about gender roles and public behavior, I do not believe this.

All three of these types of evidence are empirical claims that can be, and have been, substantiated by historians, anthropologists, sociologists, and psychologists. Although one might argue with a specific detail, in general the evidence seems strong, perhaps even undeniable. When "ethics is relative" is understood to be a descriptive claim, it seems to be highly plausible. Nevertheless, there are a number of ways we can put the claim to further testing through the dialectic method. One way is to press what the claim means or implies; another is to reformulate "ethics is relative" into a normative claim, and then see whether it is defensible as such.

Taking the first tack, we can press deeper, not by attacking the evidence but by questioning whether it supports the conclusion. In other words, one might wonder whether the diversity of belief shown by the evidence isn't superficial and misleading. Isn't it possible that universal norms underlie the seemingly disparate beliefs, rules, and practices? Universal norms may be at work in all human societies, but hidden from sight because they are expressed or interpreted in different ways in different contexts. General moral norms such as respect for human life or maximizing happiness might be operative, even though these general norms get expressed in different ways, at different times, and in different places. Anthropologists often draw attention to a seeming universal prohibition on incest although, of course, societies have very different ideas about kinship (i.e., which persons are forbidden as sexual partners). The point is that even if the "ethics is relative" claim is taken to be essentially a descriptive claim, it can be challenged and the dialectic method used to follow out the challenge. Are there any universal norms? How do we explain when individuals defy and rebel against their society's norms? How do moral norms change?

A second way to move the dialectic forward is to treat "ethics is relative" as a normative claim. In some sense, when we took the claim to be descriptive, it didn't seem to be a moral claim at all. That is, it didn't provide any recommendations or guidance as to how we "ought" to behave; it didn't give us a rule or principle that we have to use in making decisions. One way to reformulate "ethics is relative" into a normative claim is to interpret it to mean that "right and wrong *are* relative," that is, whatever is right or wrong is nonuniversal and depends on something like one's culture or when and where one is living. Here the claim might be comparable to: "what is right for you may not be right for me" or "when in Rome, do as the Romans." Sometimes ethical relativists (i.e., those who claim "ethics is relative") seem to assert that right and wrong are relative to the individual, and other times that right and wrong are relative to the society in which one lives. Each formulation would take the dialectic in a different direction.

Pursuing the latter alternative, "ethics is relative" would mean that what is morally right for me, an American living in the twenty-first century, differs from what is right for a person living in another country or in another time period. In other words, the claim seems to be that right and wrong are relative to one's society, and that one *should* act in conformance with the rules of one's society.

So our dialectic has led to a clear formulation of the claim, clear enough for it to be tested in the dialectic. When we turn a critical eye to this claim, it appears to be quite problematic. The claim that "one should act in conformance with the rules of one's society" runs into at least three serious problems.

First, although normative ethical relativists have a variety of ways to articulate and defend their claim, some versions of ethical relativism seem to slip into inconsistency and even self-contradiction. If normative ethical relativists say that right and wrong are relative to one's society, and mean by this that an individual is bound by the rules of his or her society and should follow the rules in their society, then the relativist seems to be asserting a universal moral principle. "Everyone," they claim, "ought to follow the norms of their society." So, if this is what relativists mean, they contradict the very claim they make: it is contradictory to say that ethics is relative *and* "everyone" ought to follow the same general principle. To be sure, ethical relativists can try to defend against this criticism, but notice that if they pull back from making any normative claim whatsoever, then it would seem they don't have an ethical theory at all, but merely a description of the variation in moral beliefs and practices.

Another potential inconsistency arises when one considers a common motive for making the relativistic claim. Some ethical relativists adopt ethical relativism because they are trying to stop what anthropologists call "ethnocentrism." Ethnocentrism refers to people from one culture using the standards of their own culture to judge (and likely condemn) the practices and people of another culture. Avoiding ethnocentrism means being tolerant and respectful of difference. It means appreciating the diversity and variety of beliefs and practices, including moral beliefs and practices. However, this stance against ethnocentrism is not exactly consistent with ethical relativism, at least not with normative ethical relativism. If you adopt the position that it is wrong to judge other cultures by the standards of your own, then you seem to be asserting a universal moral principle. You seem to be affirming one rule that goes beyond, or has special status beyond, all the others that you take to be relative. So, once again, it seems that there is something contradictory about normative ethical relativism, at least the versions we have considered.

Second, if the normative ethical relativist claim is that we ought to follow the rules of our society, then what is being claimed is antithetical to a good deal of human experience with moral heroes. Many of our most highly regarded moral heroes—Socrates, Martin Luther King, Ghandi, even Jesus, would, on this account, be considered wrong or bad because they did not follow the rules of their society. Adopting the normative claim that one should follow the rules of one's society seems to rule out resistance or rebellion in situations that are often considered tests of moral virtue.

Finally, the "ethics is relative" claim does not provide much help in making moral decisions, especially not with decisions in tough situations. Many ethical decisions are easy to make; we know we should keep our promises, avoid intentionally harming others, refrain from stealing, and so on. We tend to look to moral principles and theories when cultural practices are unclear or novel situations arise. Many of the most daunting and important ethical issues individuals and societies face are those arising from new technologies that create situations that humans haven't faced before—should I donate my organs for transplantation? Should we allow human cloning? Should ISPs filter child pornography and prevent their users from accessing it? These are precisely the kinds of ethical questions that cannot be decided by social convention because there are no absolute rules and practices that precisely apply. Thus, a moral principle that says right and wrong are relative or "you ought to do what is considered right in your society" just isn't very helpful.

Thus, although many other moves can be made in a dialectic about ethics, the versions of "ethics is relative" that we have considered do not seem plausible. You can now take the dialectic in another direction.

Because we have not drawn a definitive conclusion, it is important to point out that we have made progress. We have clarified the claim that "ethics is relative" by distinguishing a descriptive interpretation and a normative interpretation. We have examined evidence put forward to support the descriptive claim, and have evaluated the evidence. We have identified three problems with a normative interpretation of "ethics is relative." As a normative claim, it seems to be self-contradictory; it seems inconsistent with our ideas about moral heroes, and doesn't seem to provide the kind of guidance we often seek from ethical theories. Most importantly, we have illustrated the dialectic method that we will continue to use throughout this book.

ETHICAL THEORIES AND CONCEPTS

We turn now to several moral theories that have stood the test of time in moral philosophy. They provide frameworks and vocabulary for engaging in the dialectic process, although they are themselves subject to the scrutiny of the dialectical method. None of these theories is meant to provide an algorithm for ethical decision making; rather they provide modes of thinking, tools to use in analyzing ethical issues.

Utilitariansim

Utilitarianism is an ethical theory claiming that what makes behavior right or wrong depends wholly on the consequences. For this reason it is also often classified as a form of "consequentialism." In putting the emphasis on consequences, utilitarianism affirms that what is important about human behavior is the outcome or results of the behavior and not the intention a person has when he or she acts. In one version of utilitarianism, what is all important is happiness-producing consequences. Crudely put, actions are good when they produce happiness and bad when they produce the opposite, unhappiness. The term *utilitarianism* derives from the word *utility*. According to utilitarianism, actions, rules, or policies are good because of their usefulness (their utility) in bringing about good consequences.

According to the version of utilitarianism that we will use, individuals should adhere to a basic principle: *Everyone ought to act so as to bring about the greatest amount of happiness for the greatest number of people.* Following the dialectic method, we should now ask: What, if any, support can be given for this theory? Why should we act to bring about the greatest amount of happiness? Why shouldn't we each seek our own interest? Utilitarianism has an answer.

Intrinsic and Instrumental Value

Utilitarians begin by focusing on values and asking what is so important, so valuable to human beings, that we could use it to ground an ethical theory. They note that among all the things that human beings seem to value, we can distinguish things that are valued because they lead to something else from things that are valued for their own sake. The former are called *instrumental* goods and the latter *intrinsic* goods. Money is a classic example of something that is instrumentally good. It is not valuable for its own sake, but rather has value as a means for acquiring other things. On the other hand, intrinsic goods are not valued because they are a means to something else; they are valuable in themselves. Knowledge is sometimes said to be intrinsically valuable. So is art because of its beauty. You might also think about environmental debates in which the value of nature or animals or plant species or ecosystems are said to be valuable independent of their value to human beings. The claim is that these things have value independent of their utility to human beings.

Having drawn this distinction between instrumental and intrinsic goods, utilitarians ask what is so valuable that it could ground a theory of right and wrong? It has to be something intrinsically valuable, because something that is instrumentally valuable is dependent for its goodness on whether it leads to another good. If you want x because it is a means to y, then y is what is truly valuable and x has only secondary or derivative value.

The version of utilitarianism on which we are focusing claims that happiness is the ultimate intrinsic good, because it is valuable for its own sake. Happiness cannot be understood as simply a means to something else. Indeed, some utilitarians claim that everything else is desired as a means to happiness and that, as a result, everything else has only secondary or derivative (instrumental) value. To see this, take any activity that people engage in, and ask why they do it. Each time you will find that the sequence of questions ends with happiness. Take, for example, your career choice. Suppose that you have chosen to study computer science so as to become a computer professional. Why do you want to be a computer professional? Perhaps you believe that you have a talent for computing, and believe you will be able to get a well-paying job in computer science—one in which you can be creative and somewhat autonomous. Then we must ask, why are these things important to you? That is, why is it important to you to have a career doing something for which you have a talent? Why do you care about being well paid? Why do you desire a job in which you can be creative and autonomous? Suppose that you reply by saying that being well paid is important to you because you want security or because you like to buy things or because there are people who are financially dependent on you. In turn, we can ask about each of these. Why is it important to be secure? Why do you want security or material possessions? Why do you want to support your dependents? The questions will continue until you point to something that is valuable in itself and not for the sake of something else. It seems that the questions can stop only when you say you want whatever it is because you believe it will make you happy. The questioning stops here because it doesn't seem to make sense to ask why someone wants to be happy.

Utilitarians claim that any discussion of what you should seek in life, and what is valuable, will not stop until you get to happiness. Will a career as a computer professional make you happy? Will it really bring security? Will security or material possessions, in fact, make you happy? Such discussions always center on whether or not one has chosen the correct means to happiness. The value of happiness isn't questioned because happiness is intrinsically good.

So, when a person is faced with a decision about what to do, the person should consider possible courses of action, predict the consequences of each alternative, and *choose that action which brings about the most good consequences, that is, the most happiness*. The utilitarian principle provides a rough decision procedure. When you are choosing between courses of action, the right action is the one that produces the most overall net happiness (happiness minus unhappiness). To be sure, the right action may be one that brings about some unhappiness, but that is justified if the action also brings about so much happiness that the unhappiness is outweighed, or as long as the action has the least net unhappiness of all the alternatives.

Be careful not to confuse utilitarianism with *egoism*. Egoism is a theory that specifies that one should act so as to bring about the greatest number of good consequences for one's self. What is good is what makes "me" happy or gets me what I want. Utilitarianism does not say that you should maximize your own good. Rather, total happiness is what is at issue. Thus, when you evaluate your alternatives, you have to ask about their effects on the happiness of everyone. This includes effects on you, but your happiness counts the same as the happiness of others. It may turn out to be right for you to do something that will diminish your own happiness because it will bring about a marked increase in overall happiness.

The decision-making process proposed in utilitarianism seems to be at the heart of a good deal of social decision making. That is, legislators and public policy makers seem to seek policies that will produce good consequences, and they often opt for policies that may have some negative consequences but will, on balance, bring about more good (consequences) than harm (bad consequences). At the core, cost–benefit or risk–benefit analyses are utilitarian. Benefits are weighed against risks. For example, if a community were considering whether to allow a new waste disposal plant to be built in their area, the community would weigh the benefits of having the plant there against the risk of harm and other negative consequences to all those who would be affected.

Acts versus Rules

Because of disagreements on important details, philosophers have formulated different versions of utilitarianism. One important and controversial issue has to do with whether the focus should be on *rules* of behavior or individual *acts*. Utilitarians have recognized that it would be counter to overall happiness if each one of us had to calculate at every moment what all the consequences of every one of our actions would be. Not only is this impractical, because it is time consuming and sometimes we must act quickly, but often the consequences are impossible to foresee. Thus, there is a need for general rules to guide our actions in ordinary situations.

Rule-utilitarians argue that we ought to adopt rules that, if followed by everyone, would, in the long run, maximize happiness. Take, for example, telling the truth. If individuals regularly told lies, it would be very disruptive. You would never know when to believe what you were told. In the long run, a rule obligating people to tell the truth has enormous beneficial consequences. Thus, "tell the truth" becomes a utilitarian moral rule. "Keep your promises," and "Don't reward behavior that causes pain to others," are also rules that can be justified on utilitarian grounds. According to rule-utilitarianism, if the rule can be justified in terms of the consequences that are brought about from people following it, then individuals ought to follow the rule.

Act-utilitarians put the emphasis on individual actions rather than rules. They believe that even though it may be difficult for us to anticipate the consequences of our actions, that is what we should try to do. Take, for example, a case where lying may bring about more happiness than telling the truth. Say you are told by a doctor that tentative test results indicate that your spouse *may* be terminally ill. You know your spouse well enough to know that this knowledge, at this time, will cause your spouse enormous stress. He or she is already under a good deal of stress because of pressures at work and because someone else in the family is very ill. To tell your spouse the truth about the test results will cause more stress and anxiety, and this stress and anxiety may turn out to be unnecessary if further tests prove that the spouse is not terminally ill. Your spouse asks you what you and the doctor talked about. Should you lie or tell the truth? An act-utilitarian might say that the right thing to do in such a situation is to lie, for little good would come from telling the truth and a good deal of suffering (perhaps unnecessary suffering) will be avoided from lying. A rule-utilitarian would agree that good might result from lying in this one case, but in the long run, if we cannot count on people telling the truth (especially our spouses), more bad than good will come. Think of the anxiety that might arise if spouses routinely lied to one another. Thus, according to rule-utilitarians, we must uphold the rule against lying; it is wrong to lie.

Act-utilitarianism treats rules simply as "rules of thumb," general guidelines to be abandoned in situations where it is clear that more happiness will result from breaking them. Rule-utilitarians, on the other hand, take rules to be strict. They justify moral rules in terms of the happiness consequences that result from people following them. If a rule is justified, then an act that violates the rule is wrong.

In either case, it should be clear that the utilitarian principle can be used to formulate a decision procedure for figuring out what you should do in a situation. In fact, utilitarians propose that the utilitarian principle be used to decide the laws of a society. Or they point out that the laws we currently have can be justified on utilitarian grounds. Prohibitions on stealing, killing, breaking contracts, and fraud, for example, are justified because of their consequences for human well being. Utilitarianism is also often used as a principle for evaluating the laws that we have. If a law is not producing good consequences, or is producing a mixture of good and bad effects, and we know of another approach that will produce better net effects, then that information provides the grounds for changing the law. Punishment is a good example of a social practice that can be evaluated in terms of its utility. According to utilitarianism, because punishment involves the imposition of pain, if it does not produce some good consequences, then it is not justified. Typically utilitarians focus on the deterrent effect of punishment as the good consequence counterbalancing the pain involved.

Although we cannot pursue the link here, it is worth noting that utilitarianism might be used to return to our earlier discussion of "ethics is relative" because utilitarianism might be thought of as capturing part of the idea of relativism. Because the theory claims that the right thing to do depends on the consequences *and* because the same action performed in one context or set of circumstances may produce quite different consequences in another context, utilitarianism seems to allow that the right thing will vary with the context. For example, although in general more good may result from telling the truth, lying may be better in certain circumstances. Even rule-utilitarians must admit that the rules that will produce the most happiness may vary from situation to situation. A simple example would be to imagine that in a natural environment in which water is scarce, a moral prohibition on using water in swimming pools or to water lawns would be justified. On the other hand, in a natural environment in which water is abundant, such a rule would not be justified. So, even though utilitarians assert a universal principle, the universal principle is compatible with varying laws and moral practices at different times or in different places.

Now that the fundamentals of utilitarianism have been explained, it is worth remembering, once again, that we are engaged in a dialectic process. We have described the idea of utilitarianism and have made a case for the theory. The theory has been "put on the table," so to speak. Even though it has been developed only in its most rudimentary form, the theory can be put to the test of critical evaluation.

Critique of Utilitarianism

One of the most important criticisms of utilitarianism is that when it is applied to certain cases, it seems to go against some of our most strongly held moral intuitions. In particular, it seems to justify imposing enormous burdens on some individuals for the sake of others. According to utilitarianism, every person is to be counted equally. No one person's unhappiness or happiness is more important than another's.

However, because utilitarians are concerned with the total amount of happiness, we can imagine situations where great overall happiness might result from sacrificing the happiness of a few. Suppose, for example, that having a small number of slaves would create great happiness for a large number of individuals. The individuals who were made slaves would be unhappy, but this would be counterbalanced by significant increases in the happiness of many others. This seems to be justifiable (if not obligatory) in a utilitarian framework. Another more contemporary example is to imagine a situation in which by killing one person and using all his or her organs for transplantation, we would be able to save ten lives. Killing one to save ten would seem to maximize good consequences. Critics of utilitarianism argue that because utilitarianism justifies such practices as slavery and killing of the innocent, it has to be wrong. It is, therefore, unacceptable as an account of morality.

In defending the theory from this criticism, utilitarians can argue that utilitarianism does not justify such unsavory practices. Critics, they may argue, are forgetting the difference between short-term and long-term consequences. Utilitarianism is concerned with all the consequences, and when long-term consequences are taken into account, it becomes clear that practices such as slavery and killing innocent people to use their organs could never be justified. In the long run, such practices have the effect of creating so much fear in people that net happiness is diminished rather than increased. Imagine the fear and anxiety that would prevail in a society in which anyone might at any time be taken as a slave. Or imagine the reluctance of anyone to go to a hospital if there was even a remote possibility that they might be killed if they happen to be at the hospital at a time when a major accident occurred and organs were needed to save many victims. Thus, the good effects of practices of this kind could never counterbalance the long-term bad effects.

Other utilitarians boldly concede that there are going to be some circumstances in which what seem to be repugnant practices should be accepted because they bring about consequences having a greater net good than would be brought about by other practices, that is, because they are consistent with the principle of utility. So, for example, according to these utilitarians, if there are ever circumstances in which slavery would produce more good than ill, then slavery would be morally acceptable. These utilitarians acknowledge that there may be circumstances in which some people should be sacrificed for the sake of total happiness. The current debate about the use of torture to extract information that might prevent events such as terrorist attacks fits this form of analysis. Although most agree that torture is bad, some argue that the bad is counterbalanced by the good consequences that may result. Others argue that in the long-run it does more harm even to the torturing country because it means that their soldiers are more likely to be tortured if torture becomes a common practice. Still others argue that tortured prisoners are likely to say anything at all during torture, and that makes intelligence gathered during torture largely useless because the truth must still be sifted out from the lies.

In dialectic analysis, it is important to pick up on our strongly held moral intuitions because they are often connected to a moral principle or theory. In the case of utilitarianism, the intuition that slavery is always wrong (or that it is wrong to kill the innocent for the sake of some greater good) hints at something missing in utilitarianism and points in an alternative direction. A concrete case will help us further understand utilitarianism and introduce an alternative theory, one that captures the moral intuition about the wrongness of slavery and killing the innocent.

Case Illustration

Not long ago, when medical researchers had just succeeded in developing the kidney dialysis machine, a few hospitals acquired a limited number of these expensive machines. Hospitals soon found that the number of patients needing treatment on the machines far exceeded the number of machines they had available or could afford. Decisions had to be made as to who would get access to the machines, and these were often life–death decisions. In response, some hospitals set up internal review boards composed of medical staff and community representatives. These boards were to decide which patients should get access to the dialysis machines. The medical condition of each patient was taken into account, but the decisions were additionally made on the basis of the personal and social characteristics of each patient: age, job, number of dependents, social usefulness of job, whether the person had a criminal record, and so on. The review committees appeared to be using utilitarian criteria. The resource— kidney dialysis machines—was scarce, and they wanted to maximize the benefit (the good consequences) of the use of the machines. Thus, those who were most likely to benefit and to contribute to society in the future would get access. Individuals were given a high ranking for access to the machines if they were doctors (with the potential to save other lives), if they had dependents, if they were young, and so on. Those who were given lower priority or no priority for access to the machines were those who were so ill that they were likely to die even with treatment, those who were older, those who were criminals, those without dependents, and so on.

As the activities of the hospital review boards became known to the public, they were criticized. Critics argued that your value as a person cannot be measured by your value to the community. The review boards were valuing individuals on the basis of their *social* value, and this seemed dangerous. Everyone, it was argued, has value in and of themselves.

The critique of this distribution method implied a principle that is antithetical to utilitarianism. It suggested that each and every person, no matter what their lot in life, has value and should be respected. To treat individuals as if they are a means to some social end seems the utmost in disrespect. And, that is exactly what a policy of allocating scarce resources according to social value does. It says, in effect, that people have value only as a means to the betterment of society, and by that criteria some individuals are much more valuable than others.

In an ideal world, more kidney dialysis machines would be produced so that no one would have to do without. At the time, this was impossible (as it is now for other types of medical treatment). Because decisions had to be made, the critics of distributing access to kidney dialysis machines on the basis of social utility proposed that access should be distributed by means of a lottery that included all of those in need. In a lottery, everyone has an equal chance; everyone counts the same. This, they argued, was the only fair method of distribution.

The unfairness of the utilitarian distribution is important because it goes to the heart of the theory. Oddly, although the theory treats each individual's happiness as equal, when overall or net happiness is determined by adding up and balancing bad against good consequences, some individual's unhappiness turns out to be dispensable for the sake of the happiness of others. Critics argue that people are valuable in themselves, not for their contribution to overall happiness. They argue that utilitarianism leads to imposing an unfair burden on some individuals; it treats some individuals as means to the good of others.

Before we explore an alternative to utilitarianism, we should note that utilitarianism goes a long way in providing a reasoned and comprehensive account of many of our moral notions. It is not a theory to be dismissed lightly. Consequences seem an important element in moral reasoning and in moral practices. However, we turn now to an ethical theory that articulates the reasoning underlying the critique of utilitarianism.

Deontological Theory

In utilitarianism, what makes an action right or wrong is outside the action; it is the consequences, effects, or results of the action. By contrast, deontological theories put the emphasis on the internal character of the act itself.[1] What makes an action right or wrong for deontologists is the principle inherent in the action. If an action is done from a sense of duty, if the principle of the action can be universalized, then the action is right. For example, if I tell the truth (not just because it is convenient for me to do so, but) because I recognize that I must respect the other person, then I act from duty and my action is right. If I tell the truth because either I fear getting caught or believe I will be rewarded for doing so, then my act is not morally worthy.

We will focus here on the theory of Immanuel Kant. Referring back to the allocation of dialysis machines, Kant's moral theory justifies distribution by a lottery, or at least *not* by social value. In Kant's philosophy, one must always act according to the categorical imperative. The categorical imperative specifies that we should *never treat human beings merely as means to an end*. We should *always treat human beings as ends in themselves*. Utilitarianism is criticized because it appears to tolerate sacrificing some people for the sake of others. In utilitarianism, right and wrong depend on the consequences and therefore vary with the circumstances. By contrast, deontological theories assert that there are some actions that are always wrong, no matter what the consequences. A good example of this is killing. Even though we can imagine situations in which intentionally killing one person may save the lives of many others, deontologists insist that intentional killing is always wrong. Killing is wrong even in extreme situations because it means using the victim merely as a means and does not treat the human being as valuable in and of him- or herself.

Yes, deontologists recognize self-defense and other special circumstances as sometimes excusing killing, but these are cases when, it is argued, the killing isn't

---

[1] The term "deontology" derives from the Greek words deon (duty) and logos (science). Etymologically, then, deontology means the science of duty.

intentional. In their defense someone might say: "The person attacked me; I had no other choice but to defend myself. After all, I too am of value; I did not aim at the attacker's death, I aimed only to stop the attack."

At the heart of deontological theory is an idea about what it means to be a person, and this is connected to the idea of moral agency. Charles Fried (1978) put the point as follows:

> [T]he substantive contents of the norms of right and wrong express the value of persons, of respect for personality. What we may not do to each other, the things which are wrong, are precisely those forms of personal interaction which deny to our victim the status of a freely choosing, rationally valuing, specially efficacious person, the special status of moral personality. (pp. 28–29)

According to deontologists, the utilitarians go wrong when they fix on happiness as the highest good. Deontologists point out that happiness cannot be the highest good for humans. The fact that we are rational beings, capable of reasoning about what we want to do and then deciding and acting, suggests that our end (our highest good) is something other than happiness. Humans differ from all other things in the world insofar as we have the capacity for rationality. The behavior of other things is determined simply by laws of nature. Plants turn toward the sun because of photosynthesis. They don't think and decide which way they will turn. Physical objects fall by the law of gravity. Water boils when it reaches a certain temperature. In contrast, human beings have the capacity to legislate for themselves. We decide how we will behave. As Kant describes this, it is the difference between behavior that is determined by the laws of nature, that is, acting in accordance with law (as plants and stones do) *and* acting in accordance with *the conception* of law. Only human beings are capable of the latter.

The capacity for rational decision making is the most important feature of human beings. Each of us has this capacity; each of us can make choices—choices about what we will do, and what kind of persons we will become. No one else can or should make these choices for us. Moreover, we should respect this capacity in others.

Notice that it makes good sense that our rationality is connected with morality, because we could not be moral beings at all unless we had this rational capacity. We do not think of plants or fish or dogs and cats as moral beings precisely because they do not have the full capacity to reason about their actions. We are moral beings because we have the capacity to give ourselves rules (laws) and follow them. [Some may dispute that dogs and cats are without rational capacity; they may claim that dogs and cats and other nonhumans have the ability to conform to a conception of law. The dialectic could go off here in the direction of considering whether the rational capacity required for morality can come in degrees.]

Where utilitarians note that all humans seek happiness, deontologists emphasize that humans are creatures with goals who engage in activities directed toward achieving these goals (ends), and that they use their rationality to formulate their goals and figure out what kind of life to live. In a sense, deontologists pull back from fixing on any particular value as structuring morality and instead ground morality in the capacity of each individual to organize his or her own life, make choices, and engage in activities to realize their self-chosen life plans. What morality requires is that we respect each of these beings as valuable in themselves, and refrain from valuing them only insofar as they fit into our own life plans. In other words, morality requires that we don't treat others merely as a means to our own ends.

As mentioned before, Kant's moral philosophy centers around what he called the *categorical imperative*. Although he puts forward three versions of it, we have focused on the second version: *Never treat another human being merely as a means but always as an end*. This general rule is derived from the idea that persons are moral beings because they are rational, efficacious beings. Because we each have the capacity to think and decide and act for ourselves, we should each be treated in ways that recognize this capacity. This is precisely what it means to respect a person.

Note the "merely" in the categorical imperative. Deontologists do not insist that we never use another person as a means to an end, only that we never "merely" use them. For example, if I own a company and hire employees to work in my company, I might be thought of as using my employees as a means to my end (i.e., the success of my business). This, however, is not a violation of the categorical imperative so long as I treat the employees as ends in themselves, which involves paying them a fair wage, being honest about the dangers of the work environment, evaluating their work fairly, and so on. In these ways I respect my employees' abilities to choose for themselves whether they want to work for me and under what conditions. What would be wrong would be to take them as slaves and coerce them to work for me. It would also be wrong to pay them so little that they must borrow from me and remain always in my debt. This would be exploitation. This would show disregard for the value of each person as a "freely choosing, rationally valuing, specially efficacious person." Similarly, it would be wrong for me to lie to employees about the conditions of their work. Suppose, for example, that while working in my plant, employees will be exposed to dangerous, cancer-causing chemicals. I know this but don't tell the employees because I am afraid they will quit. In not being forthcoming with this information, I am, in effect, manipulating the employees to serve my ends. I am not recognizing them as beings of value with their own life-plans and the capacity to choose how they will live their lives.

Case Illustration

Although utilitarianism and Kantian theory were contrasted in the case illustration about the allocation of scarce medical resources, another case will clarify this even more. Consider a case involving computers. Suppose a professor of sociology undertakes research on attitudes toward sex and sexual behavior among high school students. Among other things, she interviews hundreds of high school students concerning their attitudes and behavior. She knows that the students will never give her information unless she guarantees them confidentiality, so before doing the interviews, she promises each student that she alone will have access to the raw interview data, and that all publishable results will be reported in statistical form. Thus, it would be impossible to correlate information in the study with particular students.

Suppose, however, that it is now time to code the interview data, and she realizes that it will be much easier to have graduate student assistants do this rather than doing it herself. She wonders whether she should let the graduate students handle the raw data. Should she allow the graduate assistants to code and process the data? In a utilitarian analysis, the professor would weigh the good consequences that will come from the research (and especially from getting the results out quickly) versus the possible harm to her subjects and herself if the graduate students leak information about individual students. The research will provide important information to people working with high school students and may help the professor's career to prosper. Still, she has explicitly promised confidentiality to the student–subjects and has to worry about the effects on her credibility as a social researcher, and on social science research in general, if she breaks her promise. Her subjects, and many others, may be reluctant in the future to trust her and other social scientists if she breaks the promise and information on individual interviewees leaks out. Moreover, the benefits of getting the research done quickly may be marginal.

From a utilitarian perspective, then, it would seem that the professor should not violate her promise of confidentiality. Fortunately, there are ways to code data before graduate students handle it. As well, there are many steps she can take to ensure that the graduate students are well informed about the confidentiality of the data and the consequences of their leaking information about individuals.

Interestingly, a deontologist is likely to come to the same conclusion, although the reasoning would be quite different. On a deontological analysis, the important question is not whether good and bad consequences will result from assuring the confidentiality of the data, but whether the professor treats her subjects merely as means to her end of developing new knowledge and advancing her own career. Is she recognizing the student–subjects as ends in themselves? Clearly, were she to ignore her promise of confidentiality to the students, she would not be treating them as ends. Each student decided for him- or herself whether to participate in the study, and each made his or her choice based on the professor's pledge of confidentiality. She would be treating them merely as means if she were to break her promise when it suited her. Thus, out of respect for the subjects, the sociologist must ensure the confidentiality of the data and either handle the raw data herself, or put procedures in place that will ensure that graduate students keep what they see confidential. Indeed, they should be told that the consequences of revealing confidential data will be severe.

The two theories do not, then, come to very different conclusions in this case. However, the analysis is different, that is, the reasons for keeping the data confidential are distinctive. Thus, it isn't hard to imagine that the theories lead to dramatically different conclusions in other cases.

Only the bare bones of each theory have been presented. The dialectic could go off in any number of directions here. However, in the interest of getting to the issues surrounding computers and information technology, we must move on and put a few more important ideas "on the table."

Rights

So far, very little has been said about rights, although we often use the language of rights when discussing moral issues. "You have no right to say that to me." "My boss has no right to tell me what to do on the weekends." Ethicists often associate rights with deontological theories. The categorical imperative requires that each person be treated as an end in him- or herself, and it is possible to express this idea by saying that individuals have "a right to" the kind of treatment that is implied in being treated as an end. The idea that each individual must be respected as valuable in him- or herself implies certain rights, for example, a right not to be killed or enslaved, a right to be told whether we are going to be used in research, a right to make decisions about how we will live our lives, and so on.

An important distinction that philosophers often make here is between negative rights and positive rights. Negative rights are rights that require restraint by others. For example, my right not to be killed requires that others refrain from killing me. It does not, however, require that others take positive action to keep me alive. Positive rights, on the other hand, imply that others have a duty to do something to, or for, the right holder. So, if we say that I have a positive right to life, this implies not just that others must refrain from killing me, but that they must do such things as feed me if I am starving, give me medical treatment if I am sick, swim out and save me if I am drowning, and so on. As you can see, the difference between negative and positive rights is quite significant.

Positive rights are more controversial than negative rights because they have implications that are counterintuitive. If every person has a positive right to life, this seems to imply that each and every one of us has a duty to do whatever is necessary to keep all people alive. This would seem to suggest that, among other things, it is our duty to give away any excess wealth that we have to feed and care for those who are starving or suffering from malnutrition. It also seems to imply that we have a duty to supply extraordinary life-saving treatment for all those who are dying. In response to these implications, some philosophers have argued that individuals have only negative rights.

Although, as I said earlier, rights are often associated with deontological theories, it is important to note that rights can be derived from other theories as well. For example, we can argue for the recognition of a right to property on utilitarian grounds. Suppose we ask why individuals should be allowed to have private property in general and, in particular, why they should be allowed to own software. As we will see in Chapter 5, utilitarians argue for proprietary rights in software on grounds that much more, and better, software will be created if the individuals who create it are allowed to own (and then license or sell) it. Thus, they argue that individuals should have a legal right to ownership of software because of the beneficial consequences of creating such a right.

So, rights can be grounded in different theoretical frameworks. Distinctions also have to be made between legal, moral, natural, and human rights. Legal rights are rights created by law. Moral, natural, or human rights are claims independent of law and grounded in theories that pertain to morality, nature, or what it means to be a human being, respectively. The important point to remember is that whenever an argument is framed in terms of rights, it is a good idea to identify what kind of right is being claimed, and what theory underlies the rights-claim.

Rights and Social Contract Theory

The idea that individuals have fundamental "rights" is deeply rooted in social contract theory. In this tradition, a social contract (between individuals, or between individuals and government) is hypothesized to explain and justify the obligations that human beings have to one another. Many of these theories imagine human beings in a state of nature, and then show that reason would lead individuals in such a state to agree to live according to certain rules, or to give power to a government to enforce certain rules. Theorists depict the state of nature (without government or civil society) as a state of insecurity and uncertainty. Thomas Hobbes, for example, describes the state of nature as "solitary, poor, nasty, brutish, and short" (The Leviathan). The state of nature is so miserable that rational human beings would agree (make a contract) to join forces with others and give up some of their natural freedom in exchange for the benefits of cooperation. They would agree to abide by rules and refrain from certain actions in exchange for others doing the same.

Arguments of this kind are made by several social contract theorists and each specifies the nature and limits of the obligations incurred differently. One important difference, for example, is in whether morality exists prior to the social contract. Hobbes argues that there is no justice or injustice in a state of nature; humans are at war with one another, and each individual must do what they must to preserve themselves. John Locke, on the other hand, specifies a natural form of justice in the state of nature. Human beings have rights in the state of nature and others can treat individuals unjustly. Government is necessary to insure that natural justice is implemented properly because without government, there is no certainty that punishments will be distributed justly.

In 1971, John Rawls introduced a new version of social contract theory in a book entitled simply, *A Theory of Justice*. The theory may well be one of the most influential moral theories of the twentieth century, because not only did it generate an enormous amount of attention in the philosophical community, it influenced discussion among economists, social scientists, and public policy makers.

Rawls was primarily interested in questions of distributive justice. In the tradition of a social contract theorist, he tries to understand what sort of contract between individuals would be just. He recognizes that we cannot arrive at an account of justice, and the fairness of social arrangements, by reasoning about what rules particular individuals would agree to. He understands that individuals are self-interested, and therefore will be influenced by their own experiences and situation when they think about fair arrangements. Thus, if some group of us were to get together in something like a state of nature (suppose a group is stranded on an island, or a nuclear war occurs and only a few survive), the rules we would agree to would not necessarily be just.

The problem is that we would each want rules that would favor us. Smart people would want rules that favored intelligence. Strong people would want a system that rewarded physical strength. Women and other historically disadvantaged groups would want to make sure that rules weren't biased against their group, and so on. The point is that the outcome of a negotiation would likely be distorted by past injustices, or arbitrary factors, in the preferences of particular individuals. Thus, Rawls seeks a better way to get at justice.

He asks us to imagine individuals who are behind a veil of ignorance getting together to decide on the rules of society. He refers to this as the original position, and structures the original position so that individuals are rational and self-interested but behind a veil of ignorance. The veil of ignorance is such that individuals do not know what their personal characteristics will be. They don't know whether they will be male or female, black or white, high IQ or low IQ, physically strong or weak, musically talented, successful at business, and so on. At the same time, these individuals will be rational and self-interested and know something about human nature and human psychology. In a sense, what Rawls suggests here is that we have to imagine *generic* human beings. They have the abstract features of all human beings in that they are rational and self-interested, and they have general knowledge about how humans behave and interact and how they are affected in various ways, but they have no specific knowledge about who they are or will be when they emerge from behind the veil of ignorance.

According to Rawls, justice is what individuals in the original position would agree to. Justice *is* what people would choose when they are rational and self-interested, informed about human nature and psychology, but behind a veil of ignorance with regard to their own characteristics. Rawls argues that two rules would be agreed to in the original position:

1. Each person should have an equal right to the most extensive basic liberty compatible with a similar liberty for others.
2. Social and economic inequalities should be arranged so that they are both (a) reasonably expected to be to everyone's advantage, and (b) attached to positions and offices open to all.

These are "rules of rules" in the sense that they are general principles constraining the formulation of more specific rules. These principles assure that no matter where an individual ends up in the lottery of life (i.e., no matter what kind or degree of intelligence, talents, or physical abilities one has), he or she would have liberty and opportunity. Every individual will have a fair shot at a decent life.

Although Rawls's account of justice has met with criticism, it goes a long way toward providing a framework for envisioning and critiquing just institutions. This discussion of Rawls is extremely abbreviated, as were the accounts of Kant and utilitarianism. As before, we have to stop the dialectic and note that discussion could go off in any number of directions from here. Perhaps the most important thing to keep in mind when claims about rights and justice are made is not to accept them without question. Generally, such claims presume a much more complicated set of concepts and assumptions, and you cannot know whether the claim is worthy until you examine what lies behind it and what its implications are.

Virtue Ethics

One other important tradition in moral philosophy should be mentioned. In recent years, interest has arisen in resurrecting the tradition of virtue ethics, a tradition going all the way back to Plato and Aristotle. These ancient Greek philosophers pursued the question: What is a good person? What are the virtues associated with being a good person? For the Greeks, *virtue* meant excellence, and ethics was concerned with the excellences of human character. A person who has these qualities is one who is capable of functioning well as a human being.

The list of possible virtues is long and there is no general agreement on which are most important, but the possibilities include courage, benevolence, generosity, honesty, tolerance, and self-control. Virtue theorists try to identify the list of virtues and to give an account of each. What is courage? What is honesty? They also give an account of why the virtues are important. Virtue theory seems to fill a gap left by other theories we considered, because it addresses the question of moral character, whereas the other theories focus primarily on action and decision making. What sort of character should we be trying to develop in ourselves and in our children? We look to moral heroes, for example, as exemplars of moral virtue. Why do we admire such people? What is it about their character and their motivation that is worthy of our admiration?

Virtue theory might be brought into the discussion of computers and information technology and ethics at any number of points. The most obvious is, perhaps, the discussion of professional ethics, where the characteristics of a good computer professional should be considered. Good computer professionals will, perhaps, exhibit honesty in dealing with clients and the public. They should exhibit courage when faced with situations in which they are being pressured to do something illegal or act counter to public safety. A virtue approach would focus on these characteristics and more, emphasizing the virtues of a good computer professional.

Analogical Reasoning in Computer Ethics

In Chapter 1, we identified one of the goals of computer ethics as understanding the role of computers and IT in constituting situations that pose an ethical dilemma or call for ethical decision making. One very useful way to analyze such situations is to reason by analogy, that is, consider similar (analogous) situations in which there isn't a computer or IT, and then examine whether the absence of the technology makes a moral difference. Sometimes the technology doesn't change the character of the ethical situation; other times it does. Either way, the analogy can be enlightening. Often when we reason by analogy we are able to see things in the analogous case that are relevant to the computer situation but weren't visible because we were focused on the technology. If, on the other hand, the involvement of the technology seems to make a moral difference, then we know there is something about the way in which the technology has constituted the situation that needs to be examined more carefully and linked to a moral concept or theory.

To illustrate, consider a break-in by a computer hacker. This kind of behavior will be discussed more extensively in Chapter 6, but for now let us consider a simple case. A hacker breaks into someone's system, looks around at various files, and copies some of the files that are stored locally. What should we make of this behavior? That is, how should we characterize and evaluate it ethically? Reasoning by analogy, we could consider the similarities and differences between this behavior and that of someone who breaks into an office, then into file cabinets, and then removes paper files that are of interest. Is there a moral difference between these two kinds of actions? Certainly it is true that the physical movements required to get access to electronic files are quite different from those required to break into an office and into a file cabinet. On the other hand, both sets of actions involve obtaining access to information that an individual had stored with the intention that others would not have access. An interesting difference between the two situations is that in the computer case, the files are still there and available for use by the owner, whereas in the noncomputer case, the files are gone. Does this mean the hacker case is not a case of "theft"? Is it still theft but less harmful or less bad than an ordinary break-in? Or are these morally comparable actions? If so, then "theft" must involve more than depriving the owner of access to what he or she owns. The point is that the analogy helps in teasing out what elements of the case are relevant to a moral assessment and what elements are not. If we cannot find anything morally different about the two cases, then we cannot (with consistency) claim that one type of behavior is morally permissible and the other is not.

Consider a slightly different case with a different analogy. Suppose a hacker is trying to break into systems to see whether he can do it. If he is able to break in, he looks at files but never makes copies. The behavior is mostly about the challenge of breaking in. Is this comparable to walking down a street and testing the doors of every house to see whether they are locked? Suppose someone does this and when they find a door unlocked (a file accessible), they go in and look around. They don't take anything from the house (file). They simply look at what the owner has put in her or his drawers (what she or he has stored in various files). The question is, is there any difference between these two cases? Is testing to see whether you can get access to computer systems different from testing doors on houses to see whether they are unlocked? From the point of view of the person who is being intruded upon, both types of actions may be felt to be intrusions of privacy and a violation of property rights. Whatever one says about the comparability or noncomparability of these cases, the analogy helps to focus attention on the elements of the action or case that are relevant to a moral evaluation.

Nevertheless, although analogies can be extremely helpful, they have to be used with caution. Reasoning by analogy has dangers that can be avoided only by fully developing the analogy. Analogies are useful because they allow us to draw upon situations or technologies with which we are familiar, situations in which there may be less controversy about right and wrong. This helps us to see rules or principles that might be relevant in the computer situation. The danger is that we may be so taken with the similarities of the cases that we fail to recognize important differences. For example, in arguing about online break-ins and the dissemination of computer viruses, hackers sometimes put forth the argument that they are providing a service by identifying and revealing the flaws and vulnerabilities in computer systems so that they can be fixed. Countering this argument, Eugene Spafford (1992) uses a powerful analogy. He suggests that the hacker's argument is comparable to arguing that it is morally permissible to set a fire in a shopping mall to show the flaws in the fire protection system. Launching a computer virus on the Internet has some parallels to starting a fire in a shopping mall, but this analogy is so powerful that we might immediately jump to the conclusion that because one is wrong, the other must also be wrong. We should first ask whether there are any important differences. Some might argue that lighting a fire in a shopping mall puts individual lives at risk, whereas most computer viruses do not. Both actions cause property damage, but the damage done by most computer viruses can be repaired more easily. Thus, when reasoning by analogy, it is important to identify the differences as well as the similarities between the computer and noncomputer cases.

Conclusion

The deep questions and general concerns of ethics that we have discussed in this chapter will continue to come into play in the chapters that follow. The ideas delineated in Chapter 1 as the substance of sociotechnical computer ethics will be brought together with the ethical concepts and theories discussed in this chapter. The goal of Chapter 3 and subsequent chapters will be to analyze ethical issues in IT-configured societies.

As we will see in the next chapters, IT creates a variety of situations that challenge traditional ethical concepts and theories. The dialectic method is enormously helpful in making progress on these challenges. However, it is important to note that the concepts and tools introduced in this chapter are not algorithms for solving moral problems; they are not the be all and end all of practical ethics. They are a starting place. Remember that science is never done either. In both science and ethics, we look for reasons supporting the claims that we make, and we tell stories (develop arguments and theories) to answer our questions. We tell stories about why the physical world is the way it is, why human beings behave the way they do, and why lying and killing are wrong. The stories we tell often get better over time. The stories are retold with new interpretations and in ways that fit the current context. Sometimes accounts get broader (more encompassing) and richer, sometimes more elegant. They are best when they help us to see new things we never noticed before. The stories generally lead to new questions. So it is with ethics as well as science.

Study Questions

1. How do descriptive (empirical) claims and prescriptive (normative) claims differ? Give examples of each kind of claim.
2. Describe a discussion of a moral issue that is currently receiving attention in the media. Identify different claims and arguments that were put forward and defended. List the claims in an order that illustrates a dialectic about this issue, with one claim and argument leading to another claim and another argument, and so on. Are there some claims that are still being presented in the media that have, in your judgment, already been rejected in the dialectic?
3. Explain the difference between "ethics is relative" as a descriptive claim and as a normative claim.
4. What evidence can be used to support "ethics is relative" as a descriptive claim?

5. What are the three problems with "ethics is relative" as a normative claim?
6. What is the basic principle of utilitarianism?
7. What is the difference between an instrumental good and an intrinsic good?
8. Why do utilitarians believe that happiness is the ultimate basis for morality?
9. What is the difference between act-utilitarianism and rule-utilitarianism?
10. What is the major criticism of utilitarianism? Explain it using an example other than the distribution of scaree medical resources.
11. What is the unique characteristic of human beings according to deontologists? How is this quality connected to morality?
12. What is the categorical imperative? Give two examples of violations of the categorical imperative.
13. How can rights be based on deontological theory? How can rights be based on utility theory?
14. What is the veil of ignorance in the original position in Rawls's social contract theory?
15. What are the two principles of justice in Rawls's theory?
16. How does virtue ethics theory differ in focus from other theories discussed in this chapter?
17. What is analogical reasoning? Give an example of how it can be used in computer ethics.
18. Why should we always use caution when arguing on the basis of analogies?

CHAPTER 3

Ethics in IT-Configured Societies

CHAPTER OUTLINE

SCENARIOS

Scenario 3.1 Google in China: "Don't Be Evil"

The Google search engine was created in 1998 by Serge Brin and Larry Page. Even though it was not the first widely available Web search engine (Alta Vista, Webcrawler, and Lycos were all available in 1998), Google rapidly became the most popular. Although exact figures are controversial, at this writing many estimates put Google's market share of Web searches at well over 50 percent. [http://marketshare. hitslink.com/report.aspx?qprid=4]

There are probably many reasons for Google's continued success at attracting users. Its algorithms for searching are advanced, it has invested in massive resources to increase performance, and its simple, uncluttered interface was distinctive when it first began. In addition, some also credit Google's famous motto, "Don't be evil," as part of its attraction. That slogan may have gotten Google positive free publicity, but it has also made Google vulnerable to criticisms about its policies, some of which seem to contradict its mission statement: "To organize the world's information and make it universally accessible and usable."

The most intense criticisms of Google have centered on its filtering (some would say "censorship") of particular content in particular countries. For example, in Germany and France Google filters out anti-Semitic websites to comply with laws in those countries against hate speech. Perhaps the largest controversy was over Google's entry into China, where the government requires extensive filtering, including blocking references to Taiwan, Tibet, and the Tiananmen Square massacre. Both Yahoo and Microsoft, key competitors to Google, entered the Chinese market and also agreed to these restrictions. (They, however, do not trumpet the slogan "Don't be evil.")

Google responded to the criticism about filtering by pointing out that "Don't be evil" also requires "Don't be illegal"; Google strives to obey the laws of countries where it operates. The company maintains that even limited access to the Internet is inherently democratizing, and that Google, as a public company, owes a duty to its shareholders to pursue business opportunities in China, even if that requires doing filtering that many find objectionable.

Google has tried to anticipate other possible trouble in China. For example, Google does not provide e-mail, chat, and blogging services in China (services they provide elsewhere) because they want to avoid confrontation with Chinese officials who might demand access to information about users posting content that the officials might find objectionable. (Indeed, Google and other providers have been forced to hand over such information in the United States in the U.S. government's "war on terrorism.")

Has Google done anything wrong? Is there a significant (ethical) difference between filtering hate speech in Germany and filtering political speech in China? Is the slogan "Don't be evil" appropriate for a publicly owned company? If so, is Google living up to that slogan? If not, does that mean working for a profit requires being evil?

Scenario 3.2 Turing Doesn't Need to Know

Hypothetical Situation

Indira is using instant messaging to get an answer to a question about a piece of software. She is interacting with Hal, a representative of the company that developed and distributes the software. During the exchange of text messages, it occurs to Indira that Hal could be a human (that was her initial assumption) *or* a sophisticated computer program designed to answer user questions. As Indira and Hal continue their conversation, Indira contemplates how to diplomatically ask whether Hal is human or not. Before she figures out how to bring up the subject, Indira receives a message from Hal that reads, "I'm just curious, Indira, are you human?"

What difference does it make whether Hal is human or not?

Scenario 3.3 Turnitin Dot Com

Hypothetical Situation

Giorgio Genova is a professor at a large state university. For the past several years he has been teaching a large class with well over a hundred students. Although the readings and assignments change each semester, the course objectives and main ideas that Genova is trying to get across stay the same. Hence, although Genova varies the essay questions on the take-home exams, they have been similar each semester. Genova is a fairly popular teacher; he works hard at teaching in ways that are effective. He believes, as do many of his colleagues, that it is important to gain the trust of students so that they engage with the material, feel comfortable asking questions, and come to appreciate the value of what they are learning.

With each of the take-home essays this semester, Genova has noticed that there seems to be an uncanny similarity in the opinions that the students express and the way they express these opinions. He is worried that because he has now taught the course for several years, there may be papers available from students who took the course in the past. So, Genova decides to run the papers through turnitin.com, a widely used plagiarism detection system. Turnitin.com compares the papers to content on the Web and to a database of papers that the company has accumulated as faculty have turned them in for testing.

Has Genova done anything wrong? What are the likely effects of Genova's actions on his students? How will widespread use of plagiarism detection systems affect classroom environments? Student–teacher relationships? The university environment?

INTRODUCTION: IT-CONFIGURED SOCIETIES

The term "information society" is often used to refer to societies in which IT is a critical part of the infrastructure through which economic, political, and cultural life is constituted. Although IT does not "determine" information societies, the activities, institutions, and social arrangements of these societies are configured with IT. IT shapes, and is shaped by, these societies.

This chapter is devoted to understanding the role of IT in such societies and especially IT's role in configuring ethical issues and shaping social values. This is a daunting task and the strategy we adopt here is to examine information societies from several different perspectives, each building on the previous. We begin with the idea that technology can be conceptualized as the instrumentation of human action. Second, we identify several features of IT that come into play when it instruments human action and configures societies. These features are: global, many-to-many scope; distinctive identity conditions (often referred to as anonymity); and reproducibility. Next, we examine domains of life that have been created by IT (virtual reality environments) or affected by IT (friendship) or are in the process of being reconfigured around IT (education). Finally, we consider democracy and democratic values in IT-configured societies.

TECHNOLOGY AS THE INSTRUMENTATION OF HUMAN ACTION

Human action is a central focus of ethics. As explained in the preceding chapter, moral theories often target actions and try to identify what it is that makes actions right or wrong, good or bad, admirable or despicable. Is it consequences? Is it the universalizability of the maxim of the action? To be sure, action is not the only focus of moral theories; theories of justice focus on the distribution of goods and opportunities; virtue theories focus on the characteristics of a good person; yet other theories explore attributions of responsibility or core values or rules. Nevertheless, human action is a good starting place for understanding the connection between technology and ethics generally, and IT and ethics in particular.

When human action is the focus of ethics, technology is best understood as "the instrumentation of human action." This makes the connection between ethics and technology seamless. In IT-configured societies, many (perhaps, most) of the actions of individuals and organizations are instrumented through IT; the instrumentation adds efficacy and makes a difference in what individuals and organizations conceive of as their options and what they actually do.

When human beings act, they move their bodies and what they do is a function of their bodies and the world their bodies encounter. I can throw a ten-pound object only so high and then it falls; how high it goes and how fast it falls is a function of my musculature, the size and shape of the object, friction, and gravity. Most importantly, our bodily movements have effects on others; our movements may have immediate effects on others or they may set off long, causal chains that have remote but significant effects on others. We are, perhaps, most aware of how our actions are a function of our bodies and features of the material world when we are confronted with what we cannot do. We cannot fly, leap to the top of tall buildings, and see through things (like Superman).

Technology adds to—expands, enhances—the instrumentation of our bodies. When we act with artifacts in a world filled with technological systems, our bodily movements have different and often more powerful effects than when we act without technology. I flip a switch and an entire building is illuminated; I press the trigger on a gun, and a small projectile goes faster and with more force than any human arm could ever throw; I press buttons on a phone, make sounds, and my voice reaches the ears of someone thousands of miles away. Indeed, with technology we can each, effectively, be Superman—we fly *in airplanes*, we reach the top of extremely tall buildings *with elevators*, and we can see through objects *using x-ray and magnetic resonance imaging machines.*

Technology changes what individuals are able to do and what they, in fact, do. Of course, all instrumentation is not equal. Particular technologies instrument human activity in quite distinctive ways. Automobiles instrument mobility, industrial machinery instruments manufacturing processes, eyeglasses expand vision, and thermostats control the temperature in buildings.

This is not, however, all there is to it because technology doesn't just expand human capabilities; it constitutes forms of action that weren't possible or even conceivable without the technology. "Genetically modifying food" and "watching television" were not just impossible before the development of gene theory and mass media, they were incomprehensible. It is the same for IT-instrumented actions. IT expands what individuals can do and constitutes actions that were inconceivable before the technology existed. "Sending spam," "searching the Web" and "blogging'" were incomprehensible and impossible before the creation of the Internet.

IT instruments collective or organizational action as well as individual action. Consider the case of a business that uses an IT system to instrument the work of its employees. When a company installs a performance monitoring system on its computers, data about employee behavior is automatically generated and stored while employees work. Records—of speed, accuracy, length and content of phone calls, idle time of machines, websites visited—become a seamless part of work. IT is used here to instrument the work of employees, and the instrumentation has features that were not part of the prior instrumentation. Yes, employers have always monitored the work of their employees, but the IT instrumentation changes the features and extent of the monitoring.

Thinking about IT as the instrumentation of human action has two important advantages for ethical analysis. First, it keeps humans as the agents of actions, and second, it allows us to focus on the contribution of the instrumentation to the character of human actions. In other words, this conception of technology positions human beings as central to technological outcomes—humans are the actors—while at the same time recognizing that the use of technology powerfully shapes what humans can do and what they actually do. Technology instruments what is always *human* activity, and human activity may be in part constituted by technology.

Cyborgs, Robots, and Humans

Before using this concept of technology, we can explain it further by responding to some possible objections. The account may be criticized, first, for not acknowledging the "agency" of technology. STS scholars have used the notion of "agency" to explain the role of technology in society; they argue that technology has agency in the sense that it contributes to what happens in the world. What individuals, organizations, and even nation–states do is a function of the technologies through which they are constituted. Technology has efficacy, the power to effect outcomes.

As a field, STS might be understood to have as one of its goals to draw attention to the power of technology, that is, to understand and explain how power is wielded through technology. To achieve this goal, STS theorists argue for the "agency" of technology. For example, in what is labeled "actor-network theory" (ANT), sociotechnical systems are represented as networks—networks of things and people. Each node in a network influences what happens. ANT makes the point that we shouldn't privilege the contribution of human actors to various outcomes, so the theory recommends that we refer to each node in the network as an "actant." There are human and nonhuman actants. For example, a computer program is an actant as is the human user of the program. They each behave and the interaction of their behaviors produces outcomes.

Network theorists are likely to criticize our account of technology as the instrumentation of human action on grounds that it privileges human actors and doesn't sufficiently acknowledge the contribution of technology. Our counter is that our account allows us to see both the contributions of humans and of technology, and to see them as intertwined but distinct. In identifying technology as the instrumentation of human action, we link technology and human activity tightly and inextricably. Our reasons for keeping humans as "the actors" in our conceptualization of technology reflects our concern about another set of issues and another possible line of criticism of the account.

Coming from a quite different direction, critics may think we are mistaken to keep IT (not just any technology but IT in particular) connected to human action because IT systems have the potential to become autonomous actors. These theorists see how independently computer programs, bots, and robots can function. They anticipate a future in which IT systems will function even more autonomously and to a point that humans will not be able to understand what IT systems are doing, let alone control them. Some of these scholars argue that bots and robots may in the future function so autonomously that we will be compelled to grant them the status of moral agents. They will be "artificial" moral agents and we will be obligated to refrain from turning them off—because of their moral status.

The debate about the moral status of autonomous computer programs, bots, and robots is important and will likely continue. It is important as much for what it reveals about the nature of cognition, intelligence, and morality as it is about what will happen in the future. We have adopted the account of technology as the instrumentation of human action in part with an eye to this debate, and with the intention of keeping in view that human beings are always involved in technological endeavors. When programs, bots, and robots seem to behave autonomously, it is because humans have built and deployed them to do so. If these systems function more and more autonomously, it will be because humans have chosen (by action or inaction) to put such systems in operation. Our account presupposes that technology is sociotechnical; wherever there are artifacts, there are social practices, social arrangements, and social relationships. In other words (and connecting back to the view of technology being proposed here), bots and robots *are* instrumentations of human action.

Interestingly enough, both lines of criticism—that our account doesn't sufficiently acknowledge the contribution of technology and that it keeps technology too tightly linked to human action—have a common thrust. They are both concerned to show that humans are not fully in control of what happens in the world. STS scholars are struck by the powerful way that technology constitutes the world we live in and contributes to outcomes. The autonomous moral agent theorists see that programs, bots, and robots are behaving more and more independently. In both cases, the concern is to show not just that technology is powerful but that humans are not fully in control and cannot be responsible for what happens. Both accounts seem, in this respect, to border on technological determinism; they seem, that is, to presume that technological development and technology's role in society are uncontrollable or keep going without human intentional activity.

We adopt the account of technology as the instrumentation of human action as a strategy to keep the connection between technology and human activity in full view. Our view incorporates the idea that technology is always "tethered" to human beings. Of course, everything that happens isn't intended. Unintended consequences are common, and combinations of intentional activity by different people produce results that no single individual intended. Nevertheless, technology is human-made and it doesn't come into being or get deployed without human activity. Human activity is required both for production and deployment.

So, although it may be true to say that bots and robots with increasingly greater independence are likely to develop in the future, it would be a mistake to leap to the conclusion that humans will be compelled to adopt or deploy these technologies. To adopt the inevitability of "artificial moral agents" is both to slip into technological determinism and also to presume that notions of responsibility and the need to hold humans responsible for what happens will not come into play in the future. Concerns about accountability are likely to influence the deployment (if not the development) of autonomous bots and robots, just as systems of accountability (product liability law, torts, and other legal concepts) have influenced the development of current technological systems.

One way to think through the issues here is to consider a somewhat different account of technology and its role in human activity. Some theorists have suggested that we should think of ourselves as "cyborgs," that is, human–technology combinations. This idea is most salient when we think about technologies implanted in our bodies, for example, heart monitors, replacement joints, and mind-altering drugs. Here it seems that we (or at least some of us) are cyborgs. But why restrict cyborghood to implanted artifacts? We live our lives seamlessly and intimately intertwined with technology; our lives depend on energy, transportation, and sanitation systems. Could we live as we do, be who we are, without electricity, medicine, and industrial agriculture? Without these technologies, we couldn't and wouldn't think of ourselves and our lives in the way that we do now. Thus, our being cyborgs is as much about the technologies that surround us as about those implanted in or around our bodies.

The idea that we are cyborgs is not far from our idea about technology as the instrumentation of human action. On the one hand, the cyborg idea seems to hint at the human component not being fully in control because a cyborg consists of "silicon and carbon." On the other hand, this raises a question about how to conceptualize the actions of a cyborg, especially given the centrality of agency, action, and intentionality to moral theory and moral notions. The issues here are quite fascinating.

A major challenge for morality in IT-configured societies is to develop adequate notions of responsibility, notions that hold individuals responsible for their actions, and hold those who design and deploy technologies responsible for their actions. What is clear in all of this is that whatever we think about technology—whether we use the cyborg metaphor, allow for artificial moral agents, or think of technology as the instrumentation of human action—ideas about responsibility must be taken into account.

Scenario 3.2 hints at the themes that we have just discussed. The scenario depicts what may happen as IT-configured societies increasingly adopt sophisticated programs to deal with clients and customers for interactive functions that in the past were performed by humans. We already experience situations of this kind when we send questions to websites, receive responses, and then wonder whether the response was machine generated or a human being actually read our question and customized the answer. Of course, we can question the question: What difference does it make whether the client/customer is communicating with a human or not as long as the response to the question is adequate? Is it enough to say that humans simply prefer to know whether they are communicating with a person or not? Perhaps it should depend on the context. For example, some may feel more comfortable discussing medical questions with a person; they may believe that medical issues are so complicated, nuanced, and individualized that no machine could ever do as well as a person. There are also responsibility issues here. What if the answer given is inaccurate or misleading? Will accountability differ if a human gave the answer rather than a machine? Should we have a system of accountability in which a company is responsible for answers given, regardless of whether the answer was given by a human or machine agent?

We have explored two possible criticisms of our account of technology as the instrumentation of human action in order to draw out some of its implications. Because we will continue to use this account both throughout this chapter and in subsequent chapters, the "proof" of its value will be "in the pudding" so to speak. The analyses we provide in the rest of the book will demonstrate the value of the account.

THREE FEATURES OF IT-CONFIGURED ACTIVITIES

In Chapter 1 we critiqued the standard account of computer ethics on grounds that it applies generally to new technologies and not specifically to computers or IT. The same could be said of our account of technology as the instrumentation of human action; it is an account of technology in general and although it applies to IT, it does not provide an account of what is distinctive about IT ethics. In this section we take on the task of identifying some of the distinguishing characteristics of IT systems. Although we are reluctant to generalize about IT because it is such a malleable technology, many of the ethical issues that arise in IT-configured societies seem to cluster around three features: (1) global, many-to-many scope; (2) distinctive identity conditions (in which individuals have the ability to be anonymous or pseudonymous); and (3) reproducible. For now, we will not be concerned with whether and how these features are produced; our concern is with their significance for ethical issues and their contribution to ethical dilemmas. We will begin by focusing on IT-instrumented communication, especially communication via the Internet, and will compare this form of communication with face-to-face, telephone, television, and radio communication. [Note that the comparison is a little convoluted because telephone, television, and radio are now thoroughly computerized and often instrumented through the Internet, although they were invented and functioned initially without computers.]

Global, Many-to-Many Scope

When we communicate without any form of technology, we have a fairly limited range. Whether we speak softly or yell at the top of our lungs, we can speak only to those who are geographically close. Our reach is limited by the structure of our throats and ears and how sound travels. Megaphones, telephones, and hearing aids expand the range of the spoken word. Writing makes use of technology, and the reach depends on the technology one uses—pen and ink, typewriter, and so on. Once one puts words on paper, the paper can travel great distances by means of messengers, carrier pigeons, pony express, or extremely complex mail delivery systems, for example, the U.S. Postal Service and FedEx. The reach of individual communication has been significantly expanded through IT and the Internet. With relatively little effort, an individual can with very simple movements reach others who are on the other side of the earth.

Internet-instrumented communication has a global scope. To be sure, the Internet does not allow us to communicate everywhere, and to everyone in the world, only with those who live in places where there is electricity, computers, and other technologies that receive telephone or satellite signals. Still, even with this limitation, the Internet significantly expands the scope of individual and organizational reach, and the expansion is especially significant in relation to the effort involved. That is, with the proper equipment and service, individuals achieve this expanded scope with relatively little effort.

Although the expanded scope of communication on the Internet seems enormous when we compare it to face-to-face communication, it is not so enormous when compared to the mail services, telephone, or radio and television transmission because these also have global reach. Oddly, the system with the largest scope seems to be hard mail (sometimes derided as "snail mail") because it does not depend on electricity as do telephone, radio, television, and the Internet. Letters sent via hard mail can reach many more places than the Internet. The comparison is interesting because it suggests that the importance of the global scope of the Internet is tied to its ease of use, immediacy, and low cost. We can write on paper and send our paper messages via a postal service, or we can publish our written words in a newspaper, magazine, or book that is distributed around the world. However, by comparison with the Internet, these forms of communication are cumbersome, expensive, and slow. Writing messages on paper—even if we duplicate the same message for thousands of people—takes more time and energy than moving our fingers over a keyboard and clicking on icons. Getting something published in a newspaper or magazine is quite complex and fraught with uncertainty. So, the significance of the global scope of the Internet is a function of ease, immediacy, and affordability.

Television and radio communication are similar to the Internet in global scope and immediacy. One simply speaks into a microphone and the words can reach huge numbers of people. The important difference here is that radio and television communication are one-way from station to listeners and viewers. We can refer to this as one-to-many communication to contrast it with the Internet's capacity for many-to-many communication.

It is tempting to characterize the Internet's many-to-many scope as distinctively interactive, but we have to remember that face-to-face communication is highly interactive. So, it is not interactivity alone that is the unusual feature of communication via the Internet. Nor is it ease alone or global reach alone. Rather, it is the combination of elements we have just discussed. The Internet provides to many individuals who are geographically distant from one another the capacity to communicate easily, quickly, and cheaply. It provides something to individuals that was, before the Internet, available only to a few—namely those who owned, or had access to, radio or television stations or could afford long-distance telephone calls. The Internet puts this instrumentation in the hands of many, allowing many to communicate globally with many others.

Distinctive Identity Conditions

Although it is tempting to say that anonymity is a distinctive feature of communication on the Internet, this is not quite accurate. For one thing, our communications on the Internet are monitored by service providers and can be traced by other interested parties, those who have a legal right to access the information or who have the technology that allows them to (illegally) access it (e.g., with packet sniffers). The temptation to think of Internet communication as anonymous seems to arise from the fact that we do not see each other directly when we communicate on the Internet. A famous *New Yorker* cartoon captured this idea as it depicted a dog in front of a computer thinking, "no one knows you're a dog on the Internet."

A more accurate characterization would be that communication on the Internet is mediated. A complex sociotechnical system instruments what we say to one another online. Typically, we cannot see each other directly, that is, we don't have access to visual cues about one another when we communicate via e-mail, chat, or use instant messaging. However, Web cams and other new technologies are likely to become more common, so this may change. In any case, mediation means, among other things, that there is always the possibility of intentional or unintentional distortions of identity, for example, machine-generated images that disguise the person. Humans have relied on their senses to determine the identity of others for thousands and thousands of years, and because of this, the trustworthiness or reliability of our identity in electronic communication may always be an issue, if for no other reason than that technology can be manipulated more easily than a physical presence.

The claim that Internet communication is unique because it affords anonymity is also problematic because anonymity is itself a complex concept. Anonymity seems to be contextual and relational. One can be anonymous to one person while identified to another. We can do a variety of things to make our identity more or less apparent to particular individuals. For example, you can use an e-mail address that hides your real name. You can use pseudonyms in chat rooms and virtual games. You could even have several Facebook identities, making some information available under one identity and other information available under another.

To illustrate how complicated anonymity is, consider the following situation. I get in my car and drive several hundred miles away from my home. I stop my car, enter a grocery store, and buy groceries, paying with cash. I could be said to be anonymous in this grocery store because no one in the store knows me or pays much attention to me. No one knows my name, what kind of work I do, where I live, how I feel, and so on. Oddly, while I was anonymous in these ways, I was in full view. People in the store, if they had bothered to notice, could see what I looked like, what I was wearing, and could have gauged my weight, height, age, and so on. The anonymity I had in this situation seems to have something to do with the fact that no one in the store knew my name, or could connect the information available to them (by looking), with any other information about me, for example, my address, occupation, or political affiliation.

The kind and degree of anonymity one has in any situation seems to depend on the ways in which, and extent to which, information can be linked with other information. To see this, consider one change in the situation just described. Suppose that I make a purchase at the store but use a credit card instead of paying in cash. My behavior is now instrumented through a vast and complex technological system that involves information moving from the store to a credit card company that is linked to other institutions through which I pay my credit card bill, for example, my bank and a credit rating agency. Each node in this vast financial system has information about me. Thus, once I use my credit card, my identity condition in the store has changed. If later in the day a crime is committed in the area, the police might ask whether anyone in the store noticed strangers, and if someone has noticed me, the police can ask the store to go through their transaction records, and pull my credit card information. With my credit card number, it is easy for the police to obtain a wide array of additional information about me.

Now consider a different situation. When I go to the polls to vote in a local, state, or national election, I am required to provide a form of identification that includes my name and address (to verify that I am a qualified voter). I am also required to sign the register, attesting to the fact that I am who I claim I am. I proceed to the voting machines—assume here a mechanical-lever voting machine—and cast my vote on a machine that is entirely disconnected from the book containing my name, address, and signature. My vote is anonymous in the sense that how I voted cannot be connected to me (my name, address, signature). Remember, however, that my vote was recorded—it was counted. So, whereas *how* I voted was anonymous, *that* I voted and *where* I voted is not. Here, once again, linking of information is important in the sense that the system is designed so that a link cannot be made between me and how I voted. Yet, I was not exactly anonymous insofar as there is a record of my having signed in, a record connected to my name and address. [Note that the disconnection between an individual and his or her vote is still meant to be maintained with electronic voting machines. The problem with electronic voting machines is that individuals are increasingly unsure that their vote is actually being counted.]

So, anonymity is complicated and its role in various activities is contextual. Anonymity depends on certain things being known or not known by particular others in particular contexts. Complexity aside, it should be clear that anonymity involves minimizing the kind of links that can be made to different kinds of information. In the voting case, my name and address are known but this information cannot be linked with how I voted; in the grocery store case, information about my appearance and location are known, and as long as I pay in cash this information isn't linked to other information but if I pay with a credit card, links can be made.

So, it isn't accurate to say simply that anonymity is a feature of communication on the Internet. Nor is it accurate to say that pseudonymity is a unique feature, because pseudonymity is possible in face-to-face communication and telephone communication. Individuals can disguise themselves by wearing masks and distorting their voices, or they can simply tell lies about who they are and what they want.

Perhaps the best way to characterize these aspects of Internet-instrumented communication is to say that there are distinctive identity conditions in Internet communication. The distinctiveness comes from two elements: (1) mediation—Internet communication is mediated through a vast sociotechnical system, and (2) the range of identity conditions that are available.

As already noted above, when we communicate via the Internet, those with whom we communicate do not see us directly; they see traces of us, traces that are produced in IT. Although many of us have become quite accustomed to this, it differs from the traditional mode of communication in which we use information about physical appearance (what people look like, what their voices sound like, and how they move their bodies) to identify others. Traditionally, humans have relied on this kind of information especially for continuity, that is, to know when we encounter someone we have encountered before. A person's physical appearance, voice, and facial expressions are used to fill in our understanding of one another as whole persons. The fact that the Internet does not give us this information is part of the difference between online and offline identity conditions. It seems to make some users "feel" anonymous but the feeling, as the preceding analysis suggests, may be quite misleading.

The second distinctive aspect of identity conditions in Internet communication is variability. IT instrumentation makes a variety of formats possible and these formats, in turn, facilitate and constrain identity conditions. In virtual games, we communicate through our characters (avatars); in chat rooms or social networking sites, we can, if we choose, adopt pseudonyms and remain somewhat anonymous or we can provide accurate, detailed information that is easily linked to other aspects of our identities. This array of possibilities for identity seems distinctive, and important.

One final caveat is necessary. When it comes to identity and the Internet, there is always a gap between persons and machines. Tracking and monitoring of online communication involves watching machine activity, and thus, there is almost always a question about who produced the machine activity. In Chapter 6, where we take up IT-instrumented crime, for example, we will see that even when criminal behavior is traced to a machine located in a particular place, there is still a problem in determining who was controlling the machine when the machine was used in a particular way.

Reproducibility

A third important feature of Internet communication (and IT in general) is reproducibility. Electronic information is easy to copy and there is generally no loss of quality or value in the reproduction. Moreover, because the original is left intact in the process of copying, there may be no evidence that electronic information was copied. This feature has dramatic implications for property rights and crime. When physical objects are stolen, the object is gone and the owner no longer has access. When electronic information—be it a record, a program, or a piece of proprietary software—is copied, the original is still there, the owner still has access, and there may be no indication that a copy was made.

Reproducibility is a significant aspect of Internet communication because of what it allows. When you utter words in unrecorded face-to-face communication, the listener hears the words, and then they are gone. This is not the case with Internet communication. The words endure. They endure in the sense that they exist in machines and remain there unless and until they are deleted. Indeed, deleting words exchanged in Internet communication can be no small feat. You may delete a message from your outbox, but the person who received the message may keep the message and may forward it to others who copy it and send it to yet others, and so on. As well, your service provider may maintain records of your communication.

In a sense, reproducibility expands the scope of IT-instrumented communication in time and place, but this expansion of scope means less control of written words by those who write them. The gain and loss seem to go together. Depending on how, and to whom, you send your "words," they may exist forever in someone else's machine. In a sense, endurance is the default position in Internet communication because if you do nothing, your communications continue to be available; at least until service providers delete them.

Reproducibility also expands the possibilities for disconnection between words and people. It makes it possible for one person to copy the words of another and then change them, or keep the words the same but use them as if they were their own. For example, the reproducibility of information on the Web has made it possible for individuals to copy information and claim it to be theirs, or to change the words of others so that someone else is misrepresented. This reproducibility is sometimes referred to as making possible "cut and paste" environments. [We will discuss the implications of this "cut and paste" capacity in education in a moment.]

So, these three characteristics—global many-to-many scope, distinctive identity conditions, and reproducibility—seem to distinguish IT-instrumented communication. To be sure, online systems can be designed so as to limit the scope of communication, make identity conditions similar to those offline, and prevent reproducibility, but more often than not they are features of activities in IT-configured societies. Geographic distance becomes less and less essential for everyday life and global interaction more and more common; individuals and organizations construct identities and pseudo identities online; and information gets reproduced effortlessly over and over again. In the remainder of this chapter we will see precisely how these characteristics come into play in many domains of life. In Chapters 4 and 5, we examine how they shape privacy and property rights issues, and in Chapter 6, we explore how they affect crime and security, and other issues of law and order on the Internet.

IT-CONFIGURED DOMAINS OF LIFE

To explore the implications of these three characteristics for ethical and value issues in IT-configured societies, we will briefly examine three domains of life in which IT plays a prominent role. Our aim here is to illustrate the ethical challenges and changes that occur when activities are constituted with IT.

Virtuality, Avatars, and Role-Playing Games

One of the most fascinating aspects of living in an IT-configured world is the opportunities for participation in virtual environments. Role-playing games are one such environment. In these games, players interact with one another in real time through avatars—characters created by players using the gaming software. Avatars are software constructions manifested graphically and textually. Players are able to control their avatars through a keyboard; they are able to have the avatar move and speak in ways that are unique to each game. Avatars interact with one another in worlds with qualities unlike those of the natural world. The virtual rape case described in Scenario 1.1 took place in one of the first virtual reality game sites. LambdaMOO still exists but many more sites are now available including EVE online, Everquest, and Second Life.

Although it is possible to limit access, many virtual games have global, many-to-many scope. Through their avatars, individual players interact with other players who may be anywhere in the world. However, of the three features discussed above, the identity conditions of interaction in virtual games are the most interesting because they are what make for "virtuality." In virtual environments, players experience other players through their avatars. No one playing the game may know the offline identity of any other players and they don't acquire information that is linkable with other information about the person. In this sense, players are anonymous and they are also pseudonymous insofar as their identity is in their avatar. Avatars can exist over extended periods of time and have ongoing relationships with other avatars. Players may not intend that their avatars be their "representatives"; that is, what players do outside the game and what they have their avatars do are understood to be different. Avatars are an opportunity for players to explore different identities and experience what it is like to be a particular kind of being. Nevertheless, avatars are expressions of their controllers.

Although the virtual rape case described in Scenario 1.1 took place many years ago, it continues to be useful for exploring the ethical challenges of virtual environments. The incident occurred at a time when little attention had been given to the status or meaning of avatar behavior or the attachment relationship that seems to form between player and avatar. When the virtual rape case first came to the attention of computer ethicists, the case seemed to comfortably fit the standard account. Individuals had new possibilities—manipulating avatars of their own creation in virtual games—and there was a conceptual muddle and a policy vacuum with regard to the new form of action. How could and should we think about the behavior of Bungle and/or the behavior of the person controlling Bungle? Because participants in the game expressed distress and anger about the so-called rape, what were we to make of the fact that no "real" rape had occurred? Had anyone done anything wrong? Who was wronged? What harm was done? Who and how might someone be punished?

Initially, it seemed that we might try to separate out what happened in the virtual environment from the people who were controlling the avatars. For example, it would be easy to say that because it was all virtual, any punishment or consequences should also be virtual. Punish Bungle and leave it at that. Of course, it is unclear what would be involved in punishing Bungle. Would we simply enact a virtual punishment? Put Bungle in a virtual jail for a given number of years? The problem with this approach is that the individuals who were upset and distressed about the virtual rape were the flesh-and-blood controllers of avatars. So the case cannot be dismissed so easily. To treat the wrongdoing as merely virtual and respond only within the virtual room doesn't acknowledge that virtual worlds are also "real" in important respects.

When the case first came to the attention of computer ethicists, it seemed a good candidate for analogical thinking. We might think of behavior in virtual environments as a form of expression like writing a story or making a movie. Written words and images can be harmful, as in pornography and violent films, and especially when individuals are exposed to these visual and textual forms without their consent or when they are under age. Offline, we hold individuals legally and morally responsible for exposing children to pornography and even with adults, we require that they be given warning so they have the opportunity to avoid exposure. For example, bookstores selling pornography are not allowed to display their goods as part of their advertisements; they must forewarn customers about their wares. If the wrongdoing in the virtual rape was that of exposing members to pornography and violence without warning, then clearly the wrongdoing was that of the person controlling Bungle, not Bungle. Of course, the person controlling Bungle didn't rape anyone. Because rape is one of the most serious crimes committed against human beings, it seems misleading and somewhat disingenuous to even refer to the case as a rape. Rather, Bungle's controller, it would seem, harmed the other human players by exposing them to a level of violence that they did not expect or want to see in LambdaMOO.

This preliminary analysis has the advantage of framing the game—LambdaMOO—as a sociotechnical system. The game consists of software and hardware, people interacting through and with the software, and people with ideas about what they were doing and how they should behave. The software allows players to engage in certain kinds of behavior and prevents them from engaging in other kinds. Whether aware of it or not, the players had ideas about what they were doing, and those ideas shaped the game—the virtual world. Implicitly, most players adhered to social norms of behavior similar to those they might adhere to offline. They maintained certain rules of civility. The person controlling Bungle had a different idea. He broke the norms of civility assumed by other players. Today, most role-playing games specify norms for the game through rules and contracts, and players must explicitly commit to these before they join the game.

Notice that the social norms of the game were not just in the minds of the players, they were also in the software. The game software was set up so that no one but the game wizard (administrator) could control certain aspects of the game. As well, the software had been set up so that each player could control his or her own avatar. Bungle's controller didn't just violate a norm with regard to the level of violence in the game, he or she gained unauthorized access to the system and took control of the characters that had been created by other participants. Thus, Bungle's controller violated the social *and* technological norms of the game, that is, norms embedded in the software and in the thinking and behavior of other players. The virtual rape case is, then, a good illustration of the sociotechnical aspects of morality. Moral norms can be socially and technologically constructed.

This analysis of the virtual rape is far from complete; the LambdaMOO incident continues to peak the interests of computer ethicists, and the most recent literature suggests that in analyzing role-playing games, one has to come to grips with the attachment that individuals form with their avatars. As one scholar recently explained, avatars are "the embodied conception of the participant's self through which she communicates with others in the community" (Wolfendale, 2007). The attachment relationship is important because it provides a basis for understanding why many players felt that they had been wronged or harmed by Bungle's behavior. Remember that Bungle's controller had to take control of avatars that belonged to others in order to perform the rape. We can imagine that the legitimate controllers of legba and Starspinner were angry both because their control had been taken away and because "their" avatars had been used to enact a rape. We might even say here that legba and Starspinner were demeaned and disrespected in the rape enactment, and, therefore, their creators were demeaned and disrespected. When players identify with their avatars, they have strong feelings about how the avatars are treated.

So, another way to think about the wrong done in the virtual rape case is to frame the actions of Bungle's controller as harming the other players by showing disrespect for avatars understood as expressions to which individuals were strongly attached. Although not definitive, an analogy might be helpful here. The attachment of a player to his or her avatar might be seen as analogous to a person's attachment to his or her family emblem or memorabilia of a favorite sports team. If someone were to spit on or step on your family emblem or the shirt of your favorite soccer player, you might well be offended. You might take this to be a serious personal assault.

We do not claim that any of these accounts of the virtual rape case are the final word. Virtuality is complex and its meaning is far from settled. What is clear is that IT has configured a form of interaction that is shaping, and being shaped by, several factors including moral norms and practices. Issues of this kind are likely to continue to arise as IT-configured societies evolve.

Friendship and Social Networking

In IT-configured societies, friendship is instrumented, in part at least, through a variety of IT systems including social networking sites, chat rooms, instant messaging, e-mail, cell phones, text messaging, and more. These technologies affect who your friends are, how much contact you have, when you have contact, what and how much you know about each other, and what you say and do together. In this respect, modern friendship is a sociotechnical system.

That friendship is taken up in a book on ethics may seem odd to some, but friendship has been a topic in moral philosophy going back to the ancient Greeks. Aristotle's analysis of friendship continues to be used by contemporary philosophers as the starting place for thinking about friendship, what it is, and why it is so valuable. Aristotle gave an account of friendship that may seem idealistic, although the fundamental ideas are relevant to friendship today. Aristotle believed that true friends cared about each other in a special way. Friends are those who you care about for their own sake. You care about them and their well being not because you may benefit from the friendship or because their good may somehow promote your good. Aristotle also believed that friendship achieved its highest value when friendships are based on an appreciation of the other's quality of mind and character. You choose friends because you respect their qualities and character, and the better those qualities, the better the friendship.

Friendship on the Internet has come under the scrutiny of computer ethicists, and some have questioned whether "true" friendships can be formed online. Recent research has indicated that we may be using the Internet and IT not as much to initiate friendships but to supplement offline friendships with those who we also meet face-to-face. Nevertheless, critics have raised questions about the limitations of online communication and, therefore, online friendship. As an example of the critical perspective, consider that Dean Cocking and Steve Matthews (2000) published an article titled "Unreal Friends" in which they argued that real friendships could not be established or maintained on the Internet. Building their argument on the insight that communication is affected by contextual factors. Cocking and Matthews articulate a concern about the ways in which the Internet environment structures and constrains verbal behavior. They argue that the Internet environment distorts important aspects of a person's character (that is, it distorts what individuals reveal about their character) and weakens the interactions in which persons develop a relational self through their interactions with their friends. Their argument is based on recognition of a significant difference in the kinds and degree of control that individuals have over self-disclosure in online communication as compared to offline. Their argument is connected to Aristotle's idea that friendships are better when they are based on the qualities of a friend's character. If the Internet limits what one can learn about friends, then it limits the possibility of true friendship.

Whether or not we agree with Cocking and Matthews about the Internet constraining (or distorting) friendship, their claim that communication on the Internet differs from face-to-face communication seems right and so does their focus on what individuals reveal about themselves online. Moreover, the differences between online and offline relationships are not limited to differences in self-disclosure.

Historically, individuals have had close friendships primarily with those who lived in the same geographic area because living in the same location meant frequent contact, frequent opportunities for interaction, and shared experiences. Over time and long before IT, technologies expanded the scope of friendship, if not for creating, at least for maintaining relationships. Think of friendships maintained by letter writing and how that was affected by expansion of the mail system through railroads and airplanes. Think of friendships maintained through telephones and, of course, through improvements in our capacities to travel. In the past, individuals lost touch with friends who moved away or if they didn't lose touch, communication was less frequent and this made it difficult to maintain intimacy. Social networking sites, cell phones, IM, and chat rooms have expanded the scope of friendship and increased the possibilities for frequent contact regardless of place and time zone. It doesn't matter nearly as much where your friends are, as long as they have access to the Internet and cell phone towers.

Although we shouldn't forget that individuals consciously construct their identities offline—in their choices of clothing, haircut, the car they drive, how they furnish their room or apartment—IT structures the construction of identity online. Think here of social networking sites and what the default settings have one reveal. We construct our identities as well when we make decisions about our user ID; what, if any, quotation we use in our e-mail signature; and the information and images we post on Facebook. Here we can see that the architecture of a system can make a difference in how one constructs one's identity and, in turn, the conception that friends have of us.

Reproducibility also plays an important role in Internet-instrumented friendship. Remember that in face-to-face interactions, words are spoken and then they are gone. Someone may with effort try to listen in on a face-to-face conversation but it takes a good deal of effort and technology to record what you say. Interactions with friends in IT forums are reproducible with little effort. Internet service providers often keep records and can make them available to law enforcement agencies (with or without a warrant). And, as we saw in Scenario 1.2, employers and law enforcement agencies examine information on social networking sites. As users become more aware of this, they may construct their identities differently.

It would seem, then, that friendship instrumented through IT differs from friendship instrumented through other technologies, but the significance of the differences is unclear, especially when we remember that what is at issue is not online versus offline. Most commonly, friendships are established and maintained online *and* offline. At the extreme ends of the continuum are friendships that exist only online or only offline, but in between are a wide range of hybrids. Some friendships begin online and move offline; others begin offline and move online, and in either case, the amount of offline and online can vary widely and change over time.

In Chapter 4, we will focus on privacy and there we will see that the flow of information in relationships affects the nature of the relationship. We will then raise the question whether intimate relationships can develop in environments in which there is little or no privacy. That discussion will supplement our discussion of friendship in this chapter.

Education and Plagiarism Detection

Many aspects of education have been reconfigured around IT. Think of online application processes, communications between teachers and students, record keeping, and online courses. At the most profound level, the permeation of IT in education has disrupted ideas about the purposes, values, and measures of education; in other words, the reconfiguration of education around IT has changed ideas as to what it means to be educated. This transformation has happened not just because of the adoption of IT but also because IT is seen as the infrastructure of the future. Thus, educational institutions have embraced goals that have to do with preparing students for a life, jobs, and citizenship in a world filled with IT.

As an illustration of the subtle, but profound, changes in ethical norms and values that occur when education is instrumented with IT, consider plagiarism and plagiarism-detection systems. Of course, issues of academic integrity and plagiarism predate IT; teachers have long dealt with students who cheat, and plagiarism has long been defined (in the United States and many European countries at least) to include direct copying of text that has been written by someone else.

However, because of the reproducibility of information and the accessibility of information on the Internet, it is much easier to cut and paste text (segments or the whole of an assignment) and claim it as one's own. A slightly more sophisticated form of plagiarism is to cut and paste, manipulate the text slightly, and then claim it as your own. This is a case where one of the enormous benefits of IT and the Internet are butting up against the values of a domain of life. On the one hand, it is a boon that information is so accessible, and the ability to cut and paste it makes it easy to keep and use. On the other hand, educational institutions have as goals that students master knowledge and demonstrate their mastery by producing that knowledge on their own, and that students learn to think and write and demonstrate their ability to do so by producing thought and expressing it in writing or verbally "on their own."

At the moment, we seem to be in the midst of a collision between what is possible and easy *and* the norms of education. At a deep and often not articulated level, educational goals and strategies are being challenged and rethought. Perhaps education has to change to accommodate to a world in which cut and paste is the norm. Perhaps the nature of writing is changing. Perhaps we need to rethink what and how we teach. On the other hand, it would seem that educational institutions must evaluate students and decide whether and when they have achieved certain levels of mastery. If "cutting and pasting" undermines their ability to do this, then institutions must have ways to identify and discourage illicit cutting and pasting.

The solution that many teachers have adopted is to use what are called "plagiarism detection systems." Turnitin is the most widely used system. Teachers submit student papers and Turnitin tests these papers in two ways: It checks the papers against published material and against unpublished material. In the latter case, papers are checked against a database of papers that the company has created from papers that have been turned in for testing. [This, by the way, has raised a number of legal issues about the copyright status of student papers.] The tester may find segments of a paper that are identical to published work or segments of text (or an entire paper) that are identical to a paper in its database.

It is worth noting here that Turnitin doesn't exactly find plagiarism; it finds matches between text; the matches may or may not mean plagiarism. A teacher has to review the matches and make a determination. For example, if a student quotes a paper, puts that text within quotation marks, and cites the source, then the student has not plagiarized at all. Turnitin doesn't distinguish that case from the case in which a student copies an entire paper without attribution. Thus, although it may seem a simple matter, systems like Turnitin create a form of information that has to be interpreted as plagiarism.

A major issue here is the reliability of such systems. Concerns have been expressed that some plagiarized papers are not detected, that some nonplagiarized papers are identified as plagiarized, and that the results may be skewed against students for whom English is not their first language (Introna, unpublished). John Royce (2003) argues that the reliability of such systems can be demonstrated only when papers that are known to be plagiarized are submitted and caught. He cites four studies that used this approach but the results were mixed. In his own study, John Royce found that Turnitin "found no matches for material lifted from usenet discussion groups and discussion lists."

Reliability aside, there is an issue as to how automated plagiarism detection reconfigures values. Education depends in part on trust between students and teachers. Students have to trust that teachers will teach them what they need to know, and teachers have to trust that students will tell them when they understand something and when they don't. Student–teacher relationships are not unlike doctor–patient relationships in the sense that just as doctors cannot diagnose problems and identify appropriate treatments unless patients tell them about their symptoms, teachers cannot figure out what students don't know and how best to teach them unless students are honest in their responses to homework, research papers, and tests. In other words, if students hide their lack of ability and knowledge, they won't receive the education they need.

The problem with plagiarism detection devices is that they tend to create an environment of mistrust. When a teacher runs an entire set of papers through a plagiarism detector, the teacher is assuming that each and every student is a potential plagiarist. Even if the teacher selects only certain papers for submission to plagiarism detection, the teacher runs the risk of differentially bringing certain students under suspicion. Either way, if educational environments come to be based on mistrust, students will not develop maturity or the capacity for independent learning that is so critical to their futures. This is not an argument against the use of plagiarism detectors but rather for careful usage. Plagiarism detection systems are sociotechnical systems, and attention ought to be paid to the social practices that constitute these systems. In particular, attention should be paid to how students and teachers are "constructed."

The reconfiguration of education around IT, like that of other domains of life, continues to evolve. Although it seems unlikely that plagiarism detection systems will go away, the technology and social practices of plagiarism detection have not yet stabilized; they are being worked out.

DEMOCRACY AND THE INTERNET

So far we have used several different approaches to understand the significance of configuring societies with IT—conceptualizing technology as the instrumentation of human action, identifying the significant features of IT, and examining three domains of life in which IT has an important role. We turn now to another important approach. Many computer enthusiasts, the popular media, and a number of scholars have suggested that IT and the Internet are "democratic technologies." The claim is intriguing because it seems to assert a form of technological determinism; that is, the claim seems to affirm that adoption of IT and the Internet will lead (necessarily) to the adoption of democratic practices and arrangements. If we think of democracy as a value, then, the claim is that IT somehow embodies democracy. To put this in a somewhat different way, if we think of democracy as a political form, the claim is that IT requires, necessitates, or at least facilitates democratic forms of social interaction.

So, what are we to make of the IT–democracy connection? Is IT inherently democratic? Will increasing use of the Internet lead to a more democratic world? If so, is there something about the hardware, software, and telecommunication lines—the artifactual components of the Internet—that leads to democratic social arrangements? Or is it that IT and the Internet are so malleable that they can be molded to fit democracy but could also be molded to fit nondemocratic arrangements? For example, the massive surveillance possibilities to be discussed in Chapter 4 could contribute to totalitarian control. In any case, these questions call upon us to think about democratic societies as sociotechnical systems, and then to examine the contribution of the artifactual and social components to the achievement of democratic institutions and arrangements.

From the early days of computing, social theorists suggested that IT had an enormous effect on power relations. Initially, the issue arose because computers were so large and expensive that social observers presumed that the primary users would be large institutions—governments and corporations, and these users would become more powerful. In other words, computers would lead to more concentration and centralization of power. This perception and concern changed with the invention of micro-, or personal, computers. Smaller, less expensive machines meant that more people could have the enormous power of computers, and this meant decentralization of power.

Another factor contributing to the idea that IT is democratic is directly related to reproducibility. Many believed early on that because information and programs could be copied without any loss of content or quality, and at seemingly no cost, IT had the potential to revolutionize the availability of knowledge much as the printing press did in the fifteenth century. This contributed both to the idea that the technology would be revolutionary and to the idea that it would be democratic. Arguably, the open source movement is an extension of this idea because those in the open source software movement see it as a movement that will bring the benefits of IT to many more people. We will discuss this movement in more detail in Chapter 5.

What Is Democracy?

The claim that IT or the Internet is a democratic technology raises a prior question: What is democracy? Democracy is a complex idea probably best understood as a cluster of ideas, values, and arguments and, hence, characterizing a technology as democratic raises more questions than it answers. The core idea of democracy is, perhaps, best expressed as the idea that political power should reside in the citizens of a nation, rather than in a single person (a monarch or dictator) or small group of persons (an oligarchy or aristocracy). In democracies, citizens are the ultimate authority, and the government is accountable to those citizens. This idea has been articulated and interpreted in a variety of ways, and reinterpreted and modified over time. In a sense, democracy has been embodied in somewhat different ways, at different times, and in different places. Consider the array of democracies that now exist around the world.

Democracy is a moral concept in the sense that it has an underlying moral justification. Democratic theory is built on the idea that individuals are sovereign over themselves, and to be recognized as such they must have some say in the governments by which they are ruled. This may seem Kantian because it recognizes citizens as ends in themselves, not merely as means to a monarch's or dictator's ends. Nevertheless, some democratic theorists have provided utilitarian justifications for democracy. John Stuart Mill, for example, argued that democracy is the best form of government because it has the best consequences. In a democracy, citizens are required to be involved, that is, to participate in the governance of the state. Thus, democracy calls upon the active capacities of its citizens. Moreover, individuals are the best representatives of their own interests. Democracy is, then, good for individuals and at the same time makes for a better state; citizens develop their capacities and the state benefits from the ideas that citizens contribute and from an informed citizenry.

In modern, large-scale, nation–states, democracy has meant that citizens have a right to elect representatives to the government, and these governments are accountable to the citizens. The size of nation–states has been a persistent and daunting challenge to the idea of democracy insofar as it has diluted the power of individual citizens to influence their government.

Throughout history, changes in technology have meant changes in the way democratic institutions have been constituted. Think here of how systems of communication have changed the content and speed of political decision making—not just in elections but in an array of domestic and international policy matters. For example, historically, new forms of transportation and communication have repeatedly changed the way democracies work.

A number of social commentators see the Internet as the latest technology to transform democratic practices and institutions. Perhaps the most obvious example of this is in the use of the Internet for political campaigning that now involves websites, blogs, e-mail, YouTube, and more. However, the Internet has changed many other aspects of government in addition to campaigning. Consider, for example, how many government agencies have put public records online and made it possible for citizens to perform functions online; for example, submitting tax forms and paying traffic fines.

To get a handle on this very complicated set of issues, we can focus on the Internet and consider some of the arguments that are often hinted at, if not explicitly made, on behalf of a link between democracy and the Internet.

The Arguments

Many-to-many communication is probably the most prominent feature in these arguments. As described above, any individual who has access to the Internet can, in principle, communicate with any and every other individual who has access to the

Internet. Before the Internet, this power was available only to a few, the few who had access to the broadcast capabilities of radio, television, or newspapers.

The arguments made on behalf of the democratic character of the Internet seem to link many-to-many communication to democracy in the following claims: The Internet: (1) allows individuals to be producers and distributors of information, (2) provides forums that are mediated differently than mass media, (3) facilitates access to many more sources of information, and (4) facilitates the formation of associations that are independent of geographic space. Let us consider each of these arguments in turn.

The Internet has empowered individuals to produce and distribute information by removing the traditional hurdles to doing so. Producing and distributing is easier and quicker when instrumented through the Internet. Of course, posting something on a website or distributing images through YouTube doesn't guarantee that anyone will pay attention; getting others to respond is another matter. Still, the system of information production and distribution is different and available to many more people. This is precisely the point of calling the Internet's scope many-to-many.

The Internet provides a variety of forums in which citizens can exercise their democratic right of free speech, and these forums bypass traditional media. Before websites, blogs, chat rooms, search engines, and YouTube, the primary means by which citizens could distribute information on a large scale was through mass media—newspaper and book publishers, radio, and television. As mentioned earlier, the hurdles to getting something distributed were huge—one had to buy advertising space in print and broadcast media, convince publishers to publish one's written work, or somehow get the attention of the press. The Internet has made the cost of information production and distribution so low that many can be providers as well as receivers.

It is tempting to say that the new forums differ from traditional media in being *un*mediated, but this would be misleading. Distributing and accessing information on the Internet is mediated, but it is mediated quite differently than traditional media. If in no other way, the architecture of particular systems mediates; distribution is skewed but in ways that differ from mass media. Distribution on the Internet reaches only those with Internet connections, those who understand the language in which the text is written, generally those who can see, and so on. Millions of people do not have access, and others have older equipment with reduced functionality. And this is not to mention the way the design of software packages, forums, interfaces, and service providers shape the quality and character of information. Thus, it is more accurate to say that distribution on the Internet is mediated differently than the distribution of information in mass media (rather than saying it is unmediated).

One of the consequences of lower barriers to production and distribution of information is that much more information is available. Citizens have access to more information and the information comes from a broader diversity of sources. The old saying that information is power is relevant here because those who distribute information have the power to shape those who receive the information—shape their attitudes, opinions, preferences, purchasing habits, and values. When the distribution of information is expensive and requires large institutional structures (as with radio and television), the few who control the media have concentrated power. With the Internet, that power is more decentralized and distributed among the many who produce and distribute. Of course, the power of mass media has not, by any means, been eliminated. It has a presence on the Internet but its power is diluted by the broader range of other distributors.

That citizens can more readily be distributors and receivers of diverse information connects in important ways to John Stuart Mill's theory of democracy. He argued that democracy required that citizens exercise their active capacities and in so doing citizens and the state would continuously develop. Mill thought each individual's life would, in democracy, be an experiment in living that other citizens could learn from. In free societies, the best ideas emerge from the open combat of ideas. The Internet is a forum for just this sort of exchange. In effect, the Internet instruments interaction among citizens and draws on their capacities in particular ways and to a degree that was not possible before.

Yet another way in which these new forums for communication seem to contribute to democracy has to do with the formation of interest groups online. Whether the special interest is in a particular disease, a minority political position, a fetish, love of a particular kind of music, or a controversial idea, the Internet makes it possible for individuals to find others with the same interest. Of course, a wide variety of special interest organizations existed (and will continue to exist) offline. The difference the Internet makes is that associations can form and have frequent, immediate, and intense interaction *independent of geography*. When those who have a common interest are geographically dispersed, they are unable to identify one another, and hence, cannot act collectively; they have no means of working together, keeping each other informed, and making joint decisions. Separately, such individuals or groups are ineffective minorities. When they form associations online, they form communities and can act as such.

The possibilities for interest group formation online links directly to Madisonian democracy. James Madison argued that the best way for citizens to be heard in the political process was to form interest groups to put pressure on their representatives. The Internet has instrumented new means for forming such associations.

Is the Internet a Democratic Technology?

To summarize, the Internet might be considered a "democratic technology" because it: (1) allows individuals to be producers and distributors of information; (2) bypasses the traditional, concentrated power of mass media to distribute information (although is not unmediated); (3) provides access to a broader array of sources of information; and (4) facilitates the formation of interest group associations independent of geographic space. Do these claims justify the conclusion that the Internet **is** a democratic technology? They certainly identify patterns of behavior that are important for understanding IT-configured democracies. However, before drawing any conclusions, we should consider the arguments on the other side. Are there counterdemocracy patterns of behavior? Could the Internet be said to be a non- or undemocratic technology?

In discussing the argument about access to a wide variety of information resources, we noted in passing that although individuals can be the producers and distributors of information, this didn't guarantee that everyone would be heard or noticed. On the Internet, there is a good deal of competition for the attention of users. Moreover, because humans are limited in their capacity to absorb and effectively process and use information, we tend to need or find it helpful to have information filtered, selected, and routed to us. What sort of systems we have for filtering and sorting information becomes, then, an important matter. It is not at all clear that the current systems for this purpose are democratic. Are search engines democratic? What would a democratic search engine look like? Would it treat every bit of available information equal? How could it display information? Randomly? Would democratic search engines be useful?

Search engines are mechanisms for helping users identify the information they seek. To understand the democratic/nondemocratic character of the Internet, we would have to delve into the deep Web and understand exactly how various systems and algorithms order and route information. The algorithms make value decisions; they order information presented to users in a linear hierarchy. The lower down on the list, the less likely a user is to access information. Google keeps its algorithms secret. Although it has good reasons for doing so (so competitors cannot use them, and others cannot figure out how to "game" them), without access to the algorithms, we can only guess at the values that determine which websites appear higher and lower in the list of relevant sites. On the other hand, we know that some sites are sponsored (paid for), because that information is displayed. Hence, we know that money (paying for a place) makes a difference. We would have to know much more about these algorithms to decide whether this component of the Internet is democratic. The very fact that we cannot examine these algorithms seems somewhat undemocratic.

Remember also that although the Internet facilitates many-to-many communication, it also facilitates one-to-many communication. The Internet is used by powerful institutions to maintain their power or dominance in an industry. The Internet is used as much to consolidate old associations and traditional hierarchies as it is to facilitate new forms of association. In short, although the Internet gives power to the less powerful, it also gives a new kind of power to the already powerful.

The controversy called "net neutrality" is an example of how powerful forces seek to control the Internet; in the net neutrality debate, some Internet Service Providers (ISPs) advocate that some content providers be allowed to pay for enhanced network speeds ("faster pipes"), but some large providers advocate to keep all Internet communications on equal footing ("dumb pipes" or a "neutral Net"). Although smaller content providers and individual Net users will be greatly affected by the outcome of this debate, it is the large ISPs and large providers that are contesting this issue. The chairman of the U.S. Federal Communications Commission (FCC) wrote, "This is essentially a battle between the extremely wealthy (Google, Amazon, and other high-tech giants, which oppose such a move) and the merely rich (the telephone and cable industries)." [Kennard, W. Spreading the broadband revolution. *New York Times* (Oct. 21, 2006), http://www.nytimes.com/2006/10/21/opinion/21kennard.html?_r=2&oref=slogin&oref=slogin, accessed June 5, 2008]. It was not lost on several commentators that policies of the U.S. FCC have been crucial in making the contenders extremely wealthy and merely rich. (For example, see [Lessig, L., 21st Century Reaganomics: Helping the "merely rich" so as to help the really poor (Oct. 23, 2006), http://lessig.org/blog/2006/10/21st_century_reaganomics_helpi.html, accessed June 5, 2008].) This is one example that illustrates how the Internet is used to reinforce the power of governments and corporations in a way that is not accurately described as "democratic."

We should also not forget here that the surveillance capacity of the Internet (to be discussed in the next chapter) lends itself very well to totalitarian control. Remember, everything one does on the Internet endures. Traffic patterns, as well as content, are available to service providers (and hackers) and law enforcement agencies with a warrant. Private marketing agencies also want information about individual behavior on the Internet. This information is available through cookies. And, of course, the specter of China monitoring the e-mail and Web browsing activities of its citizens is probably alone enough for us to see that the Internet is not inherently democratic.

Another interesting, although perhaps ambiguous, challenge to the democratic character of the Internet is its global scope. In facilitating communication and interaction among individuals (regardless of their geographic location or nationality), the Internet has the potential to contribute to global democracy. However, this also could mean a weakening of nation–states. For good or ill, the many-to-many and differently mediated communication of the Internet makes it much more difficult for nation–states to control the flow of information to and from citizens and to control a wide variety of unlawful behavior. Although the Google in China case suggests a problem for totalitarian regimes, problems also arise for democratic regimes, for example, in enforcing legitimate laws that citizens are able to bypass.

Moreover, an intensely global economy (facilitated by the Internet) gives new economic opportunities to all involved, but at the same time pressures nation–states to harmonize their policies with other countries. This can be seen in a variety of areas where harmonization has been undertaken, including privacy and property rights policies. Whether or not harmonization is a good thing, that is, whether or not the policies are consistent with democratic values, depends very much on the particularities of the policy. Needless to say, the processes through which policies are harmonized are complex political and cultural negotiations. Although these negotiations can lead to improvements for democratic institutions and practices, they can also go the other way. The Google in China case is, again, a good example here. (We will discuss these issues further in Chapter 6.)

Finally, it is important to remember that we have characterized the communication capacity of the Internet as many-to-many and not all-to-all. Even within a country like the United States, many individuals do not have access to the Internet, at least not convenient access. And, of course, globally the picture is even worse with billions of people without access. Thus, if democracy means that all those who are affected by a decision should be involved in the decision, the Internet has potential but we have a long way yet to go.

Is the Internet a democratic technology? This much seems clear: The Internet is not *inherently* democratic. Those who believe that it is probably think of the

Internet as an artifact or technological system, but it is a sociotechnical system. It is much more than software, hardware, and telecommunications lines. Whether or not IT and the Internet facilitate democracy depends on all of the components of the system and that means the institutions as well as the artifacts. There are, as well, other reasons for eschewing such a broad and deterministic generalization as the claim that the Internet is inherently democratic. Those who believe this are likely to think that it is just a matter of time, and little needs to be done, before the adoption and use of the Internet will bring about global democracy. Nothing could be farther from the truth. The Internet is malleable and can support democratic and undemocratic patterns of behavior and institutional arrangements.

We conclude this discussion by mentioning the connection between democracy and freedom of expression, a topic that will be taken up more fully in Chapter 6, where we discuss what might be called "law and order on the Internet." Freedom of expression is generally considered not just essential to democracy but emblematic. Some would say a society isn't democratic unless its citizens have freedom of expression, at least a high degree of it. As we just described, the Internet enormously expands the possibilities for distribution of ideas and puts this capacity in the hands of many. Some describe the Internet as inherently free and even go as far as to say that the Internet is not amenable to regulation, that is, that it is uncontrollable. We address this claim head on in Chapter 6.

Conclusion

The Internet and the World Wide Web have facilitated the formation of electronic communities, communities that transcend physical borders. As people increasingly interact via the Internet, our lives change because of choices made in configuring these online communities. Some of these choices are made by individuals, but many are made by governments, corporations, and technologists. Meanwhile, economic activities, educational activities, and social activities are all changing rapidly.

In trying to discern rights and wrongs in these new IT-enabled communities, we have used ethical analysis to examine three distinctive characteristics of IT communication: global, many-to-many scope; distinctive identity conditions; and reproducibility. We also explored the many complexities involved with the relationship between IT and democracy and IT and freedom of speech. In all these analyses, we emphasized that decisions, not "nature," drive the development of the Internet and of other IT systems. We contend that careful ethical analysis will make these decisions more visible, and will help societies make these decisions more wisely.

Study Questions

1. This chapter considers how technology should be conceptualized. What are the advantages of thinking about technology as the instrumentation of human action?
2. What is captured, and what is lost, when certain forms of IT are conceptualized as robots, and when human beings are conceptualized as cyborgs?

3. How does the scope of communication on the Internet differ from other forms of communication such as telephone, television, newspaper, and talking face-to-face?

4. Why is it not accurate to say that communication on the Internet is anonymous? What is different or distinctive about the identity conditions on the Internet when compared to identity face-to-face?

5. What is reproducibility, and why is it significant?

6. Did anyone do anything wrong in the virtual rape case? If so, who? What was the wrong-doing? Develop analogies between the behavior in this case and other kinds of behavior that occur offline.

7. Explain the statement that social networking sites shape, and are shaped by, friendship.

8. What characteristics of IT (and the Internet) change the environment for plagiarism and plagiarism detection?

9. Identify and explain the four arguments made to show that the Internet is a democratic technology.

10. Do any of the four arguments in question #9 hold up to critical scrutiny? Explain which argument you think holds up the best. Do you think that this best argument is convincing?

Information Flow, Privacy, and Surveillance

Personal Steps for All IT Users

A Note on Privacy and Globalization

Conclusion

Study Questions

SCENARIOS

Scenario 4.1 E-mail Privacy and Advertising

The following description of Gmail is taken from J. I. Miller, "Don't Be Evil": Gmail's Relevant Text Advertisements Violate Google's Own Motto and Your e-mail Privacy Rights" Summer, 2005, 33 *Hofstra Law Review* 1607:

> An attorney presses "send" on an e-mail message to a prospective client following an initial consultation. The prospective client has an e-mail account with Google's recently introduced Webmail service, Gmail. What the attorney does not know is that before his e-mail reaches its intended audience, Google will have scanned the contents of the message, found within it words and phrases such as "new client," "attorneys at law," "construction litigation," and even the name of the city in which the attorney practices, and placed along side the e-mail, contemporaneously with the client's viewing of it, advertisements for legal services offered by the attorney's competitors. This seemingly hypothetical scenario is actually an everyday occurrence that is all too real.

Is there anything wrong here? If so, what?

Scenario 4.2 Workplace Spying: The Lidl Case

On March 26, 2008, Lidl, the second-largest grocery store in Germany, was accused by a German magazine (*Stern*) of hiring detectives to spy on its employees. The detectives installed cameras and microphones throughout the Lidl stores in Germany and the Czech Republic and they filled out reports on individual employees. Apparently, *Stern* obtained copies of these reports before making its accusations. According to one account, the detectives investigated workers, "both on the job, on cigarette and coffee breaks—and even on the toilet." The detectives gathered information on the financial status, relationships, and postwork activities of employees. On one account: "The transcripts also get into employees' private lives ('Her circle of friends consists mainly of junkies') and appearances ('Ms. M. has tattoos on both lower arms'). In their tone and detail, the observation logs invite comparison to those of the Stasi, the East German secret police." Particularly controversial is a report from the Czech Republic where, according to *Stern*, female employees were allegedly prohibited from going to the bathroom during work hours—unless they had their period, which they were to indicate outwardly by wearing a headband.

Lidl (which operates approximately 17,000 stores in 17 European countries) has not denied the accusations. Indeed, according to one account the company has apologized to its employees. The company attempted to justify the surveillance in terms of protecting their stores from employee theft.

The accusations are apparently being investigated by a government ombudsman for data protection. Lidl's surveillance practices may constitute violations of personal privacy and human dignity as specified in German statutes and, perhaps, their constitution.

Based On

Anonymous. 2008. "Two More German Chains Caught Spying on Employees." in *Der Spiegel Online*, April 3. <http://www.spiegel.de/international/germany/0,1518,545114,00. html> (Accessed May 9, 2008).

—. 2008. "Discount Chain Accused of Spying on Others." in *Der Spiegel Online*, March 26. <http://www.spiegel.de/international/business/0,1518,druck-543485,00. html> (Accessed May 9, 2008).

Walderman, A. 2008. "Lidl Accused of Spying on Workers." in *Businessweek*, March 26. <http://www.businessweek.com/print/globalbiz/content/mar2008/ gb20080326_558865.htm> (Accessed May 9, 2008).

Scenario 4.3 Data Mining and e-Business

The following description of consumer profiling in e-business is taken from Oscar H. Gandy, Jr., "All that glitters is not gold," *Journal of Business Ethics* 40 (2002): 373–386:

Carol is interested in purchasing a new computer and she visits TechStation.com, an electronics e-tailer. Carol is a first-time visitor to this site. After entering a few keywords to search the site and after browsing through several of the pages she selects the model she is interested in. Carol adds a printer to her virtual shopping cart and continues browsing. The observational personalization system used by the electronics store compares her point of entry to the site, the keywords she used in her initial search, her clickstream within the corporate site, and the contents of her shopping cart to the navigational patterns of existing customers already in [the] firm's database. Through this comparison, the system fits Carol into the "young mother" profile that it developed by mining the Web navigation logs generated by previous visitors and existing customers. Accordingly, the recommendation engine offers Carol a discounted educational software package before she checks out.

Carol was, in fact, not a young mother, but a middle-aged divorcée. She purchased the computer and printer she was interested in, but did not find the time management software she actually wanted to buy. A bit frustrated, Carol leaves the site in search of the software she needs. At about the same time, Steve entered the site and selected the same computer and printer. Although he chose the same products as Carol, Steve did not receive the same offer for discounted educational software. He entered the site from a different portal than that used by Carol; he had a different clickstream pattern from hers, and he used different terms in his keyword search. Steve's navigational pattern resulted in his being assigned to a different profile. Steve fit best into the "college student" profile and, as a result, he was offered a discount on a statistical software package. In fact, Steve is an English major. Like Carol, Steve's projected needs did not accurately match his real needs.

Is TechStation.com doing anything wrong? What, if any, information would help you decide whether the company is doing anything wrong? What ethical issues does this situation raise?

INTRODUCTION: INFORMATION FLOW WITH AND WITHOUT INFORMATION TECHNOLOGY

In an IT-configured society, information flows quickly and easily and in a variety of directions. In hindsight, it seems that before IT the flow of information was "constrained" by the technologies in use at the time—mechanical typewriters produced one copy (or at most a few more with the use of carbon paper); cash registers recorded the amount of a purchase but didn't create records of who bought what; mail delivery systems were slow, cumbersome, and variable. IT changed all of that and facilitated unprecedented flows of information.

All three of the characteristics we identified in the last chapter come into play in privacy and surveillance issues. Perhaps the most prominent feature is reproducibility because if it weren't for reproducibility, information would still be difficult to distribute and manipulate. Although we emphasized in Chapter 3 that information flows globally from many-to-many, we also noted that it flows in all directions including one-to-many, one-to-one, and many-to-one. Privacy and surveillance issues are primarily concerned about *personal* information, that is, information that is about a particular person. In this respect, the identity conditions of the Internet also come into play in privacy and surveillance issues because it is difficult (and often practically impossible for most) to operate online without being tracked in several ways.

To comprehend the significance of privacy and surveillance issues, it will be helpful to compare information flow today with that before the development and widespread use of IT for personal data collection. Notice first that the *scale* of personal information gathering has expanded exponentially. In the "paper-and-ink" world, not only was it costly and labor intensive to collect information, but it might not even have been considered because the paper and ink world didn't make it ready at hand. The fact that records were paper and stored in file cabinets imposed limitations on the amount of data gathered as well as who had access and how long records were retained. Electronic records have none of these limitations; they are easy to create, store, maintain, manipulate, search, and share. Thus, many more records are created and used.

Of course, we should be careful here not to slip into technological determinism. IT didn't cause organizations to gather and process so much information. Companies have always had interests in identifying and understanding customers and clients. As well, they have always had interests in getting information about their products to potential customers. Similarly, governments have always had interests in knowing about citizens. To be sure, these interests have been shaped by the development of IT; but IT was shaped in response to the interests of corporations and governments. Database management systems, datamining tools, and cookies weren't invented out of nowhere. Software and hardware developers developed tools that business and government would want to buy and use. Thus, information gathering and manipulation practices shaped, and were shaped by, IT.

In addition to an increased scale of information gathering, IT has made for new *kinds* of information. Transaction generated information (TGI) didn't, and in some sense couldn't, exist before IT. TGI is automatic and seamless. In the past when I bought something, I gave the clerk cash or wrote a check; now I provide my credit card, the card is swiped, and a record is created. The record resides in a server (or servers) somewhere in the world; that record can be accessed from any number of places, downloaded, and forwarded.

Of course, today I may not even go into a store; I simply go online and provide my credit card information. Other important forms of TGI involve the use of cookies that record the websites people access and "clickstream," as described in Scenario 4.3. When personal information from various places is merged and mined, this also produces new kinds of information. For example, although profiles of individuals were produced before IT, profiles today are expanded and much more detailed. When matched against databases of information about others, they have much more predictive power than those of the past.

Today, distribution of personal information is broader and more extensive than it was ten or twenty years ago. Before computers were connected to telephone lines, information could not move as easily as it now does. A transaction record or change in one's credit rating can instantaneously move to anywhere in the world where there are electricity and telecommunications connections. Once information about an individual is recorded on a server, it can be bought and sold, given away, traded, or stolen. The distribution of information can take place with or without the knowledge of the person whom the information is about, and it can take place intentionally as well as unintentionally.

In addition to the scale of information gathering, kinds of information, and scale of information distribution, information tends to endure for much longer periods of time. When information is stored electronically, there may be little incentive to get rid of it. In the past, the inconvenience of paper and the cost of storage served to some degree as an inhibitor to keeping and exchanging information. This endurance is illustrated through the recent controversy over personal information and images on Facebook. Facebook maintains records of all sites and it has recently come to public attention that users—even when they cease to be users—may not be able to delete information from Facebook. There is some indication that images in particular continue to be available even after one closes one's Facebook account. [See: http://news.

bbc.co.uk/2/hi/technology/7196803.stm and http://epic.org/privacy/facebook/default.html]

Note here also that we have said nothing about the quality or accuracy of the information that flows. Errors in information arise due to unintentional human error or may have occurred intentionally, for example when someone tampers with data because they want to harm a competitor or enhance their own position. When there is an error in personal information, the effect of the error can be significantly magnified; the erroneous information may spread so quickly that it is impossible for an individual to track down all the places it exists. Of course, those who want information about individuals want accurate information, but when faced with a choice between little or no verifiable data and data that may or may not be unreliable, decision makers may prefer the latter.

So, in IT-configured societies: (1) much more personal information is collected, (2) new kinds of personal information are created, (3) personal information is distributed more widely, (4) this information endures for longer periods of time, and (5) the effects of erroneous personal information are magnified. How does privacy fit into this relatively new kind of society?

WHY CARE ABOUT PRIVACY?

All of this means that individuals in IT-configured societies are intensively tracked and monitored. Surveillance may occur: through closed circuit television cameras (CCTV) when we walk on public streets or attend events in public spaces, on the computers we use at work as supervisors monitor our work, as the navigational devices installed in our automobiles identify our location to give us directions to our destination, through our cell phones as service providers locate our phones to direct calls to us, and when websites track our browsing and searching so that they can customize assistance with our searches and shopping. The data collected in each one of these contexts can then be merged to create comprehensive profiles of individuals. Combinations of data can also be "mined" to find patterns and correlations that might not otherwise be obvious. Individuals in this age range or that income level tend to buy these sorts of items or are more likely to be terrorists or to default on loans. It is not surprising, then, that IT-configured societies are often characterized as "surveillance societies."

Our task in this chapter is not just to describe how personal information flows but to examine the significance of this flow critically and normatively. To this end we must ask questions of the following kind: What, if anything, is the value of privacy? If privacy disappears, what exactly will be lost? How does surveillance affect social arrangements, institutions, and practices? What sort of beings do we become when we live in surveillance societies?

We will begin to answer these questions by making the best utilitarian case we can *for* surveillance, that is, for the kind of personal information gathering and distribution processes that are common in information societies. As we move to the case *against* surveillance and *for* privacy, the frame of the argument will start with a utilitarian analysis and then shift away from utilitarianism toward arguments based on autonomy and democracy.

"No Need to Worry"

Those who think we need not worry about intensive tracking and monitoring of individual behavior can, it would seem, make the following arguments. First, they can argue that if you aren't doing anything wrong, you should have no need to worry about being watched. Second, they can argue that privacy is overrated; they can point out that those who live in IT-configured societies have, in fact, let privacy go and this is evidence that privacy is neither valued nor valuable. Finally, they can argue that the information that organizations gather about individuals has enormous benefits to the organizations that gather it as well as to the individuals the information is about. We will consider each of these arguments in turn with a critical eye.

According to the first argument, if you haven't broken the law—if you are doing a good job at work, paying your bills on time, not doing anything illegal online or off—then you have no need to worry; nothing bad will happen to you from being watched. Someone putting forth this argument might go as far as to say that "privacy only protects people who have something to hide."

Unfortunately, the effects of personal information flow are much more complicated and not always as benign as this argument suggests. Remember that erroneous information can dramatically affect your life even if you have done nothing wrong. Suppose you are traveling away from your home and the police begin chasing your car. They point guns and rifles at you and force you to get out of your car. They frisk you. If you panic and respond suspiciously, you could be beaten or killed. Suppose further that the police officers believe you are driving a stolen vehicle and they disregard your explanation that the car is yours. You try to explain that it had been stolen, but was found last week and returned to you by the police in the city where you live. You find out later that when you reported the car stolen, the information was put into a database available to patrol cars in several bordering states. Evidently, however, the information that the car had been found and returned to its owner never made its way into the database for the patrol cars in this state. Aside from the increased risk to which you have been exposed, we might further suppose that it takes the police officers a day to confirm the truth of your claim that you were driving your own car. So, even though you have done nothing wrong, you may spend a night or two in jail and miss out on whatever you had been planning to do. That night in jail is almost certainly recorded electronically and the record of your incarceration can itself become an issue. For example, years from now you may lose an opportunity for a new job because a prospective employer finds a record of your jail time in a database, and doesn't even interview you despite your otherwise spotless record. You have been harmed even though you did nothing wrong. You also may not even be aware of the record of that night in jail, and you may never know why your life is being changed because of it.

Lest you think that erroneous information is rare, consider that in May of 2008, the Electronic Privacy Information Center (EPIC) filed a "friend of the court brief" in the U.S. Supreme Court urging that the accuracy of police databases be ensured. Describing how unreliable government databases have become, the brief urges the Court to "ensure an accuracy obligation on law enforcement agents who rely on criminal justice information systems."

In any case, the problem is not just that erroneous information can lead to decisions that are harmful to individuals. There is also the issue of irrelevant information—information that would be inappropriate or unfair for an organization to use. Remember in Scenario 1.2 in Chapter 1 how information posted on a social networking site (so that friends might see it) is used by a company to make a hiring decision. U.S. Title VII of the Civil Rights Act of 1964 prohibits employers from discriminating against applicants and employees on the basis of race or color, religion, sex, and national origin, yet when this information is readily accessible, it can be used without impunity. To make the point salient, consider a case reported some time ago. Forester and Morrison (1990) tell the story of a woman who took her landlord to court after he refused to do anything about the pest problem in her apartment. He did not show up for court but evicted her shortly after the court date. When she went looking for another apartment, she found that she was repeatedly turned down by landlords. She would look at an apartment, fill out an application form, and within a short time be told that the apartment was already rented to someone else. She later discovered that a database of names of individuals who take landlords to court was maintained and sold to landlords. Needless to say, landlords don't want to rent to individuals who are likely to take them to court. So here we have a case in which an individual experiences severe negative consequences for exercising her legal right to take her landlord to court.

Thus, it isn't true to say that if you do nothing wrong, you have no need to worry. Use of erroneous information may result in you being denied a benefit you are entitled to—a loan, a job, an educational opportunity—or subjected to treatment you don't deserve—being held up at an airport, arrested, being harassed by a collections agency. And, even when information is accurate, it can be used inappropriately to make decisions for which the information is irrelevant or even illegal to use (for example, when your race, religious affiliation, or sexual preference is used inappropriately).

The second no-need-to-worry argument is that privacy is overrated—people have traded it off for benefits, so it must not be valued or valuable. In support of this argument, consider that many of us give up privacy with regard to our purchasing habits when we shop online or at grocery stores where we use membership cards in order to receive discounts. Of course, companies make an effort to inform customers about their privacy policies, but consumers seem largely unaware of these policies and readily trade their personal information in exchange for discounts.

Although it may be true that individuals trade off privacy for what may seem like small benefits, it is unclear how this behavior should be interpreted. The fact that individuals readily give out personal information doesn't mean, necessarily, that they don't value privacy, or that privacy isn't valuable. They may be naïve and uninformed about the choices they are making, and/or they may just be wrong. The consequences of giving up personal information may be so distant from the act of disclosing it that individuals do not accurately perceive the negative consequences. The choices available to individuals when they opt to give out personal information may be constructed in such a way that individuals may be unknowingly choosing against their own interests. For example, often we are given only the choice to take the benefit (say a discount) in exchange for disclosure of information *or* not get the benefit at all. If individuals had more options, they might well choose more privacy. The bottom line here is that it is difficult to interpret the meaning of the choices that individuals are making about their personal information.

Another problem with the privacy-is-overrated claim is that even when individuals reasonably choose to give up privacy in a particular context, they are never given a choice with regard to the overall character of their society. What seems to be a choice about a *local* sharing of information may actually be a choice for *global* sharing, and so people are making a series of seemingly small choices without realizing the large cumulative effects of those choices. The cumulative effects of giving up privacy in this or that sector may not be evident when we focus on privacy in each particular domain separately. When considered separately, giving up privacy in online shopping may look benign, giving up privacy in air travel may seem reasonable, and submitting to closed circuit television monitoring in public places may not seem problematic. However, when it is all added up, we may find ourselves with little privacy at all.

In summary, there doesn't seem to be conclusive empirical evidence to support the claim that individuals don't value privacy.

The third argument is that personal information-gathering practices can be beneficial to information-gathering organizations and to their customers and subjects. This is a strong argument. Information-gathering organizations wouldn't be gathering personal information if they didn't think it would help them, and it often helps them in ways that improve their products and services. Thus, customers and clients can both benefit. Information about individuals helps organizations to make decisions and, arguably, the more information they have, the better the decisions. For example, the more information mortgage lenders and banks have about an individual, the better they should be able to determine the applicant's ability to pay back a loan. The fewer loan defaults there are, the more efficient the service, the lower the cost to borrowers. The more information that law enforcement agencies have about individuals, the better they are able to identify and capture criminals and terrorists—something from which many of us benefit. If television stations know what we watch on television and when we change the channel, they can use that information to develop programming more suited to our tastes. If marketing companies know our income level, and tastes in clothes, food, sports, and music, they can send us customized information and special offers for precisely the products that are affordable and fit our tastes.

On the other hand, there is some question as to whether organizations use the information they collect and manipulate to *serve* their customers, clients, and citizens. Indeed, there is considerable evidence that organizations use the information to *shape* their customers. There is also some question as to whether these organizations use appropriate information when they make decisions about individuals. Whether or not their decisions are justified or fair depends both on whether the information used is accurate and whether the information is relevant to the decision. Here the matter gets complicated, because information-gathering institutions use information about us in ways that have powerful effects on our lives, and appropriate use is essential to whether we are being treated fairly.

Although we have countered the first two of the no-need-to-worry arguments, the third requires more extended analysis. The third argument is utilitarian; the claim is that the intensive and extensive gathering and flow of personal information has significantly good consequences. Remember now that in a utilitarian framework, we must consider not just the positive consequences of a practice; we must consider both the positive and negative, and not just the consequences for some of those who are affected but for all of those who are affected.

The Importance of Privacy

Why, then, should we worry? What happens when personal information flows intensively and extensively in IT-configured societies? What is at stake here? Concern about the loss of personal privacy was the first public issue to gain significant attention when computers were first developed and databases of personal information began to be used by government agencies and private corporations. Privacy continues to receive a good deal of public attention, although over the years much of the battleground of privacy has shifted to a set of debates about personal information in different domains—credit records, workplace surveillance, airport screening, medical records, and so on. There has also been a conceptual shift to focusing on surveillance—information-gathering practices—as a supplement to the focus on privacy.

Privacy as an Individual Good

When the threat to privacy from IT-based practices first came to public attention in the 1970s, the issue was framed as a public policy issue, an issue calling for a balance between the needs of those who wanted information about individuals *and* the interests, preferences, or rights of the individuals who the information was about. It is important to note that in this framework it is primarily organizations—national, state, and local government agencies and private organizations—that are interested in information about individuals, and these organizational interests were seen to be in tension with individual interests or rights.

Early concerns about privacy focused on whether individuals could be said to have a legal, constitutional, or moral "right" to privacy. Of course, the arguments for a legal as compared to a constitutional or moral right are very different. In addition, privacy in relation to government differs from privacy in relation to the private sector. In the United States, legal notions of privacy can be traced back to two of the Amendments to the Constitution. The first amendment addresses freedom of speech and the press; the fourth amendment proscribes unreasonable search and seizure, and insures security in person, houses, papers, and effects. These two amendments deal, respectively, with the relationship between the government and the press, and between the government and the individual. The American forefathers were concerned about protecting citizens from the power of government. They did not envision the enormous power that private organizations have come to have over the lives of individuals. Corporations are often treated in law as persons in need of protection from government, rather than as powerful actors that need to be constrained in their dealings with individuals. Thus, the challenges of establishing rights of privacy in relation to private corporations are especially daunting.

The arguments for a "right" to privacy have been enormously convoluted and not nearly as successful as many had hoped (with the idea that a privacy right might "trump" other interests). Establishing that citizens have a "right" to something that is not explicitly stated in a historical document, such as the American Bill of Rights, is complicated in the sense that the right must be inferred from other rights, case law, common law, or other precedents. Legal rights can be created by means of legislation and, therefore, it is true that citizens of particular countries have certain kinds of privacy rights. For example, American citizens can refer to the Privacy Act of 1974 to understand their rights, and citizens of countries that are members of the European Union (E.U.) can refer to the E.U. data protection laws.

Our strategy here is not to focus on rights—legal or otherwise—but rather to try to understand broader concerns with regard to the importance of privacy. We will not argue that all data gathering and surveillance is bad, nor will we argue that privacy should always trump other values. Rather, we will argue that privacy is a complex value that is intertwined with autonomy, equality, and democracy, and its importance ought to be recognized in IT-based practices.

To begin to make the case for the value of privacy, we can return to the distinction made in Chapter 2 between instrumental and intrinsic values. Is privacy an instrumental value or an intrinsic value? That is, is privacy good because of what it leads to (enables) *or* is it good in itself? The standard arguments that have been made on behalf of privacy as an instrumental good take privacy to be instrumental for certain kinds of human relationships or for a diversity of such relationships. Fried (1968), for example, argued that friendship, intimacy, and trust could not develop in societies or contexts in which individuals were under constant surveillance. This argument was consistent with ideas hinted at in early twentieth-century science fiction works concerned with totalitarian control, works such as George Orwell's *1984* (1949) and Zamyatin's *We* (1920). These authors envisioned worlds in which individuals were continuously watched, and they suggested that in such societies it would be difficult, if not impossible, to have truly intimate moments, moments in which an individual might reveal his or her vulnerabilities, and establish intimacy with others. When individuals are being watched, it is impossible, they suggested, to develop trust and mutual respect.

Although a threat to friendship and intimacy does not seem to be at the heart of concerns about personal privacy today, the idea that privacy plays a role in *relationships* does seem to point in the right direction. Rachels (1975) put forward another, related argument that seems to get closer to the heart of the matter. Rachels argued that privacy is necessary to maintain a *diversity of relationships*. He was thinking about privacy as the control of information about yourself, and his important insight was that the kind of relationships we have with others—our parents, spouses, employers, friends, organizations—is a function of the information we have about each other. If everyone had the same information about you, you would not have a diversity of relationships. Think, for example, about what your best friend knows about you as compared with what your teacher, your employer, or Google knows about you. Or think of the differences between friends that you know only online and those that you interact with on- and offline. If we cannot control who has what information about us, it would seem that we couldn't have the diversity of relationships we have.

Taking this a step further, suppose that you have been seeing your current dentist for the last five years and she knows relatively little about you, except, of course, when it comes to your teeth. Now suppose you need extensive work done on your teeth, and you begin to go to her office regularly at a time of the day when she is not rushed. You strike up conversations about your various interests. Each time you talk to her, she learns more about you, and you learn more about her. Suppose you discover you have several hobbies and sports interests in common. You check her out on Facebook. You begin to chat online. At some point, she suggests that if you schedule your appointment as her last appointment of the day, you could go out and have a drink together afterwards. The relationship develops from one of patient–professional, to friends, perhaps to good friends, and it might eventually develop into an intimate or lifelong relationship. Notice that the changes in the nature of the relationship are, in large measure, a function of the amount and kind of information you exchange about one another.

Rachels's argument is, then, that we need privacy (control of information about ourselves) because it allows us to have a diversity of relationships; privacy is "instrumental to" a diversity of relationships. Of course, Rachels seems to presume that a diversity of relationships is intrinsically good, or he may be presuming, like Fried, that a diversity of relationships is good because it allows for friendship, intimacy, and trust which are intrinsically good. The important point in Rachels's argument is not, however, the focus on a diversity of relationships, but rather the idea that relationships are a function of information. Rachels understands that we control the nature of the relationships we have by controlling the kind of information we reveal about ourselves.

Unless we are careful here, Rachels's account may point us in the wrong direction. It would seem that the intense and wide ranging flow of personal information in information societies tends to facilitate a diversity of relationships. Social networking sites, chat rooms, and blogs open up more avenues for relationships and therefore more diversity of relationships. Similarly, when a company acquires information about you, infers that you would like their products, and sends you advertisements and special offers, you have acquired an additional relationship. The same could be said about a law enforcement agency that finds you in a database search of individuals who belong to Muslim organizations. However, in the latter cases, although you have a wider diversity of relationships, you haven't had much say in the creation of these relationships. Adding unwanted relationships may increase the diversity of your relationships, but this kind of diversity doesn't seem valuable. The value of a diversity of relationships is more complicated than Rachels suggests.

To get to the heart of the matter, we need to take Rachels's argument a step further. Gossip provides a good illustration of Rachels' idea that when we lose control of information, we lose control of relationships. When gossip about you is being circulated, you may feel threatened by the loss of control you have over your personal information. When others are gossiping about you, you don't have any control over what is being said about you and to whom the information is being given. You cannot control what people will think about you and you cannot control how they will treat you. Individuals have an interest in being viewed and treated in certain ways, and information affects how one is viewed and treated. Once the information begins to move from person to person (and organization to organization), you have no way of knowing who has what information about you. If the information is false, you have no way of contacting everyone and correcting what they've been told. Even if the information is true, there may be individuals who will treat you unfairly on the basis of this information. Yet because you don't know who has the information and whether or how it is being used, your ability to control how you are being treated is diminished.

The gossip example suggests that control of personal information is a means by which we control the relationships we have and how we are treated in those relationships. In short, control of information about ourselves is an important component of our autonomy. If we have little say in how we are treated, we are powerless. Of course, this doesn't mean that individuals should have absolute control of all information about themselves but it points to a connection between privacy (as control of information about one's self) and autonomy. This insight can be developed in two different directions. The first emphasizes contextual norms and the second emphasizes democracy.

Although the gossip example explains why we might want to control personal information, we cannot expect others to make decisions about us without information. Information about us flows in everyday life when others see us, hear what we say, and interact with us. This information flows from one person to another and individuals have little control of how others interpret the information. Moreover, we cannot expect to hide certain kinds of information when we are in particular contexts or relationships. For example, if you apply for a loan, it is reasonable for the lender to ask about your financial condition—for example, your income, assets, and debts. If you apply for a job, it is appropriate for the employer to ask about your employment history, education, and experience. Ideally, perhaps we should be able to control information and release it only when we choose to enter a particular context, that is, when we request a loan, purchase a ticket for an international flight, or have a medical bill covered by an insurance company.

When it comes to privacy, our attention should be on information practices in particular domains rather than on privacy in some broad or amorphous sense. The simple question about the value of privacy turns into a set of questions about what kind of information should flow, where it should flow in particular contexts, and who is allowed to control it.

Privacy as Contextual Integrity

Nissenbaum's account (2004) of privacy as contextual integrity does exactly what is called for. The account begins with the insight that there are information *norms* in every domain of life. The norms vary from domain to domain but in each context individuals have expectations about: (1) what kinds of information are appropriate and inappropriate, and (2) how that information will be distributed. According to Nissenbaum, then, when information norms are violated, an individual's privacy is violated. When you apply for a loan at a bank, you reasonably expect that the bank will inquire about your salary, financial assets, and debts, but you would be surprised and dismayed if the bank asked about your ethnic background, political affiliations, medical history, or sexual preferences. On the other hand, in the context of receiving health care, you would expect to be asked about your medical history; you might even expect that some of the questions about your medical history might connect to your ethnic background or possibly even your sexual preferences (although you wouldn't expect this to happen if you went in to have a broken arm set). You would not expect, in the medical context, to be asked about the details of your financial investments or political affiliations. All of this shows that there are norms with regard to what is appropriate information in particular contexts.

Similarly, there are norms about how the information revealed in particular contexts will be distributed. In the United States, cash purchases of $10,000 or more must be reported to the Internal Revenue Service. When it comes to criminal records, there are restrictions on who can access particular kinds of records as well as requirements for disclosing records to other agencies. Distribution of medical records is also restricted. On the other hand, credit reports are widely distributed to those who request them and are willing to pay. Norms for friendship are such that when you share embarrassing information with your best friend, you don't expect to see what you said posted on your friend's blog. If you do, you may reevaluate that friendship.

Information norms—norms with regard to appropriate/inappropriate kinds of information and distribution of information—are both formal and informal. Formal norms are established and explicitly stated in legislation or specified in organizational policies that are made available to employees or customers or the public. Individuals can sue organizations that violate formal norms. Other norms are informal and conventional; they are enforced primarily by social expectations and social pressure. In the United States, for example, it is generally considered impolite to ask someone—even someone you know fairly well—how much money they make. Although you might tell your close friends about your love life, you would be surprised if someone you met for the first time were to ask you about your latest romantic entanglement. Many of these informal information norms are subtle, and often they are unclear. They can vary widely in different cultures and countries. For example, although doctors and lawyers are formally expected to keep information about their patients/clients confidential, conventions with regard to what you tell your hairdresser, car mechanic, or coach are unclear. In a small town in Italy the norms about sharing personal information may be dramatically different from the norms in Tokyo.

Norms also can change over time as institutions and practices change. To change a formal norm, a new law may be enacted or a new public statement of policy issued. Change in informal information norms is common, especially as part of broader social and cultural change. Importantly, changes in information norms are often triggered by a change in technology. Remember that IT expands the possibilities for information creation and flow. This has constituted situations that fit Moor's notion of a policy vacuum. Organizations may—with adoption of a new technology—be able to create and distribute new forms of information and there may be no preexisting norms with regard to whether or how the new type of information should be used or distributed. Often norms evolve in a rather ad hoc manner with organizations simply using whatever technology is available to them while their clients, consumers, and the public are unaware of the practices until some event occurs, such as the government demanding records of weblogs. Only then do users become aware of the data that their ISPs collect. Scenario 4.1 is a good example here. Users have only recently discovered that Google can and does search e-mail for content.

Nissenbaum's account of privacy as contextual integrity draws our attention to information norms and how they vary with context. Her account implicitly explains why privacy policy debates have centered on legislation and policies for particular domains; information norms have to be worked out for particular sectors or contexts. The account also helps us to understand why privacy is so difficult to protect. IT tools are often invisible in the domains in which they are used and they are adopted and used without public announcement. Thus, customers, clients, and citizens are unaware of information norms in many contexts. They have no reason to inquire, and no way of finding out, whether information norms are being adhered to. Without knowing the norms and whether they are being adhered to, one doesn't know whether one is being treated appropriately or not.

Were we to follow this stream of analysis further, we could delve more deeply into domains in which information is particularly sensitive or especially powerful. For example, medical information is particularly sensitive, and employee monitoring is powerful in part because individuals spend so many hours of their lives in the workplace. However, we turn now to another stream of analysis that follows from our focus on control of information about ourselves and the connection between privacy and autonomy.

Privacy as a Social Good Essential for Democracy

We arrived at this point in our analysis by thinking about privacy as an individual good and asking about its importance to individuals in their relationships with others, be it with organizations or other individuals. This strategy has recently been called into question by those who point out that, in many cases, arguing for an individual interest in (or even right to) privacy has not succeeded in convincing policy makers to give individuals control over personal information. When privacy is treated as an individual interest and then pitted against the interests of public and private organizations in a utilitarian cost-benefit framework, organizational goals and interests have trumped the interests of individuals. The U.S. Patriot Act is a good case in point. In the face of the threat of terrorism, and in the interest of security, this legislation gave enormous power to security agencies to gather information about individuals without much protection for their privacy or civil liberties.

In her 1995 book, *Legislating Privacy*, Priscilla M. Regan examined three privacy policy debates that took place in the United States—information privacy, communications privacy, and psychological privacy. She concluded that when individual privacy is balanced against social goods such as security and government efficiency, personal privacy loses. Regan suggests that instead of framing privacy as an individual good, we should understand it as a social good. As a social good, privacy would be on par with other social goods such as security or efficiency. Although privacy might not always trump the other social values, it is much more likely to get a fair hearing when it is understood as a social good. Think here of the utilitarian calculus; when social good is balanced against the good of some individuals, social good generally wins. However, when two social goods are pitted against each other, both must be taken into account.

How, then, can we make the case for privacy as a social good? We can do this by returning to our discussion of a connection between privacy and autonomy but think of autonomy not just as an individual good but rather as essential to democracy. To understand this connection, we can consider an observation that a number of privacy theorists have made about information societies. They have observed that living in an IT-configured society is similar to living in a "panopticon"—a structure designed by Jeremy Bentham (1787) to serve as a prison.

Autonomy, Democracy, and the Panoptic Gaze

Bentham's prison was designed so that the chambers in which prisoners lived would be arranged in a circle and the side of each cell facing the inside of the circle would be made of glass. The guard tower would be placed in the middle of the circle, so a guard standing in the guard tower would have full view of every chamber. The prison design did not allow for two-way observation; that is, the prisoners could not see the guard in the tower. The idea of the panopticon was picked up by Michel Foucault in 1975 and brought to wider public attention. The claim that is often made about both writers is that they both understood the power of surveillance (continuous observation). They understood that surveillance affects the behavior of those who are observed. In the panopticon, a prison guard need not even be there at every moment; as long as prisoners believe they are being watched, or at least believe that they are probably being watched, they will adjust their behavior and adhere to the norms they believe the guards want to enforce.

Although interpretations of this effect vary, part of the effect of the "panoptic gaze" is achieved by individuals internalizing the views of their watchers. When individuals believe they are being watched, they are compelled to think of themselves as their observers might think of them. Thus, they come to see themselves as their watchers see them, and this leads the individuals both to experience themselves in relation to the watchers' norms and to behave quite differently than they might if they were not aware of being observed.

In IT-configured societies, if much of what we do is recorded and likely to have future consequences in the way we are treated, then we have to consider our watchers and their norms whenever we act. On the one hand, this effect may have positive consequences; for example, we are more likely to abide by the law, be careful about our debts, stay focused at work, and so on. On the other hand, our freedom and autonomy are diminished, especially when we have had little say in setting the norms. It is not just that we have to be careful about abiding by the law or paying our debts; we also have to be careful about what we post on our Facebook sites, what we search for on Google, what law enforcement officials might make of our phone calls to the Middle East, and who knows our sexual preference, drinking habits, religion, and so on. There are at least two quite different concerns here. The first is the dampening effect on our freedom (autonomy). The second can be seen by asking who are our watchers, and how have they selected the norms of behavior by which they evaluate us?

The dampening effect on freedom is significant but it is not just a matter of narrowing our freedom. Surveillance undermines our ability and capacity for democratic citizenship. Living in a panopticon means that individuals have very little space to develop themselves independently; they have little opportunity to develop autonomy. Jeffrey Reiman (1995) puts the point sharply:

> To the extent that a person experiences himself as subject to public observation, he naturally experiences himself as subject to public review. As a consequence, he will tend to act in ways that are publicly acceptable. People who are shaped to act in ways that are publicly acceptable will tend to act in safe ways, to hold and express and manifest the most widely-accepted views, indeed, the lowest-common denominator of conventionality. . . . Trained by society to act conventionally at all times, people will come so to think and so to feel. . . . As the inner life that is subject to social convention grows, the still deeper inner life that is separate from social convention contracts and, given little opportunity to develop, remains primitive. . . . You lose both the practice of making your own sense out of your deepest and most puzzling longings, and the potential for self-discovery and creativity that lurk within a rich inner life. . . . To say that people who suffer this loss will be easy to oppress doesn't say enough. They won't have to be oppressed, since there won't be anything in them that is tempted to drift from the beaten path.

The idea of democracy is the idea that citizens have the freedom to exercise their autonomy and in so doing develop their capacities to do things that have not been thought of before. Democracy requires citizens who are capable of critical thinking, individuals who can argue about the issues of the day and learn from the argument so that they can vote intelligently. All of this makes for a citizenry that is active and pushing the world forward progressively. But if the consequences of trying something new—an unconventional idea, a challenge to authority—are too negative, few citizens will develop the capacity to take risks. Democracy will be lost.

The argument for privacy is, then, an argument for the space that individuals need to develop autonomy. When the argument for privacy is framed in this way, privacy is shown to be something that is not just an individual good that can be diminished for the sake of a social good; rather, it is shown to be a social good, such an important social good that it should not be eliminated when it comes into tension with other social goods, even if the social good is security and certainly not if it is better consumer services.

The connections between privacy, autonomy, and democracy are so close that it doesn't seem accurate to say that one is instrumental to the other. Privacy, autonomy, and democracy are so intertwined that one is inconceivable without the other. Privacy is not just "instrumental to" autonomy or democracy; it is essential to both.

Data Mining, Social Sorting, and Discrimination

We can take this argument further by noting that the problem is not just that we are being tracked and monitored; the norms by which we are being measured, evaluated, and treated are often not subject to public discussion and negotiation. Often they are invisible to the individuals being watched, evaluated, and treated. When it comes to governments and government agencies, the norms may well have been established through a political process, for example, the Patriot Act, although even then in many cases the norms are kept inaccessible in the name of security. In other cases as with online tracking and marketing, there may be no rationale given or information may be protected by trade secrecy laws. In either case, those who are watched may not know they are being watched, or may know they are being watched but not know how the information is being collected or used (i.e., they don't know the information norms in a particular context). Furthermore, with the use of data mining and neural nets, even the people tracking do not know explicitly why some people are singled out for attention and others are ignored.

What is at issue here is the practices of organizations using personal information, and with data mining it is not just the fact that individuals often don't know that they are being tracked and monitored or don't know the information norms for particular contexts. Information gathered for one purpose is merged and mined to identify patterns of behavior that no individual could have imagined they were revealing when they (intentionally or unintentionally) disclosed information. Organizations gather information about lots and lots of people, merge the information, and "mine" it for patterns of behavior that are relevant to the organization's goals. Depending on the goal of the organization, individual customers, clients, or "persons of interest" are categorized into groups and the organization treats us as a member of the group. Scenario 4.3 illustrates just this.

Organizations have goals—be it a security agency screening an airline passenger list for potential terrorists or TechStation.com looking to increase its sales—and they want to achieve their goals efficiently. In theory, the more information they have about individuals, the better decisions they can make. IT tools have been developed to create and analyze personal information to help various organizations achieve their goals, and the reproducibility of IT makes it possible to collect an inordinate amount of fine-grained information and merge it with other data. Clickstream gives Web-based companies information about how customers interact with their website, information they can use to maximize the likelihood of a visitor buying something. Data mining tools look for patterns in data that an organization might not even have thought would be relevant to their goals.

We should point out here that although we have suggested that organizations gather and process information in order to achieve their goals, information may continue to be collected even though it doesn't serve those goals. For example, although it is used abundantly in the UK, recent reports suggest that CCTV has very little effect on crime rates. As a *Guardian* reporter recently explained: "Massive investment in CCTV cameras to prevent crime in the UK has failed to have a significant impact, despite billions of pounds spent on the new technology . . . Only 3 percent of street robberies in

London were solved using CCTV images, despite the fact that Britain has more security cameras than any other country in Europe." [http://www.guardian.co.uk/uk/2008/may/06/ukcrime1]

Whether an organization is interested in consumption, terrorist behavior, or employee productivity, the "name of the game" is *prediction*. Organizations want to predict how individuals are likely to behave and treat them accordingly. A bank may want to know the likelihood of you having enough money in the future to use their investment services. If you are likely to be a long-term, profit-generating customer, they may be willing to offer you lower interest rates on loans or higher rates on interest-bearing accounts. On the other hand, if you are not likely to earn enough money in the future to take advantage of their more profitable services, then the bank may be less interested in you; it may charge you a fee for your checking account while more desirable customers are offered free checking. Similarly, the airline security system is interested in knowing whether you fit the profile of a terrorist. They sort people in a variety of ways including by the ethnicity of names. Here we see how crude the sorting can be because the probability of someone with a Middle Eastern name being a terrorist is, no doubt, so small as to be insignificant but security agencies use it anyway.

Notice that there is a conundrum here. Although these practices may seem to make sense as a way of predicting behavior, they also fit the pattern of prejudice and injustice insofar as individuals are being treated as members of a class—stereotypes—and not as individuals. The parallel between this social sorting and discrimination is well recognized and, in general, organizations avoid sorting individuals into categories such as race to avoid being accused of discrimination. Antidiscrimination laws apply to using race, gender, religion, and so on. Critics worry that even though these categories are avoided, the categories that are used indirectly lead to discrimination. Some of the literature in this area refers to this as "weblining" to show the parallel to "redlining," a practice in the insurance industry that was made illegal because it was so discriminatory.

Although the categories that organizations use often seem demeaning to individuals, the most significant criticism is that the sorting leads to inequality. Different categories of individuals are treated differently, and the differential treatment results in individuals having very different opportunities. Although this might be justified when we examine a particular context, the cumulative effects of social sorting may well be divided and segmented (if not caste-like) societies. If you fit one category, you are likely to: avoid the suspicion of law enforcement, find employment, travel without being harassed, borrow money with ease, obtain insurance, and receive preferential pricing and access. But if you fit a different category, your opportunities in all of these domains are likely to be diminished. As in our discussion of the panopticon, we see again how democracy may be undermined through these practices.

Crude Categories

To illustrate the problem further, it may be helpful to explore a radical idea. What would happen if the United States adopted legislation that prohibited organizations from using anything but the crudest (that is, broadest) categories? Suppose that all customers and clients had to be treated alike and no information could be gathered or used to sort individuals into categories. To be sure, this would create many problems but suppose it was, at least, the default position so that any organization that wanted to do otherwise had to petition an agency—call it the Category Agency—for permission to use other categories. How would this transform the flow of information?

Consider some examples. In political campaigns, information for potential voters would have to be targeted to all citizens; no distinctions could be made between citizens who lived in this or that district or who had this or that "demographic." All citizens would get the same information about candidates. Similarly, imagine that consumer-marketing firms would only be able to advertise to consumers, writ large; that is, they would have to send the same advertising to all consumers and air the same commercials in all regions of the country. Employers would have to give all employees the same benefits. Airlines would have to charge the same for a ticket from one place to another no matter who or where an individual bought a ticket.

A few advantages come immediately into view. The first, and perhaps too obvious one, is that individuals would have a good deal more privacy because there wouldn't be much fine-grained data gathered about them. There would be no use for it.

Second, individuals would be treated much more as autonomous beings. Instead of having their behavior watched with inferences made about who they are and what they want, individuals would have to be asked. That is, advertisements could be distributed and special discounts could be made, and individuals would respond—rather than their response being predicted. Surveys could be taken, but a wide spectrum of individuals would have to be surveyed and the results accumulated into one database that revealed "customer" attitudes. Individuals would, it seems, be treated as rational beings capable of thinking, processing information, and making judgments, rather than entities to be watched and manipulated. Indeed, in the process of getting information to individuals qua individuals (rather than to a category), we would all be exposed to a wider range of information—that was sent to everyone—and called upon to think about it.

Third, and related to the second point, individuals would be treated as changeable—because they have autonomy. In the fine-grained, predictive systems, organizations put us in a category and then feed us information accordingly. This makes us more and more what we already are. In a system of crude categories, individuals are exposed to a wide range of information and can do their own choosing and selecting, and over time may change their likes and dislikes, attitudes, and political beliefs. Perhaps ironically, when we treat people equally, people are more likely to learn and to grow, and are *less* likely to become homogenous.

This proposal is not without drawbacks, but it adds to the picture of the importance of privacy in the sense that it shows us that when personal information is used the way it is being used now, individuals are treated as objects, not as persons—as means to the goals of organizations, not as ends in themselves (rational beings capable of making decisions for themselves).

Summary of the Arguments for Privacy and Against Surveillance

Returning to our broad analysis of privacy, where do we stand? We have seen that personal information flows intensively and extensively in IT-configured societies. The flow of information shapes organizational practices and these practices powerfully affect the lives and experiences of individuals. The effects of these practices have been framed as issues of privacy, but we have seen that privacy is an extremely complex idea and the effects of personal information gathering practices are multifaceted, touching on other values such as autonomy, equality, and democracy.

We don't claim to have figured out the entire privacy puzzle here. But we have identified a number of accounts of the value of privacy. When personal information flows as readily as it does in IT-configured societies, privacy protection is a daunting challenge. We turn now to consider some general strategies for privacy protection.

IS PRIVACY OVER? STRATEGIES FOR SHAPING DATA FLOW

It is not uncommon to hear it said that "privacy is over; forget it." Such statements are usually followed by an explanation that there is just too much personal information available, and once it resides in a database anywhere in the world, it is impossible to control where it flows. Such statements are typically followed by an example of some form of personal information that we would want to be quickly and easily available—say you are traveling away from home and are in a car accident. "Wouldn't you want the medical staff to be able to get access to your medical records wherever they are?" Obviously, the answer is "yes." However, saying "yes" to this question does not seem equivalent to saying we should let go of privacy altogether. Rather, the example suggests that in the domain of medical records, we want the norm of distribution to be such that medical professionals, or whomever we want, to be able to get access and as quickly as would serve our interests.

The "privacy is over" claim seems too glib and overly simplistic. Of course, there are many contexts in which personal information should be readily available to certain users. Nevertheless, there is too much at stake here to throw up our hands and give up on shaping the production and flow of personal information. Privacy issues can, and should, be framed as part of the larger enterprise of structuring and constituting democratic social institutions in IT-configured societies. This is a matter of strategy as well as specifying policies for particular domains.

Our analysis above has referred to a relatively small number of the issues that are currently being debated in the United States as well as other countries. The breadth and complexity of the issues can be grasped by taking a look at several key websites on the topic. We draw your attention in particular to the Electronic Privacy Information Center (http://www.epic.org), Privacy International (http://www.privacyinternational. org), the Electronic Frontier Foundation (http://www.eff.org), the Center for Democracy and Technology (http://www.cdt.org), privacy.org (http://www.privacy. org); and the Center for Digital Democracy (http://www.democraticmedia.org). These sites provide a wealth of information on current issues, proposed legislation, court cases in which privacy issues are being contested, and news alerts. The range of issues is illustrated, for example, by the list of current issues that appears on privacy.org:

Biometrics technologies

Video surveillance

Online privacy and e-Commerce

Workplace monitoring

Wireless communications and location tracking

Data profiling

Criminal identity theft

Background checks

Information broker industry

Public records on the Internet

Financial privacy

Medical records confidentiality and genetic privacy

Wiretapping and electronic communications

Youth privacy issues

Digital rights management

Digital television and broadband cable TV

Radio Frequency Identification (RFID)

Real ID

Absence of federal-level privacy protection law

Behavioral targeting

A review of the debates over these issues reveals some common strategies that are adopted or are being proposed across different contexts. Although not trying to be thorough, we will discuss several strategies that seem important for understanding privacy debates or taking action.

Fair Information Practices

A recurrent issue in privacy debates is whether sectors or industries should be regulated with respect to their personal information practices through legislation and penalties for failure to comply *or* should be allowed to self-regulate. Most industries prefer not to be regulated by the government. They claim that they know their domain better than the government and hence, know better how to encourage and achieve high standards of performance (in many different areas, including privacy). In self-regulation, an industry will gather its members, develop a set of rules or standards, and agree to abide by those standards. If all (especially the most powerful) members agree to abide by the standards, then the playing field is level and competition will not force a lowering of standards.

Often self-regulation works, and it works especially well when the interests of the industry and the interests of the public are aligned. On the other hand, when self-regulation doesn't work and the public or a set of customers or clients are not being served, regulation is necessary. In the case of privacy, at least in the United States, there is a mixture of self-regulation and legislation, although there is some indication that self-regulation doesn't work. Consider a 2005 report from EPIC entitled "Privacy Self Regulation: A Decade of Disappointment." In the report, EPIC entreats the Federal Trade Commission and Congress to "seriously reconsider its faith in self-regulatory privacy approaches. They have led to a decade of disappointment; one where Congress has been stalled and the public anesthetized, as privacy practices steadily worsened." EPIC calls for the government to "create a floor of standards for protection of personal information based on Fair Information Practices."

We do not want to engage in the debate over self-regulation here. Whether there is self-regulation or legislation, a set of general principles are commonly used, either as the basis for structuring legislation or for specifying self-regulatory standards. The "Code of Fair Information Practices" was developed and recommended for implementation in the 1973 Report of the Secretary of Health, Education, and Welfare's Advisory Committee on Automated Personal Data Systems (titled "Records, Computers and the Rights of Citizens"). Although it was never made into law, it has served as a model and been influential in the development of privacy policy. The Code specifies that: (1) there must be no personal data record-keeping system whose very existence is secret, (2) there must be a way for an individual to find out what information about him or her is in a record and how it is used, (3) there must be a way for an individual to prevent information about him or her that was obtained for one purpose from being used or made available for other purposes without his or her consent, (4) there must be a way for an individual to correct or amend a record of identifiable information about him or her, and (5) any organization creating, maintaining, using, or disseminating records of identifiable personal data must assure the reliability of the data for their intended use and must take precautions to prevent the misuse of data.

To see how these principles have been interpreted today, consider the following statement that appears on the website of the Federal Trade Commission (http://www.ftc.gov):

> Over the past quarter century, government agencies in the United States, Canada, and Europe have studied the manner in which entities collect and use personal information—their "information practices"—and the safeguards required to assure those practices are fair and provide adequate privacy protection. (27) The result has been a series of reports, guidelines, and model codes that represent widely-accepted principles concerning fair information practices. (28) Common to all of these documents [hereinafter referred to as "fair information practice codes"] are five core principles of privacy protection: (1) Notice/Awareness; (2) Choice/Consent; (3) Access/Participation; (4) Integrity/Security; and (5) Enforcement/Redress.

Other examples of the code can be found on the Web. For example, on the website of the Center for Democracy and Technology you will find "Generic Principles of Fair Information Practices that include Principles of Openness, Individual Participation, Collection Limitation", Data Quality, Finality, Security, and Accountability [http://www.cdt.org/privacy/guide/basic/generic.html]

Thus, fair information practices might be understood as the starting place for thinking about privacy policy. However, although the principles are recognized, they have not been uniformly interpreted or implemented. Information collected for one purpose is often used for other purposes, for example, when grocery stores sell information from their loyalty cards to advertisers. In Scenario 4.1, we see that e-mail (which we might not even think of as information) is scanned for advertising purposes. Another area of slippage from the intention of the Code is the right of individuals to access personal information held in databases. Although this right may exist in theory, most of us have no idea where information about us resides and how we would go about getting access to that information, or how we could correct the information if it were erroneous.

Transparency

A review of recent debate on privacy issues suggests that a common approach being proposed is the adoption of transparency policies. One of the reasons that consumers and clients are so compliant when it comes to their privacy is that they are unaware of information practices. For example, most of those who shop online are unaware that their clickstream is being tracked and this information is being put into a pool of other data. Most Gmail users are unaware of content scanning.

Transparency would go a long way toward finding out exactly what citizens, clients, and consumers think about information practices. Earlier in this chapter we examined the claim that people don't value privacy. There we noted that because the public knows so little about information practices, we cannot say whether most people care or don't care about who has their personal information and how it is used. Making these practices transparent would be a good first step in finding out what the public really thinks about privacy.

Opt-In versus Opt-Out

Another general approach is to insist on opt-in rather than opt-out policies. This has been a topic of dispute in a recent discussion of telephone records. Evidently, the Federal Communications Commission and the National Cable and Telecommunications Association are scrabbling over whether records of whom we call should be an opt-in or opt-out. [See www.epic.org]

The opt-in versus opt-out decision was also a factor in the controversy over Facebook's Beacon program. Mentioned earlier, this was Facebook's advertising program that announced to one's friends what one had just bought. For Facebook this was an advertising schema. They could collect revenue from the companies for advertising purchases from them. Facebook users reacted with anger. As Mark Zuckerberg (CEO of Facebook) explains: "The problem with our initial approach of making it an opt-out system instead of opt-in was that if someone forgot to decline to share something, Beacon still went ahead and shared it with their friends." [http://blog.facebook.com/blog.php?post=7584397130]

The opt-in rather than opt-out strategy goes hand in hand with transparency. Indeed, given how little information consumers, clients, and citizens have about information practices, the opt-out strategy seems unfair if not deceptive. Personal information is gathered and used and if we figure out what is happening we can opt-out. By contrast, if organizations cannot use personal information about us unless they get our permission, then they have to inform us of their practices and convince us that we want to opt-in. This is consistent with our analysis above insofar as opt-in treats us as rational beings capable of making decisions, rather than passive objects to be manipulated.

Design and Computer Professionals

Rarely mentioned although sometimes implicit, we would like to call attention to the role that IT professionals can play in protecting privacy. The architecture of IT systems can make a big difference in what kind of data is collected and how it flows from place to place. This is the business of IT professionals. Chapter 7 is devoted to a discussion of IT professionals and their responsibilities, but here we want to note that they can play a role in protecting privacy in several important ways. IT professionals could collectively make a commitment to protecting privacy similar to the commitment that environmental engineers seem to adopt with respect to protection of the environment. This is not a farfetched idea because the original ACM (Association for Computing Machinery) Code of Professional Conduct (passed by the ACM Council in 1973) specified that: An ACM member, whenever dealing with data concerning individuals, shall always consider the principle of the individuals' privacy and seek to:

- Minimize the data collected
- Limit authorized access to the data
- Provide proper security for the data
- Determine the required retention period of the data
- Ensure proper disposal of the data

When the code was revised in 1992, these edicts were dropped and replaced with a General Moral Imperative specifying that an ACM member will "Respect the privacy of others." The Guidelines explain that: "It is the responsibility of professionals to maintain the privacy and integrity of data describing individuals. This includes taking precautions to ensure the accuracy of data, as well as protecting it from unauthorized access or accidental disclosure to inappropriate individuals."

Individual IT professionals can make a difference both in the way they design systems and in the way they present and discuss decisions with their clients. Because of their special expertise, IT professionals are often in the best position to evaluate the security and reliability of databases of personal information, and the potential uses and abuses of that information. Thus, they are in a position to inform their clients or employers about privacy issues and to participate in public policy discussions.

In particular, because IT professionals understand how IT systems work better than anyone else, they can use their expertise to encourage practices that safeguard privacy.

Personal Steps for All IT Users

Several of the websites we mentioned above provide recommendations for individuals and what they can do to protect themselves. EPIC provides a list of links to tools that one can use to send e-mail anonymously, surf the net anonymously, or make sure that one's computer is secure. The Center for Democracy and Technology's Guide to online privacy lists ten ways to protect privacy online:

1. Look for privacy policies on the Web.
2. Get a separate e-mail account for personal e-mail.
3. Teach your kids that giving out personal information online means giving it to strangers.
4. Clear your memory cache after browsing.
5. Make sure that online forms are secure.
6. Reject unnecessary cookies.
7. Use anonymous remailers.
8. Encrypt your e-mail.
9. Use anonymizers while browsing.
10. Opt-out of third-party information sharing. [http://www.cdt.org/privacy/guide/basic/topten.html]

The Electronic Frontier Foundation also has a list of twelve ways to protect your online privacy:

1. Do not reveal personal information inadvertently.
2. Turn on cookie notices in your Web browser, and/or use cookie management software or infomediaries.
3. Keep a "clean" e-mail address.
4. Do not reveal personal details to strangers or just-met "friends."
5. Realize you may be monitored at work, avoid sending highly personal e-mail to mailing lists, and keep sensitive files on your home computer.
6. Beware of sites that offer some sort of reward or prize in exchange for your contact information or other personal details.
7. Do not reply to spammers, for any reason.
8. Be conscious of Web security.
9. Be conscious of home computer security.
10. Examine privacy policies and seals.
11. Remember that YOU decide what information about yourself to reveal, when, why, and to whom.
12. Use encryption!

These lists and advice are relevant to taking an ethical stance. If an individual values privacy, both on an individual level and as a broader social good, then there are personal actions that can be taken to enhance individual privacy. If enough individuals protect their own privacy diligently, a society's overall privacy is enhanced. This kind of individual and collective action is an alternative to the "it's over—privacy is passé" argument described above. Individuals convinced that privacy does matter do not have to passively accept the status quo. In this way, an ethical analysis of the value of privacy leads to actions that resist information intrusions.

A Note on Privacy and Globalization

Finally, the many and complex issues of privacy that we have been discussing arise in the context of an increasingly globalized economy. This means that personal information flows across national borders. Yet privacy laws vary from country to country. It is a complex and delicate issue as to what happens to personal data when it moves from one place with one set of laws to another place with a different set of laws. Many questions arising from this situation have yet to be settled.

Conclusion

Privacy may be the single most important facet of the ethical issue surrounding IT. We have tried to show this by making clear the importance of privacy to democratic society and the subtle ways in which our lives are changed when we are being watched. Individuals who walk through life knowing that each step creates a digital record that may haunt them for years differ significantly from individuals who walk through life confident that they live in an open society in which the rules are known and fair. It is sobering to think about which kind of persons we have become in the last two decades.

Protecting personal privacy is not easy and is not likely to get easier. The most effective approach to privacy protection requires action on several fronts. One thing is for sure: The use of personal information is not going to diminish of its own accord. Information about individuals is extremely valuable both in the private and public sector. Individuals may not realize how valuable that information is, or how much is at stake if privacy is lost. It will take a concerted effort from individuals and organizations to reverse, or at least confront, the loss of privacy that has accompanied the growth of IT.

Study Questions

1. What are the significant differences between personal information flow with IT and personal information flow without IT?
2. What are three arguments that can be made for why we shouldn't worry about privacy? How can each of the three be countered?
3. Explain Rachels's argument that privacy is necessary for a diversity of relationships.
4. What does gossip have to do with privacy?
5. Nissenbaum's account of privacy as contextual integrity explains privacy in terms of two norms. Explain, and give two examples of each type of norm. Choose examples that show how the norms vary from context to context.

6. What is the panopticon? How do prisoners experience themselves differently when they are in panopticon prisons?
7. What happens to people who are watched all the time according to Reiman?
8. Pick a domain of human activity in which information about individuals is gathered (e.g., insurance, buying, political campaigning, and fund-raising), and describe how organizations in that sector sort individuals into categories and try to predict their behavior.
9. What would be the benefits and drawbacks of limiting organizations to using only crude categories in their information-gathering practices?
10. What are the five principles of the code of fair information practices?
11. How would transparency policies protect privacy?
12. What is the difference between opt-in policies and opt-out policies?
13. What do you think are the three most significant personal steps an individual can take to protect his or her personal information?

Digital
Intellectual
Property

SCENARIOS

Scenario 5.1 Obtaining Pirated Software Abroad

Carol works as a computer consultant for a large consulting company. She loves her job because it allows her to continuously learn about new IT applications and she uses many of these applications in her work. When Carol goes on vacation in Southeast Asia, she decides to check out the computer stores to see what sort of software and hardware is available. While rummaging in one store, Carol finds an office suite package. It includes a spreadsheet, word processor, presentation applications, and more. Indeed, it looks identical to a package made by a well-known American company, a package that she has been thinking about buying. The price in the United States is around $1,200, which is why she has been reluctant to buy it, but here the package costs the equivalent of $50. She has heard that countries like the one she is in do not honor U.S. copyrights. She notices that the written documentation looks like a duplicated copy; it doesn't look like it has been professionally printed. The deal is just too good to resist; she buys the software.

As she prepares for the airplane trip home, she wonders where she should put the package. She's not sure what will happen if custom officials notice it as she reenters the United States. Has Carol done anything wrong? Would it be unfair if U.S. custom officials stopped Carol and confiscated the software package?

Scenario 5.2 Free Software that Follows Proprietary Software

Bingo Software Systems has an idea for a new file organizing system that Bingo believes will be significantly more intuitive than existing systems. Bingo is a small company employing twenty people. It obtains venture capital and spends three years developing the system. Over the course of the three years, Bingo invests approximately two million dollars in development of the system. When completed, the new system is successfully marketed for about a year, and Bingo recovers about 50 percent of its investment. However, after the first year, several things happen that substantially cut into sales. First, a competing company, Pete's Software, starts distributing a file organizing system that performs many of the same functions that Bingo's software does, but has a different interface and a few new features. Pete's Software has put its software on its website for free download using a GPLv2 license (this is called "Free Software"). Pete's Software hopes to recoup its investment by selling its services customizing the software for individual clients. It appears that Pete's programmers studied Bingo's system, adopted a similar general approach, and then produced a new piece of software that provided functionality comparable to that in Bingo's software but more efficiently. As far as Bingo programmers can tell, Pete's programmers did not copy any of the source or object code of the Bingo system. Instead, it seems that Pete's software was newly built, that is, from the ground up.

According to its lawyer, Bingo would be unlikely to prevail in a copyright or a "look and feel" lawsuit against Pete's Software, and extended legal proceedings would be prohibitively expensive for a small company like Bingo. Customers, primarily small businesses, appear to be downloading Pete's software and then making multiple copies for internal use. Some of those companies hire Pete's Software to help them and many don't. But Pete's Software has plenty of business, whereas Bingo's business seems to be slipping away. Bingo is unable to recover the full costs of developing its original system, and within a few years files for bankruptcy. Pete's Software, pleased by its success, begins another project in which they target another market segment currently served by proprietary software; they plan to again develop a Free Software alternative.

Is this situation unfair? Has Pete's Software wronged Bingo Software Systems?

Scenario 5.3 Using Public Domain Software in Proprietary Software

Earl Eniac has spent a year developing a virus tester. He finally has it developed to a point where he is pleased with it. It detects all the viruses he has ever encountered and repairs his system. Earl makes the tester available from his website; anyone who wants it can download it for free. Earl wants to encourage everyone to use it, so he places a Creative Commons "public domain" license on the software. The license specifies that anyone can freely copy and use Earl's software without restrictions. Earl also publishes an article in a computer journal describing how the software works.

Jake Jasper reads the article, downloads a copy of the virus tester from the website, and figures out how it works. He thinks it is a clever, creative, and useful piece of software. He also sees how several small changes could be made to the tester, changes that would make it even better. Because the copy that Jake downloaded from the Web allows him access to the source code, Jake makes these changes to the program. He then sends the revised program to Earl with an explanation of what he has done. Jake protects his revision of the program with a copyright, and starts to sell it as proprietary software from his website. Jake's User's Manual and his website describe what he has done, and give credit to Earl for the original software. Earl is a bit miffed that Jake is selling the revised software, although Earl recognizes that what Jake has done is completely legal because Earl put his software into the public domain.

Has Jake done anything wrong? Is Earl justified in thinking that the situation is somewhat unfair? Does Jake have an obligation to offer his revision to the public for free?

INTRODUCTION: THE COMPLEXITIES OF DIGITAL PROPERTY

In this chapter, we turn our attention to a set of issues that arise around the ownership of software. When software is protected by copyright, trade secrecy, or patent law, it becomes a form of intellectual property. We will sometimes refer to it as "digital intellectual property" because its digital composition makes software difficult to protect using conventional intellectual property regimes that worked for things like books and vinyl records. As we will see, much of the problem arises because of the reproducibility of IT described in Chapter 3, the ease with which electronic information can be copied (in part or whole) with no discernable difference between original and copy. Streams of code can be cut and pasted to form new programs and data can be copied and merged with other data. Ownership and control of software differs radically from ownership and control of material objects. When a material object is stolen, the owner can see that the object is gone and is left without access to the object. In contrast, software can be stolen merely by copying, and the owner does not lose access to the software. Indeed, the owner may not even notice that a copy has been made.

Definitions

The issues surrounding software ownership are complex and before they can be explained, some background is necessary. IT systems are combinations of hardware and software. "Hardware" refers to machines; machines are tangible, material objects. "Software" refers, essentially, to sets of instructions for machine components. These instructions are sequences of data usually expressed in computer languages and reducible to machine language, a sequence of zeros and ones. Software controls and configures hardware; that is, when software is installed on a computer, it determines what the computer can and cannot do. The software sets up the computer so that it responds (in determinate ways) to inputs (from users, its own memories, sensors, or other machines), processes the input, and delivers output (to users, memory, peripherals, or signals to other machines). Computers—and here we mean hardware—consist of machines that manipulate symbols and encoding. Any machine that doesn't manipulate symbols is not a computer. The term "peripherals" refers to machines that are controlled by computers and don't themselves manipulate code.

Note that although this understanding of IT is fairly standard, the technology has evolved in ways that make it difficult to delineate where one system ends and another begins. Consider, for example, a robot with many processors and moving parts receiving wireless signals from a remote device. Is it one machine or many machines linked together? Which parts are the robot, and which parts are interacting with the robot? As well, the distinction between hardware and software can be fuzzy due to recent developments. Devices can now be created by taking what is essentially a software program and etching it into a silicon chip. The microchip that is created is a hybrid between software and hardware.

In order to understand digital intellectual property issues, we must press further into the nature of software. In particular, we have to distinguish algorithms, object code, and source code because, as we will see later on, intellectual property laws treat each of these aspects of software differently. Any piece of software can be described (expressed) in three different ways or at three different levels of understanding: as an algorithm, in source code, and in object code. Most software consists of many algorithms. An algorithm is a step-by-step method for solving a particular problem. In general, an algorithm is more abstract than a particular program written for a particular computer in a particular programming language. The same algorithm can be implemented in many different programs. Each particular program is expressed as "source code." Source code refers to the program (that configures a computer) expressed in a programming language, and object code refers to the binary expression of that program in the machine language of a particular machine. Programmers trained in the programming language can read source code relatively easily, but object code is much harder for humans to read. Software is generally created first by expressing it in source code, that is, writing it out in a language such as Java or C. The program is then "compiled" into object code, a form in which a computer can use it. Source code is, then, a "before compilation" version of the program and object code is an "after compilation" version of the program. (Interpreted programming languages are slightly different; a simplified explanation is that they are translated line by line in a similar way.)

Setting the Stage

We can set the stage for exploring digital intellectual property by considering Scenario 5.2. Bingo Software is unable to sell its system because Pete's Software was able to replicate the functionality of Bingo's system, improve upon it, and then make the new software available for free. From Bingo's perspective, this is unfair because they invested an enormous amount of effort and money into the development of their system and now they cannot recoup their investment, let alone make a profit. In its defense, Pete's Software can argue that they did nothing wrong because they didn't copy Bingo's source or object code; they simply used ideas that anyone who studied the system could have discovered.

At first glance, this may seem a problem with an easy solution. All we have to do is give Bingo a legal right to own the software it creates, a legal right that would exclude others from doing what Pete's Software did. This, however, turns out to be much harder to do than one might imagine at the onset. Moreover, as we will see, there are good reasons for not giving Bingo's Software the kind of protection they would need to ensure that Pete's couldn't study the system and build on what they learned.

When software was first created, it was considered a new type of entity. The closest parallel was scripts for player pianos because these, like software, controlled how a machine operated. With software, however, machines are controlled through digital information, ultimately binary code, and that was new. The value of software was quickly recognized and this value created an intense interest in control and ownership. To be sure, issues have been, and continue to be, raised about ownership of hardware, but software has posed the more difficult challenge to conventional notions of property.

Digital intellectual property rights issues arise both at the micro and macro level. Scenarios 5.1 and 5.3 describe situations in which individuals must make, or will have to make, personal decisions. Carol decided to buy software that would be illegal to obtain in the United States and she is now confronted with the implications of that decision in choosing how to handle her entry back into the United States. Earl and Jake each made individual choices about what to do with the software they created. Of course, these micro-level issues are embedded in contexts shaped by law and policy. Carol makes her decisions against a backdrop of laws and policies and likely repercussions for her behavior. Earl and Jack make their decisions in an environment with two quite different systems for the production and distribution of software—

one proprietary, the other open source (in this case, public domain/open source). Scenario 5.2 poses a macro-level issue in the sense that it calls upon us to ask whether current laws are fair and whether they effectively structure software markets.

This is an enormously complex area of IT ethics, and the law continues to be contested. The courts and law journals are filled with case after case in which property rights are being claimed and accusations of infringements are being made. The music, film, and television industries have challenged various online schemas for downloading of music, movies, and television. Use of wireless connections (WiFi) are being framed as theft. American television writers recently went on strike to win more financial rights to Web-based distribution of the shows they had written. Add to the mix that many of the issues arise around international law and agreements because the Internet makes it so easy to move copyrighted materials and patented processes across national boundaries.

We will, in this chapter, cover only a small subset of this vast array of issues. Our focus will be primarily on U.S. law although many countries have similar laws. We will try to get to the heart of the matter by focusing on foundational, philosophical issues. In doing this we will neglect many current and important topics, but our analysis can easily be supplemented with up-to-date cases found in law journals, on the Web, or in newspapers.

PROTECTING PROPERTY RIGHTS IN SOFTWARE

We begin here by describing three forms of legal protection that are now widely used to own and control access to software: copyright, trade secrecy, and patent. These legal tools create proprietary software (PS). From its first creation, however, software never fit neatly into these legal forms and the result has been a plethora of court cases contesting claims to this or that application, and a good deal of uncertainty about what can and cannot be protected. After discussing these three forms of legal protection, we will take up the Free and Open Source Software (FOSS) movement, which is based on an entirely different vision of how software can be developed and distributed. FOSS programmers cooperate to develop and maintain software and then encourage users to copy and distribute the software, often free of charge. (Pete's did exactly this.)

Copyright

In the United States, when a software developer creates an original piece of software, the developer can use copyright law to obtain a form of ownership that will exclude others from directly copying the software without permission. That is, others are not permitted to reproduce a copyrighted work, distribute copies of it, or display or perform the copyrighted work publicly, without first obtaining permission from the copyright holder. (The author is often the copyright holder, but not always; for example, a company can hire you as a programmer and by contract hold the copyright to any software you write for them.) Until 1998, copyright protection extended for the life of the author plus fifty years. In 1998, the law was amended to extend the term of coverage to the life of the author plus seventy years.

In the United States, copyright protection is rooted in the U.S. Constitution where article I, section 8, clause 8 specifies that Congress shall have the power "To promote the progress of science and useful arts, by securing for limited times to authors and inventors the exclusive right to their respective writings and discoveries." The Copyright Act protects "original works of authorship fixed in any tangible medium of expression, now known or later developed, from which they can be perceived, reproduced, or otherwise communicated, either directly or with the aid of a machine or device." (17 U.S.C. Section 102(a) (1995))

Although copyright provides a significant form of protection to authors, when it comes to software, the protection is limited and complex issues of interpretation often arise. At the heart of copyright law is a distinction between ideas and expression. An idea cannot be copyrighted; the expression of an idea can be. The distinction between idea and expression makes sense when it comes to literary works. When an author obtains a copyright, the author does not own and cannot control the use of the ideas in his or her writing. Rather, the author owns and can exclude others from using his or her unique expression of those ideas. With this form of protection, authors are able to stop others from reproducing their writings without permission. Notice that this form of protection makes it possible for authors and publishers to make money from the sale and distribution of their writings. They can grant permission to others to use their works, for a fee.

To be sure, copyright protection can be problematic for literary works. Claims to a number of famous literary works have been contested and authors have learned the hard way that the line between idea and expression is not so easy to draw. However, these kinds of problems are even more complex when it comes to software because copyright does not seem to protect the most valuable aspect of a piece of software: the algorithm underlying the code. Algorithms are generally thought to be the ideas expressed in a program and, hence, they are not copyrightable. When expressed as source and/or object code, however, the programs are copyrightable. Both the source code and the object code are understood, in copyright law, to be "literary works," that is, formal expressions of ideas. The problem is that it is often sufficient for a competitor to study the software and with minor effort, and without directly copying, create comparable, and sometimes better, software (as we saw in the case of Bingo's file organizing system). The task of creating new source and object code may be negligible once the algorithms, ideas, or approach taken in the software is grasped from extended use of the program.

The inadequacy of copyright to protect what is valuable in software is not something that can be fixed by tinkering with copyright law. The problem is much more fundamental; it has to do with the distinction between idea and expression. Software is like literary works in being expressive, but unlike literary works in that it is also useful (functional). Software produces behavior; that is, when put into a machine, it performs tasks in a determinate way. The distinction between idea and expression doesn't capture functionality or behavior. Thus, competitors can "read" a piece of software, comprehend its useful behavior, and then develop new software that behaves in the same way but has been produced by entirely different source and object code.

Another problem with copyright is uncertainty as to what counts as an infringement. Of course when large sections of proprietary source code are copied character-by-character without the permission of the copyright holder, infringement is clear. But often it isn't clear whether something has been created anew or taken as a whole and then significantly modified. For example, the names given to variables are useful for humans reading source code, but when source code is transformed into object code, the variable names are no longer significant. Imagine that someone copies the source code, makes global changes to all the variable names, and then recompiles the source code into object code. The resulting source code is no longer identical to the original source code, but the resulting object code could be identical! Similarly, there are many cosmetic changes to the source code that would make the "changed" program look distinct from the original without substantially changing the functional behavior of the object code. When these kinds of changes are used to circumvent copyright, copyright holders generally have to take violators to court where decisions are made as to whether there has been an infringement or not. The burden of proof is on the copyright holder to prove infringement. This is not a simple matter because the copyright holder must show that there is a "striking resemblance" between the copyrighted software and the infringing software, a resemblance so close that it could only be explained by copying. If the defendant can establish that she developed the program at issue on her own, without any knowledge of the preexisting program, then she will win the case. In other words, a copyright does not give its holder a monopoly on the work. If someone else independently (without any knowledge of a preexisting work) writes something similar or even identical, there is no infringement. [Later we will see that this is an important difference between copyright and patent.]

Copyright infringement disputes often hinge on whether it is plausible to suppose that someone would come up with an identical program on his or her own, or whether the resemblance between the programs is so close as to be explainable only by direct copying. This is an extremely difficult hurdle for a copyright holder to overcome in pursuing an infringement action. A famous and important early case in the legal history of software ownership was the case of Franklin v. Apple, decided by the U.S. Supreme Court in 1984. Apple was able to show that Franklin copied Apple's operating system (the object code of their operating system) because Franklin's operating system contained line after line of identical object code. Franklin had not even bothered to delete segments of code that included Apple's name. Franklin v. Apple is also important because it established that computer programs expressed in object code are copyrightable. Before this case, no one was sure whether object code would count as expression because object code cannot be easily "read" with understanding by humans. (There may be specialists in a particular computer's hardware instructions who can discern the meaning of small pieces of object code, but these exceptions prove the rule: Object code is for computers, source code is for humans.)

If a copyright holder goes to court to prove infringement and establishes only that there is a resemblance but not a "striking" resemblance between the copyright holder's software and the defendant's software, then the copyright holder can try to win the case in a different way. The law allows copyrighted material to be appropriated by others without permission if something significant is added to the copyrighted material, such that a new expression is produced. This is referred to as "proper appropriation." You are entitled to draw on a copyrighted work as long as you use it in a way that creates or adds something new. Although improper appropriation is not a precise notion, it is meant to define the line between "taking" another's work and "building on" another's work. A copyright holder can stop an infringer if the copyright holder can show that the accused relied heavily on the copyright holder's program and did not add anything significant to it.

In either case—whether a copyright holder demonstrates a striking resemblance or improper appropriation—the copyright holder must also show that the defendant had access to the program. This casts doubt on the possibility that the defendant created the program on his or her own. As already explained, if the defendant produced a similar program on his or her own, then there is no infringement. In the case of computer software, access is often easy to prove, especially if the copyrighted software has been widely marketed. If, on the other hand, the software has been kept out of the marketplace, as, for example, when a company produces software for its own internal use, the burden of proof is on the accuser to show that the defendant obtained access to the software.

Copyright continues to be an important legal mechanism for protecting software, although, as you can see, it is far from an ideal form of protection. One response to these limitations has been to supplement copyright with "digital rights management" (DRM). That term encompasses a number of technological mechanisms built into hardware and software and designed to prevent copying automatically. DRM is used not just to protect software but all forms of digital information that can be copyrighted, including music and movies. DRM is used by PS developers, content providers (prominently entertainment companies), and governments to more effectively protect the rights of producers against those who would copy. However, hackers and users have become adept at figuring out and thwarting these mechanisms. So the corporations using DRM sought legal support for their DRM activities, and in 1998 a federal law known as the Digital Millennium Copyright Act (DMCA) was passed to support digital rights management. This legislation criminalizes circumnavigation of copyright protections. It makes it a crime not only to copy copyrighted material, but also to investigate or explain to others how to get around DRM algorithms.

Since its passage, DMCA has been controversial. Unlike copyright, DRM is not limited to a certain number of years and the sanctions for violation are heavy. Researchers in computer science, especially those studying encryption and copy protection mechanisms, have concerns about their vulnerability to prosecution for their publication and public speaking about DRM algorithms. In 2001, a Russian programmer, Dimitry Sklyarov, was arrested in the United States after speaking at a conference about these algorithms, and was held for months. Moreover, although there are explicit exceptions for some reverse engineering attempts to integrate systems, the intent of the person doing the engineering often determines whether a particular action is legal or illegal. Many IT professionals object to DMCA specifically, and to DRM mechanisms in general.

Trade Secrecy

Trade secrecy laws vary from jurisdiction to jurisdiction but in general what they do is give companies the right to keep certain kinds of information secret. The laws are aimed specifically at protecting companies from losing their competitive edge. Thus, for example, a company can keep secret the recipe of foods that it sells or the formula of chemicals it uses in certain processes. Google, for example, is able to keep the algorithms used in its search engine secret.

To hold up in court, what is claimed as a trade secret typically must: (1) have novelty, (2) represent an economic investment to the claimant, (3) have involved some effort in development, and (4) the company must show that it made some effort to keep the information a secret. Software can meet these requirements. Many software companies try to keep their software secret by using nondisclosure clauses in contracts of employment and by means of licensing agreements with those who use their software. Nondisclosure clauses require employees to refrain from revealing secrets that they learn at work. For example, employees promise in these agreements not to take copies of programs or reveal the contents of programs owned by their employer (even when they leave the company to take another job). By licensing the use of their software, developers are able to make money from their software without giving control to the customers; customers who license the use of the software agree not to give away or sell copies.

In addition to employment contracts and licensing agreements, software developers have employed a variety of technical devices to protect their secrets. Such devices include limiting what is available to the user (i.e., not giving the user access to the source program), or building into the program identifying codes so that illegal copies can be traced to their source.

Although this form of protection is used by the software industry, many complain that even with improved technical devices for maintaining secrecy, trade secrecy is not an adequate method for protecting software. For one thing, trade secrecy laws are not uniform throughout the United States or internationally, and this makes it difficult for businesses that operate in multiple jurisdictions or countries. For another, the protection provided is uncertain because the laws were not designed for IT. Companies take a risk that the courts will support their claims when and if they are ever tested in the courts.

Most problematic is the matter of meeting the requirement of maintaining secrecy. Enforcing employment and licensing agreements can be challenging. Violators can be caught taking or selling direct copies of programs, but there is nothing to stop an employee of one firm from taking the general knowledge and understanding of the principles used in a program to a new job at another firm. Likewise, someone who works with licensed software may grasp general principles that can be used to create new software.

These problems are not unique to software. In competitive environments, companies have an interest in keeping many aspects of their operation secret. What is somewhat unusual about software is that often the secret must be revealed in order to license the software. That is, in order to be useful to the licensee, the software must be modified to fit the licensee's unique needs. Sometimes the only way to do this is to give access to the source code. The licensee can, then, alter the source code to fit its situation. However, once the source program is available, the secret is less likely to remain secret and because the secret (the source code) is out, trade secrecy law may not protect the software. Even if only the object code is available to a licensee, specialists can obtain information about the software just by looking at the object code. Although this information is more limited and much harder to obtain than the information from the source code, it is still nontrivial; and a user cannot run software on his or her machine without object code.

In Scenario 5.2, trade secrecy law would have been helpful to Bingo, but only to a point. Bingo could have kept the design of its software secret during its development by means of nondisclosure clauses in employment contracts. Once the system was ready for marketing, however, keeping it a secret would have been more difficult. In showing the system to potential users, some information would be revealed, and once the system was in widespread use, Bingo's ability to control access to its system would be significantly weakened. It isn't easy for client-companies to police their employees in terms of copying, and they cannot prevent their employees from seeing and grasping the general principles used in the software.

Recently, some companies have been using the Web to protect their trade secrets. They keep their software on their own servers, and invite customers to use the software remotely—essentially users send their data or instructions to the server where the company's software processes the data and sends the output back to the customer. Web search engines, for example, offer their services this way without distributing either source or object code to users.

Web use aside, when companies license custom software, the licensing agreement generally includes provisions for the software company to modify the system for the licensee's needs and to do all repairs and maintenance of the software. This minimizes the licensee's exposure to the source code. However, for small, less complicated programs sold in mass quantities (often called "shrink-wrapped software"), it is impractical for the software company to modify every copy sold.

In summary, in allowing software developers to keep their software secret, trade secrecy law provides a powerful form of protection. The problem is that it is often impossible, or at least impractical, for software developers to use trade secrecy because in order to be licensed and used, some form of the software often has to be put into the public realm.

Patent Protection

In principle, patent protection offers the strongest form of protection for software because a patent gives the inventor a monopoly on the use of the invention. A patent holder has the right to exclude others from making, using, or selling the invention, and the right to license others to make, use, or sell it. A patent gives the patent holder a monopoly in the sense that even if someone else invents the same thing independently, without any knowledge of the patent holder's invention, the secondary inventor is excluded from use of the device without permission of the patent holder.

Referring back again to Scenario 5.2, patent protection could give Bingo Software the power to prevent Pete's from marketing its system if important aspects of Bingo's system were deemed patentable. [If only it were that simple!]

There are three types of patents: utility patents, design patents, and patents on plant forms. The primary concern here is with utility patents because utility patents hold the most promise of protecting software. Utility patents are granted for a term of seventeen years, although the term may be extended for an additional five years. When it comes to software, the problem with patent protection is not in the kind of protection it provides, but rather in whether or not patents are appropriate for software. For several years, U.S. courts were reluctant to grant patents on software, and for good reason. But many U.S. software patents have now been granted, much to the chagrin of many in the field of computing.

The aim of the patent system is not simply to ensure that individuals reap rewards for their inventions. Rather, the motive underlying the patent system is to create a system that leads to the advancement of the useful arts and sciences. The goals of the patent system are to foster invention, promote disclosure of inventions, and assure that ideas already in the public domain remain there for free use. Achievement of these goals is, in turn, expected to improve the economy, increase employment, and make better lives for citizens. Of course, an important way of fostering invention is to reward it. Patent protection does not guarantee that individuals will be rewarded for their inventions, but it provides a form of protection that makes reward possible. In other words, if you have a monopoly and your invention has commercial value, then you (and no one else) will be in a position to market the invention. In this way, patent protection fosters invention and innovation. It is important to keep in mind, however, that rewarding successful inventions is a means, not an end, as far as the public is concerned.

The patent system recognizes that inventions brought into the public realm are beneficial not just in themselves but also because others can learn from and build on these inventions. If new ideas are kept secret, progress in the useful arts and sciences is impeded; others are prevented from seeing, learning from, and building upon the new ideas. Patent protection encourages the inventor to put her ideas into the public realm by promising her protection that she wouldn't have if she simply kept her ideas to herself. Moreover, if an inventor chooses to keep her patent secret, then she has no legal recourse (no legal claim) if someone else comes up with the same idea or copies the invention.

These two arguments—that patents encourage invention and encourage bringing inventions into the public realm—also lead, however, to important restrictions. In the patent system, abstract ideas, mathematical formulae, scientific principles, laws of nature, and mental processes cannot be patented. To give someone the exclusive right to control these kinds of things would inhibit further invention rather than fostering it because these things are the building blocks of invention. If individuals had to get permission from a patent holder to use an idea, a mathematical algorithm, or a law of nature, invention would be significantly impeded. Imagine, for example, the enormous power of the person who held a patent on the law of gravitational pull or the mental steps involved in addition or multiplication!

Although this restriction on what can be patented seems essential, it creates problems for patenting software. A patent claim must satisfy a two-step test before a patent can be granted. The claim must: (1) fall within the category of permissible subject matter, and (2) it must: (a) have utility, (b) have novelty, and, (c) be nonobvious. The latter three tests are not easy to pass, but they have not been problematic for software. That is, software can be and often is useful, novel, and not so simple as to be obvious to the average person. Software has, however, had difficulty passing the first test, qualifying as permissible subject matter.

The subject matter of a patent is limited to "a process, machine, manufacture or composition of matter or an improvement thereof." Generally, software has been considered a process or part of a process:

> A process may be patentable, irrespective of the particular form of the instrumentalities used. A process is a mode of treatment of certain materials to produce a given result. It is an act, or a series of acts, performed upon the subject matter to be transformed and reduced to a different state or thing. If new and useful, it is just as patentable as is a piece of machinery. (Cochrane v. Deener, 94 U.S. 780, 787–788:161876:17)

One difficulty in extending patent protection to software is in specifying what subject matter is transformed by software. However, this problem is secondary to a larger issue. In the 1970s and 1980s, there was reluctance to grant patents on software or software-related inventions for fear that in granting patents on software, ownership of mental processes might, in effect, be granted. Each of the steps in an algorithm is an operation a person can, in principle at least, perform mentally. If a series of such steps were patented, the patent holder might be able to require that permission or a license be sought before those operations were performed mentally. Needless to say, this would significantly interfere with freedom of thought.

Another difficulty with patenting software has to do with algorithms. Granting a monopoly on the use of a software invention could lead to a monopoly on the use of a mathematical algorithm. This is explicitly prohibited in patent law as inappropriate subject matter. The problem is, what is a software invention if not an algorithm—the order and sequence of steps to achieve a certain result. The issue goes to the heart of what exactly one owns when one has a patent on a piece of software.

Before the Diamond v. Diehr case was settled in 1981, very few patents had been granted on software (Diamond v. Diehr, 1981). There had been a struggle between the U.S. Supreme Court, the Patent Office, and the Court of Customs and Patent Appeals (CCPA), with the first two resisting granting of patents and the latter pressing to extend patent protection to software. In Diamond v. Diehr, the Supreme Court, in a 5 to 4 vote, denied a patent to Diehr. Even though it was a close and disputable decision, the Patent Office and especially the CCPA interpreted the court's reasoning so as to justify granting patents on software inventions. Although only a handful of software-related patents had been granted before Diamond v. Diehr, many thousands have been granted since. Gregory Aharonian (1993) reported that more than 9,000 software patents were granted between the late 1960s and the end of

1992, and 1,300 were issued in 1992 alone. Statistics vary widely but the Goodwin Proctor IP Advisor (2006) reports that in the U.S. "the number of patents issued in 2004 was about *five times* the number issued in 1990 (about 11,600 vs 2,400)." One estimate for 2007 is that 40,000 software patents were issued in the United States alone. (http://www.codinghorror.com/blog/archives/000902.html)

Concerns are now being expressed that too much software is being patented and that patents are getting in the way of development in the field. These concerns go to the heart of the patent system's aim, because they suggest that because so much is owned, innovation is being constrained. The subject matter limitation on what can be patented aims to insure that the building blocks of science and technology are not owned so that continued development will flourish, yet complaints suggest just that: The building blocks of software are becoming proprietary via patents.

The situation can be described roughly as follows: Because so many patents have been granted, before putting new software on the market, a software developer must do an extensive and expensive patent search. If overlapping patents are found, licenses must be secured. Even if no overlapping patents are found, there is always the risk of late-issuing patents. Hence, there is always the risk of a lawsuit due to patent infringement. A software company may invest a great deal in the development of their software, invest more in a patent search, and then find at the last minute that the software infringes on something already claimed. These factors make software development a risky business and constitute barriers to the development of new software. The costs and risks are barriers especially for small entrepreneurs. The situation seems to call for change. Yet, at this point, change may be difficult simply because the software industry has grown and solidified in an environment structured by this form of protection.

FREE AND OPEN SOURCE SOFTWARE

Despite the problems with copyright, trade secrecy, and patent law, these forms of protection are used. However, partly as a result of their limitations and partly because of an alternative vision of how software can be developed, there is now what might be called a two-track system for control and distribution of software. PS protected by copyright, trade secrecy, and patent law is one track; the other is software that is produced and distributed under one of the categories of Free and Open Source Software (FOSS). The vision of software development embraced by FOSS is one of transparent software, software that users can modify to fit their needs, and software that is widely available (including those who cannot afford to buy PS). FOSS programmers do nothing illegal but they make their software available to the public, often for free and often under a license that allows users access to the source code. Much (although not all) FOSS encourages users to run, redistribute, and modify the code although there may be user agreements with restrictions on reuse of the code.

In order to understand the FOSS movement, we should distinguish between three important approaches to digital "sharing": Free Software (FS), Open Source Software (OSS), and the Creative Commons (CC). An important difference between FS and OSS is how each handles the situation in which someone modifies the software (code) and then redistributes it. With FS, users have the freedom to run, copy, distribute, study, change, and improve the software. When FS is licensed, the license requires that if the code is incorporated into another program, the new program must also be FS. Richard Stallman, the founder and continuing spokesperson of the FS Foundation (FSF), calls this licensing scheme "copyleft." In other words, when software is distributed as FS, the license stipulates that its copyright owner allow users to redistribute the software only if they redistribute it with the same license. This is sometimes characterized as a "viral" scheme; the free quality of the code "infects" whatever other code it touches.

FS is committed to four freedoms for software users:

1. The freedom to run the program, for any purpose.
2. The freedom to study how the program works, and adapt it to your needs. Access to the source code is a precondition for this.
3. The freedom to redistribute copies so you can help your neighbor.
4. The freedom to improve the program, and release your improvements to the public, so that the whole community benefits. Access to the source code is a precondition for this. (see http://www.gnu.org/philosophy/free-sw.html)

Open Source Software (OSS) does not include the same restrictions as FS, although the Open Source Initiative (OSI), the organization most closely associated with OSS, accepts FS as OSS. OSI accepts many other software licensing agreements than Stallman and FSF accept as FS. The debates between FS advocates and OSS advocates have at times been acrimonious, suggesting significant differences in these two strategies for maintaining software freedoms. Our interest here is in contrasting FS and OSS with PS.

A common misconception is that FOSS is never distributed with a cost. Although this is true for some FOSS, for example, Open Office and Apache Server Software, other FOSS is distributed at a cost, for example, Red Hat Unix. It is the rights that come with the software that distinguish FOSS from PS, particularly the right to view and modify the source code. Software developers can still make money selling and customizing FOSS. Indeed, in the last few years, some major corporations such as SUN and IBM have begun to develop and distribute FOSS. Interestingly, many of the difficulties discussed above with regard to protecting software become moot with FOSS. The source and object code are not protected from users at all, so the difficulties of doing so disappear. Prices for FOSS are modest or zero because communities of programmers volunteer their services to develop and improve the programs in an ongoing process. The culture of FOSS has been extended using the Web, although FS predates widespread availability of the Web.

Perhaps unsurprisingly, corporations with heavy investments in PS have not been uniformly enthusiastic about FOSS. FOSS represents a threat to PS, and some PS developers have long argued against FOSS, claiming that it is unreliable, illegal (because of alleged patent and copyright infringement) and "communistic." FOSS advocates are vocal in their opposition to these claims and claim alternatively that corporations marketing PS are using software patents and DRM technologies to enforce unfair and illegal monopolies. Despite this resistance to FOSS, in recent years some major corporations and small businesses have begun to incorporate FOSS either by using it or by trying to make money by providing services that involve customization or maintenance of FOSS.

With this backdrop of the current environment for software development, we now want to step back and explore the most basic questions of property. Software as we are using the term here didn't exist before computers. From an STS perspective, what it "is" has been socially constructed through debates and decisions—by judges, courts, programmers, corporations, and users, to name only a few—and there continues to be a struggle over its meaning and how it will evolve in the future. Much of this struggle takes place around social conceptions of property. Hence, it will serve us well to consider foundational thinking about property rights.

THE PHILOSOPHICAL BASIS OF PROPERTY

Property is by no means a simple notion. It is, effectively, created by laws specifying what can and cannot be owned, how things may be acquired and transferred, and what owners can and cannot do with their property. Laws define what counts as property and create different kinds of property. The laws regulating ownership of land, for example, are quite different from those regulating ownership of an automobile. In the case of land, there are rules about how far the land goes down into the ground and how far up into the air space above, about what can and cannot be constructed on the land, and when the land may be confiscated by the government. To own a car, one has to acquire a piece of paper referred to as the "title" and even with a "title," the owner may not be able to take possession of the car without proof that the car is insured. Then, even with a title and proof of insurance, ownership does not mean that you can legally drive the car on public roads; you first need a driver's license. Ownership of "intellectual" property is even more complicated, as we saw in the previous section with copyright and patent law specifying the conditions for ownership of the expression of ideas and inventions.

Building on two of the ethical theories introduced in Chapter 2, we can distinguish two broad theories of property that often are hidden beneath the surface of debates about ownership of software. One theory is utilitarian and the other is a natural rights theory that might loosely be associated with Kantian theory although it originated with John Locke. As our earlier discussion indicated, the reasoning behind patent and copyright law is utilitarian. These systems aim at fostering creativity and innovation, and encouraging disclosure. However, despite the utilitarian foundations of copyright and patent law, proprietary rights in software are often defended as a matter of natural right. For this reason, we begin here with an examination of the natural rights arguments for and against ownership of software.

Natural Rights Arguments

Drawing on the natural rights tradition, an argument on behalf of software ownership might be made as follows. Because individuals own themselves, they own their labor. Thus, individuals have a right—a natural right—to what they produce with their labor. This is the core idea in John Locke's labor theory of property, although he specifies a number of conditions on this argument, conditions that we will not discuss here. According to a Lockean analysis, in a state of nature (before laws and civilized society), an individual who came upon a stretch of land and spent months turning the land into a garden (by planting seed, tending to the plants each day, nourishing them, and protecting them from bad weather) would have rights in the crops that grew. The laborer would have a right to the crops because they would not have existed without the individual's labor. The force of the argument becomes most salient when we imagine that someone comes along and seizes the crops without permission from the laborer. There seems to be something unfair in the second person acquiring the fruits of the first person's labor. Indeed, some might say that this is plain and simple theft even though there are no laws in a state of nature.

This Lockean argument is intuitively appealing. The person who takes the crops has effectively made the laborer his slave. The argument is built on the idea of individual sovereignty and self-ownership and one's labor is an extension of one's self (one's body); to seize the products of someone's labor is to render the person a slave.

Using this Lockean account, it would seem that software developers could argue that the software they create is rightfully theirs because they produced it with their labor (both intellectual and physical). Remember that it seemed unfair for Bingo Software, in Scenario 5.2, to invest its resources and labor in software only to have it used by Pete's. Pete's Software used the work of Bingo and was able to make money from the work, yet they paid Bingo Software nothing. Using the Lockean argument, we might say that Pete's effectively made Bingo their slave. This seems a powerful argument for granting some sort of property right in software, a property right that Bingo could use to prevent Pete's from appropriating its labor.

Critique of the Natural Rights Argument

Despite its appeal, the natural rights argument has several flaws. The first applies to property rights in general and the second specifically to intellectual property. The first flaw goes to the heart of the labor theory of property by calling into question the "naturalness" of the connection between property and labor. Nozick (1974) raises the question in the following way:

> Why does mixing one's labor with something make one the owner of it? . . . why isn't mixing what I own with what I don't own a way of losing what I own rather than a way of gaining what I don't? If I own a can of tomato juice and spill it in the sea so that its molecules (made radioactive, so I can check this) mingle evenly throughout the sea, do I thereby come to own the sea, or have I foolishly dissipated my tomato juice? (Nozick, *Anarchy, State, and Utopia*, pp. 174–175)

Notice that Nozick is not questioning ownership of one's self or one's labor, only what happens when one mixes one's labor with something else. Although this is merely a question, it weakens the claim that we have a "natural" right to that with which we mix our labor. The question raises doubt about the "naturalness" of the connection between labor and ownership rights. Property rights, it would seem, could go either way—one could lose or gain rights in a mixed product. Interestingly, the FOSS "viral" schema mentioned earlier seems to be an example of a property schema in which one loses rights to one's labor when one mixes it with the products of others' labor. The agreement specifies that when one uses free code, the free quality of the code "infects" whatever other code it touches.

To push our critique of the labor theory further, imagine a society in which individuals acquire no property rights in what they create with their labor. Suppose further that no one in this society can own the products of anyone else's labor. Would such a society necessarily be unjust? To be sure, it would be unjust if some individuals acquired rights to what other individuals had created, but if there are no property rights (except in one's self), then where is the injustice? Consider also that individuals would know in advance that their labor would not lead to ownership, so they would decide what to do (where to invest their labor) informed by the likely consequences of doing so. Such a society would not, it seems, be vulnerable to the claim that it was unjust. To be sure, from a utilitarian perspective, the society might be a disaster, but here we are concerned only with whether natural rights would be violated and that does not seem to be the case.

Returning to Scenario 5.2, if there were no laws prohibiting copying of software, then when Pete's copied the software developed by Bingo and let others make copies, there is no natural injustice. This is precisely what at least some advocates of FOSS would like to become the norm.

A second flaw in the labor theory relates to software being nontangible (intellectual) and goes directly to the notion of confiscation. Returning to the earlier example, when someone comes along and takes the laborer's crops, the laborer loses the products of his labor. However, when it comes to intellectual products such as ideas, musical tunes, and mental steps, the laborer does not lose access to the products of the labor. If I labor in creating a song or formalizing an abstract idea such as the Pythagorean theorem, and someone hears the song (even memorizes it) or comprehends the idea in the theorem (and can remember it and use it), I don't lose the song or the theorem. I can continue to have and use the intellectual results of my labor while others have and use them. Thus, there is no confiscation.

This is precisely the issue with software. Software experts can examine software, comprehend the idea in it, including its functionality, and then use this understanding to write original software (source code). Moreover, once a piece of software is developed, many others can make identical copies of the software and yet not deprive the developer of the original.

If software developers aren't deprived of the use of the software they create, what then is the problem? The problem has been lurking beneath the surface and we can now bring it to "the light of day." What PS software developers want is not just a right to own, in the sense of possess and use, their software, they want a right to control their software for economic gain in a market environment. They want an economic right. Notice that they cannot claim a right to make money from their software because that depends on the market. They want the ability to put software on the market and make money if consumers like the product.

Once we see that what is at issue is an economic right, we can specify important differences between PS developers and FOSS developers more clearly. Although there are variations in FOSS advocates, at least some are in favor of markets around software but they don't think the software itself—algorithms, source code, and object code—should be owned. Markets can be developed around supporting the software, for example, customizing, documenting, maintaining, training users, and so on. In this respect, it seems both PS and FOSS advocates want the capacity to do something in the marketplace but each group has a different vision of how the software market should be structured. PS developers think markets should be structured by granting intellectual property rights in algorithms, source code, and object code, whereas FOSS developers think these aspects of software should be free. This strategy, FOSS advocates believe, will create an environment with the four freedoms described above.

The dispute between PS and FOSS is largely, then, a dispute about which system is the best system for the production and distribution of software. The debate is essentially utilitarian in the sense that the issue is which system will produce the best consequences. Which system will create the most robust environment for software development? Which system will produce the best—most useful—software? Which system will lead to the most widely accessible software?

A Natural Rights Argument Against Software Ownership

Before we dig further into the utilitarian aspects of this debate it may be important to mention another natural rights argument. Earlier we referred briefly to the possibility that software programs might violate what in patent law is called "the doctrine of mental steps." This doctrine states that a series of mental operations, like addition or subtraction, cannot be owned. When software was first being considered for patents, lawyers initially expressed concern that ownership of software might violate this doctrine. They acknowledged that there are an enormous number of "steps" in a computer software program and the steps are performed extremely quickly. Nevertheless, these operations are in principle capable of being performed mentally by a person. Thus, they thought there was the possibility that ownership of programs could lead to interference with freedom of thought. Of course, patents wouldn't be granted with that possibility in mind, but down the road those who were granted patents on programs might, through a series of court cases, effectively acquire a monopoly on mental operations. So the argument went.

This concern—that granting ownership to programs might interfere with freedom of thought—could be understood to be a natural rights argument against ownership of software. Individuals, the argument would go, have a natural right to freedom of thought. Ownership of software would seriously interfere with freedom of thought. So, ownership of software should not be allowed.

Although the argument doesn't seem to come into play in the current legal environment, we mention it because of its important implications. For example, some advocates of FOSS suggest that freedom of thought should extend to software.

Software can be characterized as formalized ideas or forms of expression (of ideas). Thus, a relationship between software and thinking is not implausible. Moreover, expert systems and artificial intelligence are likely to become more and more sophisticated and as this happens, the difference between software ownership and ownership of modes of thinking could become blurry and legally problematic. Indeed, some of the tasks now performed with IT systems were, before the twentieth century, thought to be the unique province of human beings. Today a variety of "artificial agents" (as discussed in Chapter 3) are in use and increasingly more sophisticated versions are being developed. There are good reasons for not allowing the ownership of thought processes, so we have to be careful about the legal status of machines that "think" (in some sense of that term). Concerns about the ownership of mental operations should not be dismissed as fanciful or irrelevant.

PS VERSUS FOSS

Our analysis suggests that we might best think about the difference between PS and FOSS as a difference about the best system for the production and distribution of software wherein "best system" is a matter of which produces the best consequences. Which system will create the most robust environment for the development and distribution of useful software? Although this frames the issue as an either/or matter, the current environment has both systems and it might be argued that having both is best—as long as we can work out the problems that arise when they bump into each other. The problems that arise when the systems collide are not insignificant as illustrated in Scenarios 5.2 and 5.3.

The standard arguments for PS presume that software is produced in a market environment like the current environment and the only possibilities for ownership are the traditional forms we discussed—copyright (supplemented by DRM), trade secrecy, and patent, or no software ownership whatsoever. In this context, the argument for ownership is straightforward: Individuals and companies will not invest their time, energy, and resources to develop and market software if they cannot reap rewards (make money) from their investment. Why develop software if the moment you introduce it, others will copy it, produce it more cheaply, and yours will not sell?

This is an important argument although it can be challenged in a variety of ways. For one, it presumes that software will not be developed unless developers have an incentive and the only incentive is making money. The FOSS movement constitutes a counter example to this argument; that is, FOSS shows that software continues to be developed by those who are not motivated by money or, at least, don't make money by owning the software as PS. Most (but not all) of FOSS is supported in whole or in part by unpaid programmers; entire operating systems and suites of applications are widely available that have been produced this way and can be downloaded for free.

Ensuring that software developers make money from their inventions is not the only way to reward invention. One alternative would be a credit system. Indeed, credit is already a part of some FOSS. Programmers or designers are given credit for the work they do; the programmer's name is attached to an algorithm, program, or sequence of code, and if others like what has been created, the programmer's reputation is enhanced. The good reputation can serve the individual in a variety of ways, even ways that indirectly affect the ability to make money. A credit system is used in science for the production of scientific knowledge. Individuals are recognized for their publication of what they have discovered, so that a scientist's publication record becomes a major factor in obtaining employment as well as winning research grants and awards.

Credit may not motivate everyone and it may not create enough of an incentive to promote the development of many expensive and elaborate systems. Still, the very existence of FOSS demonstrates that making money is not the only incentive for software development.

Framing the PS versus FOSS debate in a utilitarian framework means that the central question, as we explained above, is which system will produce better consequences. This framework puts the focus on deciding ownership issues in terms of effects on continued creativity and development in the field of software. This framework suggests that the courts will have to continue to draw a delicate line between what should be ownable and what should not be ownable, probably along the lines already delineated in patent and copyright law.

We are not going to take a position on this issue here. At the moment it seems fortunate that we have both systems so that we can observe how they work and learn which system produces what kind of results.

IS IT WRONG TO COPY PROPRIETARY SOFTWARE?

Whatever conclusion you draw from the previous discussion, currently there is a good deal of legally protected PS. Individuals and companies can obtain copyrights and patents on the software they develop or keep their original software as a trade secret. This means that a person who makes a copy of PS without purchasing the software (or in some other way obtaining permission from the copyright or patent holder) is breaking the law. The person is violating the legal rights of the patent or copyright holder. Similarly, a person who uses FOSS in a way that violates its licensing agreement is also infringing on the author's legal rights. The question to which we now turn is: Are such actions morally wrong? Is it wrong for an individual to make a copy of PS? Is it wrong for an individual to violate an FS license?

First, a clarification: Making a backup copy of PS you have purchased (for your own protection) is, generally, not illegal. (This is not universally accepted by PS companies, but those who don't accept it are the exceptions.) In any case, that is not the type of copying we will examine here. Second, although the issue to be taken up here is a micro or individual moral issue, the individual at issue could be a collective unit such as an organization or corporation. Companies engage in copying when they buy a software package, don't obtain a license for multiple copies, and then make multiple copies for use within the company.

Making copies of PS is not uncommon. Based on behavior it would seem that many individuals do not think it is wrong to copy PS (or violate an FS license). Indeed, it seems that individuals who would not break other laws will make illegal copies of software. It is interesting to speculate on why this is so. Is it because it's so easy to do? Is it because the copier sees no visible sign that he or she is doing harm? Unlike stealing a car or a television, you don't deprive the owner of their possession. Is it because those who copy are so rarely prosecuted? Whatever the reasons, they are irrelevant to the question whether the behavior is immoral.

Consider a possible defense of software copying. We can formulate the gut feeling that it's okay into an argument with two parts as follows: Software copying is okay (not wrong) because: (1) there is nothing intrinsically wrong with copying, and (2) copying does no harm. The first part of the argument seems true. That is, if there were no laws against copying, the act of copying would not be wrong. Earlier we argued that intellectual property rights are not natural but a matter of social utility, and that argument seems to support this idea that there is nothing intrinsically wrong with the act of copying. In a state of nature, copying would have no moral significance. Only when there are laws against it does copying have moral significance.

The second claim is similar to the first in the sense that if we imagine people in a state of nature, it would seem that no harm is done by copying. Copying is not like coercion or physical assault in the sense that these are harmful whether unlawful or not. Copying software doesn't even deprive the possessor of access to his or her possession so it doesn't harm the possessor in that respect.

Nevertheless, both of these arguments have limited application when copying takes place in societies with laws—laws that create PS. Once legal rights are created, when an individual is deprived of one of his or her rights—be it life, a vote in an election, possession of a material object, or control of intellectual property like PS, the individual is harmed. Thus, in societies that establish PS, the act of copying PS without permission of the copyright or patent holder is illegal and harms the owner of the PS in the sense that it deprives the owner of his or her legal right to require payment in exchange for the use of the software.

A similar argument applies to violation of an FS license. If you have agreed to abide by an FS license in exchange for access, then violating the agreement is wrong. Even if the agreement was made in a state of nature so that there is no one to enforce the agreement, or court of law to go to, when you violate the agreement, you treat the licensor merely as a means to your own end. When one willingly accepts FS, one makes a commitment to abide by the copyleft restrictions.

In arguing that it is wrong to copy PS without permission and wrong to violate an FS license once there are laws and agreements, we are, in essence, arguing that it is immoral to do something illegal. We do not want our claim to be misinterpreted. There are cases in which illegality and immorality are separate matters. For example, the act of intentionally killing another person would be immoral even if it were not illegal. By contrast, violating intellectual property rights falls into a category of cases in which the immorality derives from the illegality.

You might be reluctant to concede this argument because you think the laws protecting software ownership are bad laws. Given the discussion in previous sections, you might be worried that we are putting too much weight on the illegality of software copying. After all, you might argue, the laws creating property rights in software are not very good. They don't succeed in protecting software developers very well; they don't take advantage of the potential of software to be available to so many people at so little cost; and they lead to bad consequences when they grant ownership of the building blocks of software development. Furthermore, FOSS provides software that explicitly encourages its users to copy the software. If it is legal and moral to copy FOSS, why are the laws for PS so different?

The problem with this counter (counter to our argument that it is immoral to copy) is that it implies that it is permissible to break laws whenever they are bad. Although there may be cases in which individuals are justified in breaking a bad law, it overstates the case to claim that it is permissible to break any law one deems not good. Indeed, a rich philosophical literature addresses this question of why citizens have an obligation to obey the law and when citizens are justified in breaking the law. The literature recognizes that there are circumstances in which citizens are justified in breaking the law, but such circumstances are limited. The literature suggests that citizens have what is called a prima facie obligation to obey the laws of a relatively just state. Prima facie means "all else being equal" or "unless there are overriding reasons." A prima facie obligation can be overridden by higher order obligations or by special circumstances that justify a different course of action. Higher order obligations will override when, for example, obeying the law will lead to greater harm than disobeying. For example, the law prohibiting automobiles from being driven on the left side of the road (as is the case in many countries) is a good law, but a driver would be justified in breaking this law in order to avoid an accident. On this account of a citizen's obligation to obey the laws of a relatively just state, one has an obligation to obey property laws unless there are overriding reasons for breaking them.

Most cases of PS copying do not seem to fall into this category. Most of those who make illegal copies of software do so because it is so easy and because they don't want to pay for the software. They don't copy software because an overriding moral reason takes priority over adhering to the law. Furthermore, the existence of FOSS alternatives to many PS applications removes a possible ethical argument for copying PS. Copying a PS application for which a FOSS alternative exists is particularly hard to defend ethically because the FOSS alternative could, arguably, provide almost all the functionality a user could claim was vital, and copying FOSS is not only permissible, it is encouraged. So, ironically, the existence of FOSS strengthens the ethical claim that copying PS is unethical.

Still resisting, you might try to frame software copying as an act of civil disobedience. The United States and many other countries have a tradition of recognizing some acts of disobedience to law as morally justified. However, acts of civil disobedience are generally justified on grounds that it would be immoral to obey such laws. Obedience to the law would compel one to act immorally or to support immoral institutions; thus, disobedience is justified.

It would take us too far afield to explore all the possibilities here but let us suggest some of the obstacles to making the case in defense of software copying. You would have to show that: (1) the system of property rights for software is not just a bad system, but an unjust system; and (2) adhering to those laws compels you to perform immoral acts or support unjust institutions. Making the case for (1) will not be easy. The critique would have to show either that all copyright and patent laws are unjust or that these laws when extended to software are unjust, or that these laws when interpreted in a certain way (for example, giving Microsoft control of so much of the market) are unjust.

If you can make the case for (1), then (2) will become more plausible. That is, if the system of property rights in software is unjust, then it is plausible that adhering to such laws might compel you to act immorally. But this will not be an easy case to make because adhering to the law simply means refraining from copying. In other words, you would have to show that refraining from software copying is an immoral act or supports an immoral institution.

Several authors have made just this sort of argument although the conclusions of these arguments apply only to copying in restricted circumstances. Stallman (1995) and Nissenbaum (1994) both hypothesize situations in which a person is having a great deal of trouble trying to do something with computers and a close friend has software that will solve the problems. Stallman and Nissenbaum both make the point that not helping your friend in such a situation—when you know how to help and have the means to help—seems wrong. Insofar as PS prohibits you from giving a copy of your software to your friend in need, PS discourages and prevents altruism.

Neither author seems to recognize the harm done to the copyright or patent holder when a copy is made. In fact, the situation they hypothesize sets up a dilemma in which an individual must, it seems, choose one harm over another—violate the right of the software owner or fail to help your friend. This takes us back to the idea that overriding circumstances sometimes justify breaking the law. There probably are some circumstances in which making a copy of PS will be justified to prevent some harm greater than the violation of the software owner's property rights. However, those cases are not the typical case of PS copying; that is, typically, people make illegal copies for their convenience and to save money, not to prevent serious harm from occurring.

The case for the moral permissibility of software copying would be stronger if the system of property rights in software, or all property rights, were shown to be unjust. Stallman seems to hold a view that is close to the latter. At least in some of his writings, he seems to argue that all property rights promote selfishness and discourage altruism. He might well be right about this. However, if that is the case, why pick on PS copying as if it were a special case of justified property rights violation? Wouldn't the argument apply to taking cars, computers, and money? It would seem that laws making these things private property also discourage altruism in certain circumstances.

We are quite willing to grant that there may be situations in which software copying is justified, namely when some serious harm can be prevented only by making and using an illegal copy of PS. In most cases, however, the claims of the software owner would seem to be much stronger than the claims of someone who needs a copy to make his or her life easier.

In order to fully understand our argument, it will be helpful to use an analogy. Suppose I own a private swimming pool and I make a living by allowing others to use the pool for a fee. The pool is closed on certain days, and open only for certain hours on the other days. You figure out how to break into the pool undetected, and you break in and swim when the pool is closed. The act of swimming is not intrinsically wrong, and swimming in the pool does no visible or physical harm to me, or to anyone else. Nevertheless, you are using my property without my permission. It would hardly seem a justification for ignoring my property rights if you claimed that you were hot and the swim in my pool made your life more tolerable and less onerous. Your argument would be no more convincing if you pointed out that you were not depriving me of revenues from renting the pool because you swam when the pool was closed. Note the parallel to justifying software copying on the grounds that it does no harm, makes the copier's life better, and doesn't deprive the owner of revenue because you wouldn't have bought the software anyway.

The argument would still not be convincing if instead of seeking your own comfort, you sought the comfort of your friend. Suppose, that is, that you had a friend who was suffering greatly from the heat and so you, having the knowledge of how to break into the pool, broke in, in the name of altruism, and allowed your friend to swim while you watched to make sure I didn't appear. In your defense, you argue that it would have been selfish for you not to use your knowledge to help out your friend. Your act was altruistic.

There are circumstances under which your illegal entry into my pool would be justified. For example, if I had given permission to someone to swim in the pool while it was closed to the public and that person, swimming alone, began to drown. You were innocently walking by and saw the person drowning. You broke in and jumped into the pool in order to save the drowning swimmer. Here the circumstances justify your violating my property rights.

There seems no moral difference between breaking into the pool and making a copy of PS. Both acts violate the legal rights of the owner—legal rights created by reasonably good laws. We grant that these laws prevent others from acting altruistically. We concede that private property can be individualistic, exclusionary, and even selfish. Nonetheless, it is prima facie wrong to make an illegal copy of PS because to do so is to deprive the owner of his or her legal right, and this constitutes a harm to the owner. Returning to our analogy, the ethical case for breaking into the proprietary swimming pool would also be greatly diminished if there were an alternative swimming pool open to the public and readily accessible to you and your friend; that "extra" swimming pool is analogous to FOSS.

BREAKING RULES, NO RULES, AND NEW RULES

Throughout this chapter our primary concern has been software. There are, however, several other forms of digital intellectual property that are equally controversial. We will briefly examine two other forms, music and movies, before concluding this chapter. Although important in their own right, the controversies over music and movies reinforce several of the ideas we explained in relation to software ownership.

Unauthorized copying of copyrighted music was an issue before music was routinely digitized, but when music became digital, making multiple "perfect" copies became easy and cheap. When the Web and a new encoding standard (MP3) made it even more convenient to download music, copying became a common practice, especially among young people such as college students who had convenient access to the Internet. In 2000, a service called "Napster" started to become wildly popular. The system allowed peer-to-peer file sharing, which (not coincidentally) was used almost exclusively for sharing of unauthorized copies of copyrighted music. After a lengthy battle in the U.S. courts, Napster was shut down, although it has since reopened as a pay service for obtaining music.

Napster was an IT invention designed explicitly for the purpose of bypassing the system through which copyright holders controlled the use of their intellectual property. Legally producing and distributing a proprietary recording required seeking the permission of the copyright holder and usually paying a fee for use. Napster bypassed that system, so most users were breaking the law. We say "most" because some of the files shared via Napster were *not* copyrighted. The music was not proprietary. These particular music files are an example of a new idea about how to share intellectual property.

Consider the case (now common) of a band without a contract with a music company. The band wants people to hear their music, perhaps to increase the number of people willing to pay to attend their live performances, perhaps only because they want to be heard. The band places a recording on the Web and declares it free for the taking so that individuals can download it, and share it with many more people. No rules restrict this sharing; no rules require it. Even established bands have used the Internet in creative and nonregulated ways. In 2007, more than one band put an entire album on the Web, allowed people to download it, and invited them to voluntarily pay whatever they thought the music was worth. Here we see that "no rules" didn't seem to interfere with the free flow of digital music.

Of course, this idea of "no rules" is actually an illusion. As Lawrence Lessig (1999) has famously pointed out, on the Internet, computer code is a type of law. Rules are embedded in the architecture of programs and the Internet, and those rules are very hard to break and rarely challenged. There are the laws of protocols, bandwidth, and physics, all of which limit the number of bits you can download in a given period of time with a given computer and a given Internet connection. To participate in many social websites, you have to follow the protocols—the law—or you cannot join in.

Thus our final thought about laws on the Internet is that in reality, instead of no rules there are new rules, some of which are implicit in the technology, and others that are made explicitly. Lawrence Lessig (mentioned above) has spearheaded an effort through a nonprofit organization, called Creative Commons, to encourage and facilitate the sharing of digital information. Creative Commons makes available to anyone (for free) automatically generated licensing language and symbols so that users can label digital data they are willing to share. The extensively researched licenses permit users to allow or disallow commercial use, sampling, to require attribution, or charge for use, mixing and matching restrictions and permissions. The FS licenses described earlier are one option for software in Creative Commons, but there are many more possibilities. Creative Commons licenses are not exclusively for software, but also (some would say primarily) for music, graphics, text, and presentations of all sorts. The Creative Commons project is a way of facilitating new rules and new attitudes about not only restricting and charging for reuse, but also for encouraging reuse among individuals and organizations.

The growing popularity of Creative Commons, as well as sites featuring volunteered content (such as YouTube) demonstrate that the Internet and the Web are not used merely to break the rules (although this certainly happens too); the Internet also facilitates new ways to interact, new ways to create, and new ways to distribute intellectual property. In some cases, the "middle man," so powerful in traditional entertainment, has not exactly been eliminated but replaced by an automated "middle thing." When the Web and the Internet serve in this "middle thing" role, old rules need not be followed. It's not that old rules have to be broken, just that new directions can be taken.

Notice a parallel here between FOSS and what is happening with Creative Commons. Voluntarily, software developers are connecting with each other and with users to create and distribute useful intellectual property, and they are doing so while circumnavigating traditional corporations, economic motivations, and media. FOSS need not oppose PS, just as YouTube need not "oppose" commercial TV or movies. Instead, authors of intellectual property can merely avoid the old ways by "patronizing" authors and developers willing to play by the new rules. Sometimes the new rules bump up against the old and there is trouble; for example, some broadcast television shows object to their content being placed on YouTube without compensation. We saw this as well in Scenario 5.3.

This is not to say that the new rules are always the best way to go, or that everyone participating in the Internet acts ethically. Rather, the point is that technology and notions of right and wrong are intertwined. FOSS and Creative Commons are new systems for producing and distributing creative works and they have been shaped by IT, law, and notions of right and wrong. IT, the Web, and the Internet afford us many opportunities to think creatively, and FOSS and Creative Commons are two creative responses to perceived weaknesses in traditional ideas about property applied to digital information.

Conclusion

The issues discussed in this chapter are fascinating and important. Our ideas about property are tied to deeply ingrained notions of rights, fairness, and economic justice. Law and public policy on the ownership of software and digital data structure the environment for software development, so it is important to evaluate these laws to insure the future development of IT. The issue of the permissibility of making personal copies of PS and copyrighted intellectual property is also fascinating and important but for different reasons. Here we are forced to clarify what makes an action right or wrong. We are forced to come to grips with our moral intuitions and to extend these to entities with the unique characteristics of software.

The thrust of this chapter has been to move the discussion of property rights in software away from the idea that property rights are given in nature, and toward the idea that we can and should develop a system of property rights that serve us well in the long run. Our analysis suggests that although it is generally unethical to copy proprietary software, alternative systems of production and distribution are evolving. Instead of depriving authors of their legitimate rights under the old rules, with FOSS and Creative Commons, users can choose to connect to authors willing to play under new rules. The new systems are constituted with distinctive moral rules and obligations and involve interesting relationships between authors and consumers.

Study Questions

1. What is software? What is hardware?
2. What are the differences between object programs, source programs, and algorithms?
3. What is the aim of the U.S. copyright system?
4. Why is copyright problematic for protecting software ownership?
5. What does a copyright holder have to show to prove infringement?
6. What must copyright holders show in order to prove that they had a legitimate trade secret?
7. Why is trade secrecy problematic for the protection of software ownership?
8. How is a patent a monopoly?
9. What tests must a patent claim satisfy to obtain a U.S. patent?
10. What cannot be patented in the United States? Why?
11. What are the three different forms of digital sharing discussed in this chapter?
12. What are the four freedoms that FS advocates try to preserve?
13. What is Locke's labor theory of property? Why doesn't it necessarily apply to ownership of computer software?
14. What natural rights arguments can be made for and against ownership of software?
15. The authors argue that software copying is immoral because it is illegal. List the logical steps they used to arrive at this conclusion. Is the argument valid?
16. What is Creative Commons?

Digital Order

CHAPTER OUTLINE

SCENARIOS

Scenario 6.1 Bot Roast

The following news release was issued by the U.S. Department of Justice, FBI on November 29, 2007:

> The FBI today announced the results of the second phase of its continuing investigation into a growing and serious problem involving criminal use of

botnets. Since Operation "Bot Roast" was announced last June, eight individuals have been indicted, pled guilty, or been sentenced for crimes related to botnet activity. Additionally, 13 search warrants were served in the U.S. and by overseas law enforcement partners in connection with this operation. This ongoing investigative effort has thus far uncovered more than $20 million in economic loss and more than one million victim computers.

FBI Director Robert S. Mueller, III said, "Today, botnets are the weapon of choice of cyber criminals. They seek to conceal their criminal activities by using third party computers as vehicles for their crimes. In Bot Roast II, we see the diverse and complex nature of crimes that are being committed through the use of botnets. Despite this enormous challenge, we will continue to be aggressive in finding those responsible for attempting to exploit unknowing Internet users. [www.fbi.gov/pressrel/pressrel07/botroast112907.htm]

A botnet is a collection of compromised computers under the remote command and control of a criminal "botherder." A botherder can gain control of these computers by unleashing malicious software such as viruses, worms, or Trojan horses. By executing a simple task such as opening an attachment, clicking on an advertisement, or providing personal information to a phishing site (a fraudulent site that mimics a legitimate site), an individual computer user has unintentionally allowed unauthorized access. Bot operators will then typically use these compromised computers as vehicles to facilitate other actions such as commit identity theft, launch denial-of-service attacks, and install keystroke loggers.

Although it may seem appropriate to condemn the botherders who use other people's machines to perpetrate cyber crimes, a more subtle issue is lurking here. What is the responsibility of computer owners (organizations and individuals) to keep their systems secure from the attack of botherders? Is a computer owner who refuses to purchase or use software and hardware to block attackers complicit when a botherder attacks, captures, and then uses an unprotected computer to commit a crime? Do software developers shoulder some of the blame when they distribute operating systems and applications that include security flaws that make computers vulnerable?

Scenario 6.2 Wiki Warfare

Background

Wikipedia is a free encyclopedia available on the Internet. Operated by the nonprofit Wikimedia Foundation, Wikipedia is available in many different languages. Entries are written by volunteers and involve a form of collaboration created through the website. Once an entry is written and posted, it can be edited by anyone who has access to the Internet. As the Wikipedia entry on Wikipedia explains, only registered users may create a new article, but articles can be edited anonymously or with a user account. Edits are posted immediately, but an entry may quickly be changed if another user thinks the edit is inaccurate or misleading. Although some articles change very little from day to day, articles on controversial topics may change second by second. Wikipedia has a mechanism for dealing with disagreements; a discussion board at each entry allows users to discuss their disagreements and reach consensus so that the article stabilizes. In addition to discussion boards, Wikipedia uses programs to monitor the site for obscenities and other malicious activity.

Real Event

During the 2008 presidential campaign in the United States, Wikipedia became a site for political battles. The encyclopedia includes biographical entries on political candidates and these were highly contested during the campaigns. Several news stories reported on the struggles over the entries for Hillary Clinton and Barack Obama. Although some of the contention may seem minor, the nuances of language become important in a campaign. Thus, describing one of the candidates for nominee of the Democratic Party as "a leading candidate for the Democratic nomination" versus describing the person as simply "a candidate" became a point of contention. Other struggles were not so subtle. At various points in the battle, Barack Obama's entry falsely described him as a "Kenyan–American politician" and as a Muslim. A self-appointed volunteer monitoring the Obama article was so frustrated by what she characterized as attacks on the Obama article that she contacted Wikipedia administrators. The user who kept adding these false claims was booted from access. However, as the news reports explained, those who attack entries often do so with a false identity so although booted, the user could have come back under some other user name.

[Based on Eve Fairbanks, "Wiki Woman," *The New Republic*, April 9, 2008, p. 5; Alison Stewart and Rachel Martin, "Obama, Clinton Wiki-Warfare," The Bryant Park Project. National Public Radio (NPR), April 3, 2008; and Jose Antonio Vargas, "On Wikipedia, Debating 2008 Hopefuls' Every Facet," *The Washington Post*, September 17, 2007, p. A1.]

Scenario 6.3 Yahoo and Nazi Memorabilia

In 2000, the Union of Jewish Students in France (UEJF) and the League Against Racism and Anti-Semitism (LICRA) sued Yahoo in a French court; they charged that Yahoo violated a French law banning trafficking in Nazi goods in France.

Yahoo initially shrugged off the suit. The company seemed confident that such charges could not be upheld because Yahoo is an American company with its website located in the United States. It seemed unlikely that French law could apply in the United States. However, as the case proceeded it became clear that Yahoo had underestimated the power of sovereign nations. Lawyers argued that France had a sovereign right to defend itself from the sale of illegal Nazi merchandise from the United States. As one lawyer put it: "French law does not permit racism in writing, on television or on the radio, and I see no reason to have an exception for the Internet."

Yahoo put forward what was essentially an "impossibility" defense. Company lawyers argued that Yahoo adhered to French law in its French language website. [The problem was that the French could visit its U.S. website.] They argued that the website could not detect where a visitor was from. If the U.S. website had to comply with French law, then "it would need to remove the Nazi items from its U.S. server, thereby depriving Yahoo users everywhere from buying them, and making French law the effective rule for the world."

The court battle raged for some time with Yahoo and its defenders standing firm on the principle that the law of one country could not determine content on the Internet. Eventually, however, Yahoo caved and removed the Nazi items and content from its website. A number of factors seemed to lead to this decision. Although Yahoo thought France could not exercise power in the United States, the company realized that it had assets in France including a French subsidiary that would be at risk of seizure if Yahoo didn't comply with French law. During the trial a new technology had been introduced that would allow Yahoo to detect the location of visitors; it could block visitors from France. Moreover, Yahoo had begun to negotiate with China and had agreed to China's demands to inspect and monitor information that would be accessible to its citizens. As Goldsmith and Wu 2006 put it, "The darling of the Internet free speech movement had become an agent of thought control for the Chinese government."

Even so, Yahoo later sued UEJF and LICRA in the United States to have the French court's verdict declared unenforceable in the United States, arguing that it violates the right to free speech. In January, 2006, the Ninth U.S. Circuit Court of Appeals in San Francisco dismissed Yahoo's appeal.

[Based on the account given by J. Goldsmith and T. Wu in *Who Controls the Internet?* Oxford University Press, 2006.]

INTRODUCTION: LAW AND ORDER ON THE INTERNET

In 1991 John Perry Barlow, a cofounder of the Electronic Frontier Foundation, wrote the following:

> . . . for all its importance to modern existence, Cyberspace remains a frontier region, across which roam the few aboriginal technologists and cyberpunks who can tolerate the austerity of its savage computer interfaces, incompatible communications protocols, proprietary barricades, cultural and legal ambiguities, and general lack of useful maps or metaphors.
>
> Certainly, the old concepts of property, expression, identity, movement, and context, based as they are on physical manifestation, do not apply succinctly in a world where there can be none. . . .
>
> But Cyberspace is the homeland of the Information Age, the place where the citizens of the future are destined to dwell. We will all go there whether we want to or not and we would do better to approach the place with a settler's determination to civilize it as rapidly as possible.
>
> What would it mean to civilize Cyberspace? To some, the answer to this question is simple and historically familiar: exterminate the savages, secure the resources into corporate possession, establish tariffs, and define culture strictly in terms of economy.

[John Perry Barlow, "Coming into the Country" *Communications of the ACM* 34 3 1991: 19–21].

Barlow's account exemplifies the awe and anticipation that many who were involved in the early development of the Internet had at the time. Although his thinking is a good example of technological determinism—"We will all go there whether we want to or not ..."—these excerpts capture Barlow's (and others') sense that the Internet's development was going to be revolutionary and transformative and that it was going to involve a collision of powerful interests. They likened the Internet to a new frontier on the model of the American Wild West. It was an uncivilized, free, and open territory that had to be settled; the process of settling the new territory would involve individuals and groups vying to have their visions realized and their particular interests served. Continuing with the metaphor of the Internet as a frontier, we can think of the early days of its development and the process of civilizing the Internet as a process of establishing "law and order." However, as the chapter proceeds, we make clear that law is only one of several means by which order is established and maintained. "Order" is the theme that organizes this chapter.

Chapters 4 and 5 can be read as accounts of the struggle over order with regard to personal information and property rights. In both cases, law and order have been created. Of course, law and order are never set in stone for all time. Many of the big issues have been settled but these are open to renegotiation and much is yet to be settled. Again, Chapters 4 and 5 illustrate ongoing negotiation and debate; neither property nor privacy rights on the Internet have been settled permanently. The Internet is, and perhaps always will be, a work in progress. In this chapter we consider a number of issues—in addition to those discussed in Chapters 4 and 5—that have to do with how the Internet should be ordered.

In Scenario 6.1 we see one of the most powerful means by which order is created—criminalization. Behavior of a particular kind is declared to be a crime and the criminal justice system is used to respond to transgressors. Scenario 6.1 illustrates the challenges of criminalizing behavior on the Internet; novel forms of behavior have to be conceptualized and classified, crimes must be detected, and violators caught. Doing this is enormously complicated given that the crimes are committed remotely under various "shrouds of anonymity."

Crime and security go hand in hand. In this respect, Chapters 4 and 5 set the scene for this chapter. Law defines property rights and privacy rights and these rights are protected through the criminal justice system. Of course, crime prevention and security go beyond the criminal justice system; IT systems are designed to prevent crime, so order is created in the architecture of IT systems. We saw in Chapter 5 how digital rights management mechanisms are put into software and hardware to stop copying of digital intellectual property. Security aims at protecting privacy as well as property.

Scenario 6.2 illustrates a somewhat new form of order facilitated by the Internet. Wikis are used to produce and share knowledge in collaborative arrangements that were practically impossible before. Perhaps the best example is Wikipedia because it is an encyclopedia of knowledge produced by thousands of individuals making contributions and reviewing and editing the contributions of others. Because knowledge is powerful, this mode of production has broad implications for many domains including the election of a president. Globalization may also be thought of as order, an order that is being instrumented through the Internet.

Scenario 6.3 illustrates how individuals and nation states "bump into" one another on the Internet and this puts pressure on the order that prevailed before. Censorship is one of the most challenging issues of Internet order. The right of free expression collides with the openness of the Internet challenging democratic principles. How can we allow freedom of expression and simultaneously protect individuals from offensive behavior? Another example of this is the challenge of protecting children from pornography and predators while at the same time protecting the right of adults not to have their access censored.

SOCIOTECHNICAL ORDER

We can begin to get a handle on these issues by reflecting briefly on order and chaos. Although the Internet may, at one time, have been free and open, wild and anarchical as John Perry Barlow describes above, there is now a good deal of order, order that is achieved through a combination of sociotechnical elements. In Chapter 1, we suggested that the Internet, like all technologies, is a sociotechnical system, a combination of artifacts (software, hardware, and telecommunication connections), social practices, social institutions, and social relationships and arrangements. In earlier chapters, we mentioned Lessig's account of code as a form of regulation and we can now focus more carefully on his account. Lessig (1999) argues that human behavior is regulated by law, markets, social norms, and architecture. Most of us would readily acknowledge that our behavior is influenced by the first three; we know that we are affected by laws, that we adhere to social norms and conventions, and that we are influenced by market incentives and disincentives. It is Lessig's fourth form of regulation that is surprising because we generally incorporate technology into our lives without thinking that we are subjecting ourselves to regulation when we do. Consider the following illustrations of all four forms of regulation.

Law: Scenario 6.1 illustrates how law shapes behavior on the Internet in the sense that it points to prohibitions on unauthorized access and control of privately owned systems. Of course, the scenario also illustrates attempts to violate the law and then initiatives to enforce the law by capturing and punishing those who break it. Chapters 4 and 5 were filled with discussions of the laws that pertain to privacy and property. These laws regulate behavior on the Internet and more broadly behavior involving IT.

Markets: The market shapes Internet activity in a number of ways but perhaps the one users encounter the most is the system of Internet service providers (ISPs) through which one must go to get access to the Internet. ISPs vary in the way they make money. Some offer their service for a monthly fee; others offer particular services such as free e-mail, and try to make money through advertising. The schemas by which companies make money affects the choices users make and in that respect regulates behavior. As discussed in Chapter 5, Google offers free e-mail through its Gmail system but it tries to make money through advertising. By offering this type of service, Google gives users an incentive to put up with (and potentially be influenced by) paid advertising. If, on the other hand, a country like the United States were to make the Internet a public infrastructure (like the American federal system of roads), user behavior would be regulated quite differently.

Social norms: Most Internet users adhere to informal social rules whether they are aware of it or not. Users adopt conventions for politeness and expressing emotions that parallel those that they use offline. A good example is "emoticons" like the smiley face (☺ and ☹). This is an informal convention that has been adopted. [Of course, it wouldn't be possible were it not for the code in our word processing programs that converts semicolons and parentheses to the smiley face.]

Architecture: The smiley face example illustrates how code facilitates the use of an informal convention, but perhaps the most powerful example of how code and computer architecture regulate behavior is the TCP/IP protocol that underlies the Internet. Many laud this architecture because it allows for the open nature of the information exchanges that the Internet facilitates. However, critics argue that TCP/IP does not allow specialized "pipes" that some bandwidth providers want to establish in order to make new applications available and (perhaps not coincidentally) that the providers want to provide to "preferred customers" for increased fees. Advocates for the current system of "dumb pipes" that are available to everyone (a concept now called "net neutrality") contend that innovation should occur at the edges of the Internet, not in the pipes. Thus, the hardware, software, and protocols that coordinate our use of these resources act as "laws" that help determine what we can and cannot do.

These four forms of regulation sometimes work together and sometimes are at odds with one another. For example, legal disputes persist about the liability of ISPs for the content that their customers distribute. The outcomes of these *legal* cases will shape the *market* for Internet access. For example, were ISPs to be held liable for content, customers would likely see monitoring and filtering of their communications; we can even imagine different ISPs employing different filtering standards with the market being affected by what sort of filtering customers preferred and how much they are willing to pay for unfiltered communication. An example of law and architecture working together is seen in Scenario 6.1 where law and architecture are both targeted to prevent security violations.

As we examine issues in this chapter, it will be important not to assume that the prevailing order is, by definition, the only possible order or best order that can be had. Our goal here is to draw attention to the order that has been created, and to try to understand *how* it has been created, so that we can ask normative questions. Is this order fair? Does it embody, reinforce, or counteract important social values? Can the Internet be changed to be more secure, more evenly accessible, more conducive to human creativity and democracy? It is these broader social values that we want to keep in mind as we explore law and order on the Internet.

ONLINE CRIME

As mentioned above, criminalization—declaring certain forms of behavior illegal and imposing fines or jail terms for failure to comply—is one of the most powerful ways to regulate behavior. When it comes to computer crime, a distinction is often drawn between: (1) new versions of old crimes—crimes that were done before and are now done using computers, for example, theft, fraud, stalking, libel, and defamation; and (2) crimes that couldn't exist without computers or are directed at computers, for example, sending a virus, a denial-of-service attack, inappropriately pinging, or using a "botnet" to spy on Web transactions. To put this in the language of instrumentation, there is a distinction between old crimes instrumented in new ways and crimes that attack or make use of the instrumentation to do what couldn't be done before. This sort of distinction was particularly important in the early days of computing when we were trying to figure out whether current law could be applied to what seemed to be novel acts *or* new laws had to be created.

The distinction seems less important now, because even old crimes instrumented with IT have features and characteristics that distinguish them from acts of the same type without computers. Consider, for example, the difference between the act—refer to it as A—of stealing from a bank by physically entering the bank, putting a gun to the bank teller's head, and asking for the money behind the counter. Here the thief uses the threat of shooting the teller if he or she does not comply. Now consider the act—refer to it as B—in which a thief steals from a bank by remotely (although still physically) accessing the bank's computer system, manipulating code, and in so doing transfers money from the bank to the thief's own account in a Swiss bank. B is an example of an old crime instrumented in a new way and it is tempting to say that A and B are morally equivalent acts because they are both "bank robberies." Treating A and B as morally equivalent seems, however, to ignore relevant features that are different because of the instrumentation. In A, a gun was used and human beings were put at physical risk; in B, no humans were physically threatened. To be sure, in both cases money is stolen—the legitimate rights of a bank and its depositors are violated. Nevertheless, the difference in instrumentation does seem to affect the moral character of the crime. So, classifying B as a new version of bank robbery doesn't seem to help much in the moral evaluation.

On the other hand, the distinction has a role when it comes to crimes that couldn't exist without computers or are directed at computers. Here the challenge is the kind that Moor characterized as a conceptual muddle and also the kind that lends itself to analogical reasoning. Before we can figure out whether current law is relevant or a new kind of law is needed, we need to some way of thinking about (conceptualizing) the new behavior. Take phishing, for example. Wikipedia (http://en.wikipedia.org/wiki/Phishing, accessed January 7, 2008) defines a phishing attack as "an attempt to criminally and fraudulently acquire sensitive information, such as usernames, passwords, and credit card details, by masquerading as a trustworthy entity in an electronic communication." Phishing might be thought of as comparable to someone going house to house or calling on the phone trying to find customers interested in products that will never be delivered. The thief uses the sales pitch as the opportunity to get inside the person's house and scope it out for a future break-in or simply uses the sales pitch as an opportunity to obtain personal information that will be used for future crimes. Here it is tempting to say that phishing is simply a form of fraud, although before drawing that conclusion we would want to consider whether there is anything morally different about phishing and offline fraud. There are differences in the behavior involved— phishing is done remotely and, therefore, anonymously. Is this relevant? Phishing can be done on a larger scale. Does this make it morally different?

Now consider the behavior described in Scenario 6.1. Notice that the challenge is not in figuring out whether the behavior is undesirable; we know it is undesirable.

Rather, we need a way of thinking about the activity to help us figure out the nature of the wrongdoing and what might be appropriate in the way of sanction. We want to see whether the new activity fits standard categories of crime. Again, an analogy is useful. Was the crime in Scenario 6.1 equivalent to stealing the tools (shovels, drills, lockpicks, etc.) that are used to break into a bank? Or was it equivalent to breaking into a series of buildings in order to get to the bank building? Or what? Of course, the notion of "equivalence" is tricky here. The question can misdirect our thinking because what we are looking for is "moral equivalence" and yet, as suggested earlier, the instrumentation may make a moral difference. Thus, seemingly analogous behavior could be morally different because of the different instrumentation.

A review of the literature on computer crime suggests that both types of crimes are of concern; that is, law enforcement agencies pursue old crimes now instrumented through the Internet as well as new crimes inconceivable without IT. The crimes that are typically mentioned in lists of "computer crimes" are hacking, viruses, pirating, illegal trading fraud, scams, money laundering, libel, cyber stalking, cyber terrorism, identity theft and fraud, and wireless theft. According to the Internet Crime Complaint Center (IC3), a partnership of the FBI and the National White Collar Crime Center, the most common crime on the Internet is Internet auction fraud, comprising 44.9 percent of referred complaints (2007) [http://www.fbi.gov. majcases.fraud.internetschemes.htm].

Computer crime—whether a new version of an old crime or a new type of crime—has the features we identified in Chapter 3 as distinctive to IT: global, many-to-many scope, special identity conditions, and reproducibility. Because of the global scope of the Internet, criminals sitting alone anywhere in the world can move their fingers over keyboards, stare at computer screens, and steal from those in distant places, and they can wreak havoc on the lives of people across the globe by launching viruses or denial-of-service attacks. The global reach of crime also means that crimes cross criminal jurisdictions and this makes enforcement especially challenging. Because of reproducibility, criminals can makes copies of credit card numbers with ease and with little evidence that the numbers have been taken (copied). Stalkers can maintain a form of anonymity and pseudonymity. At the same time, reproducibility can be used against thieves and stalkers because records of their computer usage may help in tracking them down.

Crime on the Internet is important for understanding the order that has been created on the Internet. It is also important for ethics because, as we saw in Chapter 5, the fact that behavior is illegal is a prima facie reason for thinking it is immoral. However, as already indicated, although the law can be a starting place for understanding order on the Internet, it isn't the ending place. The interesting and challenging ethical issues are normative and concern what sort of order there *should* be. We turn now to some ideas that challenge the prevailing order.

HACKERS AND THE HACKER ETHIC

Crime on the Internet has a history that is quite telling in terms of the culture of computer programmers and "hackers." In the early days of computing, many of the pioneers in the field had a sense of the importance of the technological development that was underway and had distinctive ideas about how the Internet should develop. Some early pioneers called themselves "hackers" but what they meant by this was that they were computer enthusiasts. "Hacking" referred to the feats such enthusiasts were able to accomplish; they would spend hours figuring out how to do clever things with the new technology, things that had never been done before. Usually hackers were young men who had acquired a good deal of knowledge about computers, and they shared this knowledge with one another through the first electronic bulletin boards. Hackers organized computer clubs and user groups, circulated newsletters, and even had conventions. Aspects of this culture are still prevalent today. Indeed, the FOSS movement might be seen as an evolution or extension of this community.

Later the term "hacker" acquired negative connotations. "Hacker" began to be used to refer to those who use computers for illegal actions, especially gaining unauthorized access to computer systems, and stealing (and then sharing) proprietary software. Resisting this change in usage, many old-line computer enthusiasts pushed for a distinction between "crackers" and "hackers." "Hacker", they hoped, would continue to have its original, heroic meaning, whereas "cracker" would refer to those who engage in illegal activities—cracking into systems.

This distinction has not, however, taken hold. "Hacker" is now routinely used to refer to those who gain unauthorized access to computer systems and engage in disruptive, illegal activities. Whatever they are called, we want to focus here on the discussion that hackers and hacking has generated because in a number of subcultures there seems to be ambivalence about the immorality of disruptive behavior on the Internet. The ambivalence goes to the heart of the rightness-wrongness of hacking. Although some hacking behaviors—such as intentionally sending viruses or worms that damage computer systems, denial-of-service attacks, and unauthorized taking control of a website—undermine the security and integrity of the Internet, hackers have long had a defense of their behavior. We turn now to that defense as a way of exploring some of the issues of "order" on the Internet.

What hackers said in defense of their behavior in the early days of computing can be sorted into four arguments. The first argument is that "all information should be free." We have, in some sense, already discussed this claim in Chapter 5 where we explored whether information—in the form of computer programs, data sets, and so on—should be owned. The "information should be free" argument is also connected to our discussion of privacy in Chapter 4. But, what does it mean to say that information should be free?

Let's try to make the best case possible for the claim that information should be free. We can start from the idea that motivates the creation of libraries. National or state libraries are created because of the belief that at least some information should be accessible to all. If a nation wants its citizenry to be well informed, then it is essential that information be available. Moreover, if that society is democratic and wants as many as possible well-informed citizens, then it cannot allow information to be available only in the marketplace. Market distribution means uneven distribution; only the rich get access to certain kinds of information and the poor get very little and different access. This undermines equality and democracy.

Early hackers recognized the enormous potential of the Internet for making information available; they envisioned universal access to the Internet and, hence, universal access to information posted on the Internet. Hackers argued that too much information was becoming proprietary. The Internet was (and still is) often compared to the printing press and the great thing about the printing press is that information can be produced easily, cheaply, and on a grand scale. So, the Internet was seen by hackers as having enormous potential for making information available to the many. However, this would happen only if information is free, and by "free" hackers seemed to mean both without cost and without restrictions due to ownership or censorship.

Of course, even if it is true that "information should be widely available," it doesn't follow necessarily that *all* information should be *free*. A counter to the hacker claim is that if all information were free, then there would be no market and no incentive to develop information. We elaborated this argument in Chapter 5 in relation to programs, software, databases, or anything that might be appropriate for copyright, patent, or trade secrecy protection. Moreover, if *all* information were free, then individuals couldn't have the right to keep some information—personal information— private. So, it seems that the argument has to be qualified or made more modest. Hackers can more effectively argue that *certain kinds* of information should be free, but then the issue becomes a matter of distinguishing what information should be free (freely accessible) and what information may be owned and protected from wide distribution.

The second hacker argument has nothing to do with information per se, but rather with access to files. The argument is that attempts by hackers to break into computer systems are often beneficial because they illustrate security problems to those who can do something about them. Here the argument refers to hackers who break into systems for the sake of breaking in and not to steal or do damage. In other words, their point is that hacking isn't so bad and sometimes does some good. Consider the first case of hacking of this kind to reach national attention. On November 2, 1988, Robert T. Morris, Jr., a Cornell computer science graduate student launched a computer "worm" that spread across the Internet. Initially, attempts by various computer wizards were ineffective at stopping the worm; it was the most sophisticated and fastest worm to hit the Internet at that time. After completing infection of a site, the worm would replicate itself and go to another system. When a site was successfully infected, the worm would send a signal to "Ernie," a popular computer system at Berkeley. To avoid quick detection, the worm program would, in effect, role a 15-sided die to see whether it should infect a new system. A positive role, a 1-in-15 chance, would instruct the worm to go ahead. Unfortunately, the program was faulty and was infecting on a 14-in-15 chance instead. This caused systems to slow down and operators took notice.

Within 48 hours, the worm was isolated, decompiled, and notices had gone out explaining how to destroy it. Although the worm did no permanent damage, it slowed systems to a standstill and acquired passwords in these systems. Morris was suspended from Cornell by a university board of inquiry for irresponsible acts, and went to trial in January 1990. A federal court in Syracuse charged him with violating the Federal Computer Fraud and Abuse Act of 1986. During the trial, Morris revealed that he had realized he had made a mistake and tried to stop the worm. He contacted various friends at Harvard to help him. Andrew Sudduth testified at the trial that he had sent messages out with the solution to kill the program, but the networks were already clogged with the worm. Morris was found guilty, was placed on three years' probation, fined $10,000, and ordered to perform 400 hours of community service. He could have been jailed for up to five years and fined $250,000.

In his defense, Robert Morris claimed that he was trying to expose a flaw in the system. He had tried other means to get the problem fixed but system administrators had not listened to him. Hence, he defended his action on grounds that he was doing a service to computer system administrators and users by demonstrating the seriousness of the problem. In fact, he confessed that he didn't mean to do as much damage as he had done; the worm got out of control. The case is illustrative because although it suggests that Morris had good motives, his goodwill led to an out-of-control worm that wreaked havoc on the Internet.

Morris' act might be understood as an act of whistle blowing. Individuals "blow the whistle" on illegal or dangerous activities so as to draw attention to a situation, prevent harm, and get the situation fixed. The literature on whistle blowing suggests that whistle blowers should always try to fix a problem through internal channels because it is better to get a bad situation fixed with the least risk or danger (to those who are in danger as well as to the whistle blower). Yes, we can imagine cases in which an individual is frustrated in her attempts to get a flaw fixed and in which the flaw is serious enough for severe action. Still, such cases are likely to be rare, and not the typical motive for most break-ins.

Arguing by analogy, Gene Spafford (1992) gave a convincing counter to the whistle-blowing argument by suggesting that the hacker defense amounts to saying that vigilantes have the right to attempt—on a continuing basis—to break into the homes in a neighborhood in order to demonstrate that the homes there are susceptible to burglars. This argument hardly seems acceptable in the case of a neighborhood so we shouldn't accept it when it comes to the Internet. Spafford also points out that online break-ins, even when done to call attention to flaws in security, waste time and money, and pressure individuals and companies to invest in security. Many do not have the resources to fix systems or implement tighter security, yet the "vigilante behavior" compels such investment. Resources that might be put to other developments are, because of all the break-in attempts, invested in security.

So, although it is unquestionably a good thing for those who become aware of flaws in the security of computer systems to inform computer administrators and urge them to fix these flaws, it is not a good thing for individuals to try to break into systems just to show that they can do it or even just to show a flaw in the system. To be sure, there may be cases in which the flaws in security are extremely serious and an individual's reports of the threat to security fall on deaf ears. Nevertheless, it is difficult to imagine a case that justifies using viruses, denial-of-service attacks, or accessing private files as a means to get the problem fixed.

The third argument that hackers make still focuses on break-ins but here the argument is that gaining unauthorized access to computer systems does no harm as long as the hacker changes nothing. And, if the hacker learns something about how computer systems operate, then, something is gained at no loss to anyone. A little thought reveals the weakness of the first part of this argument, because individuals can be harmed simply by the unauthorized entry. After all, nonphysical harm is harm nonetheless. If individuals have proprietary rights and rights to privacy, then they are harmed when these rights are violated, just as individuals are harmed when they are deprived of their right to vote or their right to due process. Moreover, hackers *can* do physical harm. Hackers can gain access to computer systems used in hospitals where patients are at risk or systems running industrial processes where workers are at physical risk from dangerous chemicals or explosions. Suppose a hacker were to access and tamper with the computer system used to match donated organs with those in need of organs. Here time is absolutely critical. A slowdown in the system caused by tampering could make the difference between life and death. At the very least, hacker intrusions "steal cycles" of the compromised machine, using resources to which the hacker has no moral claim.

Hackers may well learn a good deal about computing and computer systems by attempting to break in, but the fact that one learns from an activity doesn't justify it. Giving electric shocks to learners when they make mistakes may promote learning, but this doesn't make it a good teaching method—especially when there are other ways to learn the same thing without causing as much pain and stress. Hackers may argue that there are some things a computer science student—say one who is studying security—can learn only by trying to break into real systems. This seems to ignore the creative approaches that teachers have developed for just this purpose. For example, some schools build sophisticated, lab-based intranets available for students to break into in controlled experiments; these systems are otherwise realistic, but are disconnected from the wider Internet.

The fourth argument that hackers make—heard less frequently today—is that hackers help to keep Big Brother at bay. Responding in part to concerns about privacy (described in Chapter 4), the thrust of this argument is that hackers have the expertise to find out about illegal or immoral uses and abuses of IT. Covert illegalities and abuse of personal information can be detected by hackers and reported to the public. In effect, the argument is that hackers can serve as good vigilantes. Think of the politics of search engine algorithms, Google's scanning of Gmail, or Lidl's records of its employees' activities. Although most computer users are unlikely to think about, let alone be able to figure out, what is happening inside the code that makes the Internet work, hackers can provide protection against these activities because of their specialized knowledge. So, the argument goes.

The argument is correct in suggesting that the public needs protection against abuses and inappropriate use of information, but whether hacking and hackers are the best form of protection seems another matter. Is the cost of tolerating hackers worth what is gained in protection? Do hackers solve the problem or make it worse? There are other ways to monitor and protect against computer abuse and illegal surveillance. A national data protection commission could be created to monitor information practices, propose legislation, and prosecute violators. Better laws and clearer guidelines could be developed. Computer professionals could be assigned a role in this. Users could be expected to report suspicious behavior.

Condoning attempts to break into computer systems—even when they are done for our benefit—seems a bad idea. We would be trading one problem for another.

We might get some protection against information abuse and covert surveillance, but in exchange for this, we would make ourselves vulnerable to our vigilantes. Self-chosen vigilantes could take a look at any of our systems or files.

Although each of the hacker arguments is faulty, the thrust of hacker concerns should not be dismissed lightly. The hacker arguments point to problems in the way that IT and the Internet are currently ordered, that is, they point to problems that need to be addressed. They remind us that the Internet could be configured differently than it is now. The hacker arguments suggest that the Internet has enormous potential for providing access to information and we ought to figure out ways to take advantage of that potential. Reproducibility makes it possible for information to be copied endlessly and at negligible cost; in theory, this means information and knowledge could be spread across the globe inexpensively. Already, organizations such as Project Gutenberg (http://www.gutenberg.org/wiki/Main_Page) and the U.S. National Library of Medicine (http://www.nlm.nih.gov/medlineplus/) offer high-quality information to the Internet public at no cost beyond a connection. Perhaps many more such projects should be initiated. Hackers also draw our attention to the unreliability and vulnerability of computer systems. This vulnerability is often underappreciated when important information and activities are put online without adequate security. So, although hacking can be disruptive, dangerous, and unjustified, it represents an important countercurrent in the development of the Internet. To take advantage of the enormous potential of the Internet, it behooves us to listen to such countercurrents, even when we don't agree with them.

SOCIOTECHNICAL SECURITY

Whether it is hackers or ordinary thieves, protecting IT systems from intruders is a central focus of security. Because IT constitutes so many activities, the reliability of IT systems is critical to information societies. Reliability is broader than security; reliable computing depends both on security and well-designed IT. Poorly designed, bug-ridden systems are unreliable and inefficient. Bugs and other kinds of flaws in the production of hardware and the programming of software can be dangerous and undermine the functions of the IT systems of which they are a part. We will focus in this section on security and deal with some of the issues involving poorly designed hardware and software in Chapter 7.

We can begin here by asking the same question we asked about other values. Is security an intrinsic or instrumental value? To be sure, there are many different kinds of security—bodily security (protection from bodily harm from others or from nature), financial security, job security, national security, and so on. Arguments might be made for the intrinsic value of certain kinds of security, especially bodily security, but computer security is an instrumental value. It isn't instrumental to one specific end; rather, security is instrumental to whatever good is aimed at in the particular IT system. Computer security in transportation systems is instrumental to safe and reliable transportation; the security of financial systems is instrumental to the protection of financial resources and the accuracy of accounting; and the security of personal computers is instrumental to personal privacy. So, security is a means to a wide variety of goods and is targeted to protect IT systems from intruders, and the disruption they can cause.

Security is achieved sociotechnically. A good deal of effort is put into developing hardware and software techniques for achieving security, but these tools and techniques work in conjunction with policies and practices that regulate (in Lessig's sense of the term) human behavior. A simple example is the use of passwords to protect against intruders. A computer system using passwords can include software to encrypt stored passwords and to not display the password characters when a user logs in. And the computer system can automatically require "strong" passwords (that are more difficult to crack using brute force algorithms), and can require that users change them periodically. But all of those safeguards are useless if authorized users are careless about protecting their passwords. If even one user writes his or her password on a post-it and sticks the post-it on a monitor, then anyone entering the office (e.g., a visitor, delivery person) can easily obtain access to the system. A single careless user compromises the security of the system.

To illustrate, consider a rough account of how security is achieved in a small company. Suppose the company has a server that supports 30 computers. The IT staff maintains an intranet and company employees who have access to the company intranet can also access the broader Internet. How does the company secure itself against intruders? They might build into the hardware and software various authentication techniques, including the aforementioned passwords, but perhaps also including biometrics such as fingerprint readers. They might monitor all traffic inside the intranet and particularly scrutinize traffic to and from the Internet. In addition, they might use a swipe card system for entry and exit to the company building.

Many of these security measures protect the system against intruders from outside the company; others protect the system from employees who might violate social norms. Of course, even if these measures are completely successful, the system is still vulnerable to the employees who run the IT system. Furthermore, security measures are rarely 100 percent effective. Users find work-arounds for security measures, not necessarily to intentionally compromise security, but just to make things more convenient. Office workers prop a door open for a pizza delivery; a manager lends his password to his daughter so she can get faster access to the Internet on "take your daughter to work day"; and an IT security expert uses his wife's first name for his root password. Security has to be implemented sociotechnically to achieve its goal. It is achieved through a combination of social and technical means, and any missteps in either arena make the system more vulnerable.

Security illustrates the STS coshaping theme; on the one hand, ideas about who is a threat and how they can undermine security shape the design and development of computer hardware and software; on the other hand, security tools and techniques shape crime and criminals. The latter point becomes clear when we consider how the design of computer systems determines what intruders have to do in order to break in. Those who want to break in must become knowledgeable about certain techniques, write particular kinds of programs, or become adept at "social engineering" tricks to fool people into revealing security information. The interaction here might be characterized as a "security arms race"; intruders develop devices and techniques that assist them in breaking in; security experts figure out and deploy techniques to prevent the use of these devices; intruders find ways to get around the new security techniques; security experts come up with counters to the new criminal techniques; and so on. In a race of this kind, combatants are compelled to invest time, money, effort, and attention to defeat the other side.

But what, you might ask, does security have to do with ethics? This is a good question, although a question with several answers. A simple answer is that our discussion demonstrates that it is wrong to break into IT systems. It is wrong, that is, to gain access to systems one is not authorized to access. In our discussion of hacker ethics we considered the defenses that might be offered for breaking in, and it seems that the very least we can say is that prima facie (all else being equal) it is wrong to break in to systems that you are not authorized to access.

There are, however, more challenging, complicated, and nuanced ethical issues in security. We have included security in this chapter, entitled "digital order" because we recognize that security influences order. Security measures—technical and social—shape computing environments. Here we will take up two particularly thorny issues. One has to do with responsibility for security breaches, and the other has to do with the trade-offs that are made in security.

Who Is to Blame in Security Breaches?

Typically, when security is breached, questions of blame and accountability are raised. Although the intruder is obviously at fault, attention may also turn to those who were responsible for security. In a company or other kind of organization, this means individuals who have been specifically assigned responsibility for security. When it comes to the security of personal computers it will usually be the individual computer owner. No matter who is responsible for a machine's security, the question whether those responsible are partially to blame for the breach may be raised. This is a complicated dilemma.

We might think of the installation of security mechanisms as a burden or cost, one that is created by those who would break in—criminals with malicious intent or those who are curious as to whether they can break in. Either way, computer owners choose whether they want to invest (time, money) in security or not. The question is: If someone chooses not to take steps to protect a system from intruders, are they, partially at least, to blame when an intruder breaks in?

Analogical thinking is illuminating here. Isn't breaking into a computer system comparable to breaking into someone's home? In both cases, we can imagine people who break in and steal as well as people who break in and simply look around. Suppose a house owner leaves his or her doors unlocked, and an intruder discovers an unlocked door (be it a thief who has been watching the house for days or a teenager testing doors to see what he or she can find). Either way, suppose the attacker finds the door unlocked. Is the homeowner, therefore, partially at fault because he or she left the door unlocked?

We can follow the analogy further. Note that it seems reasonable that homeowners don't want intruders, whether they steal or not. The intrusion may be experienced as a violation of something even more basic than privacy—perhaps closer to bodily integrity. In any case, the analogy allows us to think about protection strategies. What should individuals be expected to do to protect themselves, and what are their best options for achieving security? No doubt, most people would prefer to live in areas with low crime rates, and reasonably prefer preventive strategies such as laws prohibiting break-ins and law enforcement efforts to prevent criminals from roaming in the neighborhood. When these strategies fail, homeowners resort to other methods. They put locks on their doors, and develop the habit of checking the locks each time they leave. They may invest in security cameras and alarm systems; they may even organize neighborhood watch committees or move to a gated community. Some people hire private guards or insist on more police patrols in their neighborhood. There are parallels for each of these strategies in computer security.

What does this tell us about the question of fault? It is not unreasonable for individuals to prefer to live in an environment in which they don't have to worry about their security, and a variety of strategies can be adopted to protect security at a level other than individual computers. On the other hand, it is smart for individuals to protect their own systems. In certain environments, we might even say that it is "foolish" not to protect your system (because lack of security increases the probability of intrusion). Nevertheless, it seems wrong to blame those who don't install security. Why? Because we don't know the details of their circumstances. Very few people have unlimited resources. Installing security mechanisms (on houses or computer systems) involves investments of time, money, and effort. They involve choices, and we have no way of knowing whether individuals are or aren't deploying their time, money, and effort rationally when they opt not to invest in security. To be sure, if someone had sufficient time, money, and energy to invest in security and didn't, then when their system is attacked, we would reasonably say that they had been foolish. But it is hard to say that they contributed to the wrongdoing.

However, there is yet again a complication. (These kinds of complications are a theme in this book as we try to understand the nuances of IT-configured societies.) If a computer A is part of a larger system of computers X, then not securing A also puts all the computers and users of X at risk. Thus, an individual's behavior has potential consequences for a much larger group of people than just A's owner. An example of this aspect is when a hacker hijacks an unprotected computer and uses it as a "drone" to attack other computers. Clearly the hacker is being unethical; but is an owner who facilitated the hijacking also culpable? Depending on the owner's circumstances, perhaps yes and perhaps no. But in the IT-configured societies of today, it seems difficult to defend the idea that a user with means has *no* responsibility for trying to secure a computer on the Internet, if only because of the illicit uses for which the machine might be used if turned into a drone. We expect people who own guns to have trigger locks on the guns; perhaps we are now at the point that we should expect people who have computers on the Internet to use strong passwords.

Trade-Offs in Security

Returning now to the idea that security is a matter of protecting and achieving an order that has been decided upon through law and other decision-making processes, the most controversial ethical issue in security has to do with trade-offs. How far should security and law enforcement go to ensure order? Can any means be used to achieve the goal of security? The issue in the previous section focused on a micro issue: What should individuals be morally required to do with respect to security? In this section, we will explore a macro issue: What should we as a society allow our governments to do with respect to security?

A salient example of the trade-offs involved in security is the controversy around the USA Patriot Act. After the September 11, 2001 attacks at the World Trade Center and the Pentagon in the United States, there was widespread fear of further terrorist attacks. In this atmosphere, the Patriot Act was quickly passed, granting the U.S. Federal Government broader powers for, among other things, electronic surveillance. In 2007, the Justice Department found that the FBI had "improperly and in some cases illegally used the USA Patriot Act to secretly obtain personal information" about U.S. citizens. [http://www.guardian.co.uk/world/2007/mar/09/usa. FBI abused Patriot Act powers, audit finds (March 9, 2007), accessed May 31, 2008]. The number of times the powers were invoked is striking; in a three-year period, the FBI used more than 143,000 national security letters to obtain data from businesses about customer purchases. The Act is written in such a way that nonterrorist-related activities can now be investigated without the same judicial oversight that was required prior to the Act; for example, §217 allows government surveillance of "computer trespassers without a judicial order, without notice to the person being monitored, and without reporting to a judge after the fact." [http://www.cdt.org/security/usapatriot/031027cdt.shtml. Setting the record straight (October 27, 2003) accessed May 31, 2008.]

We can see here that the value of security comes into conflict with the value of privacy. The challenge and importance of finding a good balance cannot be overstated. Critics of the Patriot Act are convinced that several provisions of this law go much too far in favoring security to the detriment of privacy. The United States has a long tradition of safeguards protecting its citizens against government intrusions; these safeguards are consistent with America's history and identity. The government reports of its own activities seem to confirm that excesses even beyond what the Patriot Act authorizes have become commonplace.

Thus, achieving adequate security involves balancing the good at which it aims against other social values and individual rights. Security shouldn't trump any and every other value. On the other hand, security is critical to the smooth and reliable functioning of information societies. Remember that computer security is an instrumental value. Although no simple or absolute rule can be provided to achieve the optimal balance between security and other values, any serious ethical analysis of security must include consideration of the values at which it aims (i.e., what it seeks to secure) and other values (especially privacy). When these values are articulated and taken into account, better trade-offs can be made.

WIKIPEDIA: A NEW ORDER OF KNOWLEDGE PRODUCTION

In our discussion of security, we emphasized that security is aimed at reliable computing and that information societies are critically dependent on reliable computing. Reliability is also a value when it comes to knowledge production in information societies. Wikipedia is an example of a new form of knowledge production. Wikipedia "orders" the production of knowledge by taking advantage of IT features that facilitate collaboration and consensus. Scenario 6.2 provides an unusual perspective on these processes because it involves the production of highly politicized knowledge.

As explained in the background for Scenario 6.2, Wikipedia is a free encyclopedia available to anyone who has access to the Internet. According to the site, 684 million people now use it each year. Wikipedia articles are produced by a process in which a user submits an article and others edit and supplement the piece. If the article is popular or contentious, it may be edited and changed frequently; other entries may be more stable. The procedures that users must follow are facilitated through the architecture of the system. The architecture includes a discussion or talk page through which contributors can discuss disagreements about editing. This explains why Wikipedia is sometimes characterized as a system of knowledge by "consensus." In the talk pages, contributors discuss their views on why a sentence is incorrect or explain why they think information is accurate/inaccurate; such discussions may go on for a long time before consensus is reached.

Wikipedia is not without problems and critics, and its own article on itself (i.e., Wikipedia's article on "Wikipedia") identifies these criticisms. The article mentions accusations of bias, inconsistencies, policies that "favor consensus over credentials," and worries that the site is susceptible to vandalism and may contain "spurious or unverified information." In its defense, Wikipedia responds to the claim of unreliability in a number of ways, suggesting that Wikipedia may be no more unreliable than paper-based encyclopedias.

At the core of controversy about Wikipedia is a deep question about the nature of knowledge and truth. The characterization of Wikipedia as knowledge production by means of "consensus" as opposed to "credentials" captures this tension. The word "credentials" refers to the traditional way that knowledge is produced, that is, before the Internet. In traditional knowledge production, published information is filtered by means of a system that involves the use of established authorities. Although details vary with the type of publication and type of knowledge, credential systems typically involve editors, publishers, and reviewers. For example, in book publishing the common practice is for an author to submit a manuscript to an editor (employed by a press); the editor then decides whether to reject the manuscript outright or send it out for review. Typically, editors select as reviewers individuals who are recognized as authorities on the topic of the book. Editors want reviewers who are able to evaluate the quality of the manuscript and to identify errors and falsehoods. Even when it comes to a topic that doesn't involve truth or falsehood, as in the case, say, of a novel, editors want reviewers who have the experience to tell good writing from bad or to tell what is likely to sell. In short, editors turn to and rely upon individuals with "credentials."

Although not beyond criticism, the credential system has a strategy for achieving reliability. Publishers have an incentive to make sure that the books they publish are accurate. They can be sued if a published work is slanderous or if readers relied on information that turned out to be false or misleading. Even if they aren't sued, the reputation of a publisher can be severely damaged by the publication of unreliable information. They turn to authorities in the field to protect their companies.

Wikipedia stands in sharp contrast to the traditional, credential system. It also has a strategy for achieving reliability, a strategy that also involves filtering. Wikipedia, as described above, draws on the knowledge base of all Internet users—not just those with credentials. Wikipedia allows all users to contribute to the encyclopedia; only registered users may submit new articles but all users, registered or not, can edit existing articles. As we saw in Scenario 6.2, the changes that a user makes to an article may remain or be altered in an ongoing iterative and collaborative process.

So Wikipedia provides an alternative filtering system, an alternative ordering aimed at reliability. Critics argue that it is not a good means for achieving reliable knowledge. Wikipedia argues that the "proof is in the pudding." We will not take a position on this debate for several reasons. First, to assert that Wikipedia is good or bad seems to oversimplify; it may well be good for some kinds of knowledge and not others. More important, Wikipedia is still in the early stages of its development and may change as IT changes. Unless the encyclopedia is demonstrably harmful, why not have multiple systems for knowledge production? To be sure, when Wikipedia users understand how Wikipedia produces knowledge, they are in a better position to determine when to rely on the site and when not. However, the same can be said for knowledge filtered through the credential system. Users are better off when they understand the systems by which information has been filtered and produced.

Wikipedia involves knowledge production by "the many" rather than "the few," so some may leap to the conclusion that it is a democratic form of knowledge production. We saw in Chapter 3 that claims of this kind are much too simplistic. Although we will not examine this issue of "the wisdom of the crowd" extensively, we do want to return to our earlier discussion of democracy. Remember that Wikipedia and traditional forms of knowledge production involve filtering. What, we must now ask, is the difference between filtering and censorship? Clearly, we need filtering to achieve reliable knowledge, but censorship is generally considered a threat to democracy. To get a handle on this, we turn now to freedom of expression.

FREEDOM OF EXPRESSION AND CENSORSHIP

Freedom of expression is one of the central issues of order on the Internet. In Chapter 3 we mentioned that freedom of expression is emblematic of democracy, that is, nation states that do not provide their citizens with a relatively high degree of freedom of expression are not considered democracies. Democratic nations and international organizations often have formal specifications (laws or documents) guaranteeing this right to citizens. In the United States, for example, the First Amendment specifies that:

> Congress shall make no law respecting an establishment of religion, or prohibiting the free exercise thereof; or abridging the freedom of speech, or of the press; or the right of the people peaceably to assemble, and to petition the Government for a redress of grievances.

The Universal Declaration of Human Rights (UDHR) adopted by the United Nations specifies in article 19 that:

> Everyone has the right to freedom of opinion and expression; this right includes freedom to hold opinions without interference and to seek, receive and impart information and ideas through any media and regardless of frontiers.

Formal specifications or not, freedom of expression is a complicated matter, and the Internet has made it even more complicated. Scenario 6.3 illustrates this challenge, although free speech advocates might identify two different issues in this scenario. The first is France's decision to ban the sale of Nazi memorabilia, because this, in itself, is a decision that suppresses speech; it suppresses the expression of ideas about Nazism. The possibility that French law might lead to censorship on the Internet, suppressing speech in the United States and depriving users across the globe from access to ideas, is another issue.

Freedom of expression is an important value and a lofty ideal, and it is important to understand why. Although many defend this freedom simply as a fundamental right, there are powerful reasons for recognizing such a right. We turn to John Stuart Mill, one of the founders of utilitarianism, for one of the best accounts of the importance of freedom of expression ever written.

John Stuart Mill and Freedom of Expression

In his essay "On Liberty," John Stuart Mill provides powerful arguments for freedom of expression. He summarizes the arguments simply and eloquently in the following passages:

> . . . the peculiar evil of silencing the expression of an opinion is, that it is robbing the human race; posterity as well as the existing generation; those who dissent from the opinion, still more than those who hold it. If the opinion is right, they are deprived of the opportunity of exchanging error for truth: if wrong, they lose, what is almost as great a benefit, the clearer perception and livelier impression of truth, produced by its collision with error. . . .
>
> We have now recognized the necessity to the mental well-being of mankind (on which all their other well-being depends) of freedom of opinion, and freedom of the expression of opinion, on four distinct grounds; which we will now briefly recapitulate.
>
> First, if any opinion is compelled to silence, that opinion may, for aught we can certainly know, be true. To deny this is to assume our own infallibility.
>
> Secondly, though the silenced opinion be an error, it may, and very commonly does, contain a portion of truth; and since the general or prevailing opinion on any subject is rarely or never the whole truth, it is only

by the collision of adverse opinions that the remainder of the truth has any chance of being supplied.

Thirdly, even if the received opinion be not only true, but the whole truth; unless it is suffered to be, and actually is, vigorously and earnestly contested, it will, by most of those who receive it, be held in the manner of a prejudice, with little comprehension or feeling of its rational grounds.

And not only this, but fourthly, the meaning of the doctrine itself will be in danger of being lost, or enfeebled, and deprived of its vital effect on the character and conduct: the dogma becoming a mere formal profession, inefficacious for good, but encumbering the ground, and preventing the growth of any real and heartfelt conviction, from reason or personal experience.

[John Stuart Mill, *On Liberty*, Chapter II]

Although 150 years old, Mill's arguments have surprisingly strong relevance to issues of free speech on the Internet. In his day, it required courage to allow the rancorous debate introduced by free speech; in our day, it requires courage to allow free electronic speech on the Internet. The Internet is potentially an enormous forum for the "contest of ideas." But the same openness that facilitates a robust exchange of ideas also brings people with varying sensibilities, values, and interests closer together, and that can mean conflict, misunderstanding, offense, and bad feelings. As a forum for the exchange of ideas, the Internet is a place where ideas are vigorously debated, a place of conflict, disagreement, and competition. It can also be a forum for hate speech, defamation, and pornography.

Offline and on, the reality is that although the value of free speech is recognized and protected, it is rarely recognized as an absolute value. Restrictions are placed on speech when other important values are at stake. In the United States, for example, a complicated patchwork of exceptions to free speech includes cases of obscenity, fighting words, commercial speech, and libel/slander. Although it is difficult to make generalizations, two principles seem to come into play when it comes to such restrictions. The first, and perhaps strongest, is the harm principle. In general, individual freedom is understood to extend only as far as another's harm. Free speech is, then, restricted when it threatens to cause harm. Of course, the harm has to be provable but the harm that comes from defamation and from exposing children to pornography have, indeed, been taken seriously by courts of law.

The second principle that comes into play in debates about free speech is the offense principle. The question is, can speech be suppressed because it is offensive to others? If this principle is used lightly, it would, of course, bring an end to free speech because individuals are offended by all sorts of things and some people are easily offended. Nevertheless, the courts have recognized some kinds of offense as justifying restrictions on free speech as in the case of "fighting words." More often, however, what is at issue is the line between harm and offense. For example, hate speech is restricted because it is considered harmful, not just offensive.

Although we will not be able to completely explore these challenges to freedom of expression here, a real case may be helpful to illustrate the deep sensibilities that can be disturbed in online free speech. Consider the following delicate case. A 2004 CNN article (http://edition.cnn.com/2004/LAW/01/13/killers.online.ap/index.html) told the story of convicted murderers whose writing and drawings about their crimes were placed on the Internet to the distress of the victims' families. At least one convict is described as "taunting" the parents of a victim, describing in lurid detail how he killed their daughter. The parents requested that the prisoner's mail be more strictly screened, and prison officials complied with the request. However, the convicts were not posting the material directly themselves; the materials were mailed or smuggled out of prison to friends on the outside, and the friends posted them. ISPs removed some of these materials, but the materials keep reappearing on the Web at different sites. Experts quoted in the article contend that the First Amendment of the U.S. Constitution protects this kind of electronic information. Whether these materials fall under the First Amendment or not, the case illustrates how speech can touch deeply felt human sensibilities. The murderers, and the people who assist them in posting the materials, cause a good deal of pain to the families of their victims.

The easy accessibility of pornography to children on the Internet is one of the most challenging of free speech issues online. Indeed, it was this issue that first drew public attention in the United States to the potential for censorship of the Internet. In 1996, the U.S. Senate passed what was referred to as the Communications Decency Act (CDA). The CDA would have made it a crime to use telecommunications devices and interactive computer services to disseminate "indecent or patently offensive sexually explicit material" to children less than 18 years of age. The U.S. Supreme Court ruled that the Act was unconstitutional, but its initial passage by the Senate demonstrated that legislation *could* significantly dampen free speech on the Internet.

Because the CDA targeted the protection of children, the issue is far from simple. Those who want to regulate pornography on the Internet emphasize how harmful and disturbing pornography can be to children. Generally, those who oppose censorship don't disagree about this. Rather, they are concerned about what is often referred to as a "slippery slope." If we grant to the government the power to censor in this case, we will take the first step down a slope that will end in much more dangerous forms of censorship. Once we allow one form of censorship, a precedent will be established and future attempts will build on the precedent.

As we have already suggested, steps down the slope have already been taken so the daunting question is how to draw the line and ensure that freedom of expression is not entirely eroded. Although we can't decide that matter here, it returns us to the value of the sociotechnical systems perspective and brings us full circle back to Lessig and the four forms of regulation. The discussion of free speech has largely been focused on law. However, in the absence of legal prohibitions, efforts have been made to address this issue by means of technical devices that will allow parents to restrict their children's access. The Yahoo case also points to technical fixes because part of the reason Yahoo lost its case was that a new technology had been created that would allow the website to identify the location of visitors. Although technical strategies may succeed in addressing the challenge of protecting children from online pornography, the important point is that the challenge of protecting values such as free speech online are recognized as sociotechnical. Recognizing these challenges as sociotechnical will lead to more creative and multipronged solutions.

Of course, there is also bad news in this because acknowledging that free speech is sociotechnical also means acknowledging that it can be addressed through private mechanisms that bypass public discussion and decision. Although emphasizing the mistake of thinking that the Internet is a place of free expression, one legal scholar explains the problem:

> With the government's withdrawal from management of the Internet, private entities assumed control. The end result is that the vast majority of speech on the Internet today occurs within private places and spaces that are owned and regulated by private entities such as Internet service providers (ISPs) like America Online (AOL) and Yahoo!, Internet access providers like employers and universities, content providers like washingtonpost.com and nytimes.com, and pipe line providers like Comcast and Verizon.
>
> [Nunziato, 2005]

Because online free speech is critically important, it would seem a mistake to leave it entirely to private institutions.

Adding to the complexities already mentioned is the global scope of the Internet. Scenario 6.3 illustrates how the sovereignty of national governments can be threatened through an online free speech issue. The case takes us back to the beginning of this chapter. The Internet, we see, is not open, chaotic, and free. It is ordered and there are many extremely important issues about how it is ordered.

Conclusion

We began this chapter with a quotation by John Perry Barlow, a pioneer and visionary of the Internet. The analysis provided in this chapter suggests that the Internet is no longer the free and open place that Barlow described almost twenty years ago. However, the Internet is enormous and remarkably diverse; thus, it is quite possible to find pockets and remnants of unsettled territory. Moreover, the Internet continues to evolve. What it will become in the future is not already determined. In fact, the points of conflict that we have described in this chapter—crime, security, reliable knowledge production, and freedom of expression—are important precisely because how these tensions are managed will make a difference in the Internet's order.

In this chapter we explored a rather diverse set of issues connected only in the sense that they affect what we have called "digital order." We used "order" rather than "law and order" to avoid the trap of thinking that law is the only means by which order is created. Our emphasis on sociotechnical order, that is, on order being achieved through law, markets, social norms, and architecture, persisted in our discussions of crime, security, knowledge production, and freedom of expression.

In Chapter 7, we turn our attention to IT professionals. The chapter can be seen as an extension of our discussion of reliability and trustworthiness because security and reliability cannot be achieved without the work of IT professionals. Of course, the work of IT professionals isn't just technical, and security cannot be achieved unless they, too, engage in social practices that contribute to the security of the systems on which they work.

Study Questions

1. What is the difference between security and reliability? How are they related?
2. If you own a personal computer, how secure is that machine? How did you decide how much security was enough?
3. If you use a computer system that is run by an organization (a university or a corporation), have you ever carefully read the security policies that you are supposed to know as a system user?
4. If your machine is being used as a drone by a hacker to send spam e-mails, are you a victim, a perpetrator, or both?
5. If you make a living by selling security software to individuals who own personal computers, are you happy or sad when hacker activity increases?
6. Have you ever received an e-mail that indicated someone else had sent out spam with your return e-mail address on it? How would you feel about that?
7. Have you ever compromised physical security for convenience? If so, what did you do? If not, have you seen anyone else do this?
8. Why is the issue of children being exposed to pornography online a difficult one to resolve? Is this the only reason, in your opinion, that this issue has received so much publicity?
9. Do you think that the 9/11 terrorist attacks have substantially changed people's attitudes toward the trade-offs between privacy and security? Do you think that the current trade-offs, as embodied in legislation, are appropriate?
10. Go on the Web and find a website that is fully accessible to the general public online (e.g., it cannot be password protected) and contains material that you personally find offensive (for this exercise, the more offensive to you, the "better"). Having viewed this material that you find objectionable, would you favor legislation to ban this kind of material from the Web? If not, why not? If so, how would you envision the law would be enforced?

CHAPTER 7

Professional Ethics in Computing

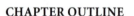

CHAPTER OUTLINE

SCENARIOS

Scenario 7.1 Software Safety

Carl Adonis is an experienced systems designer working for the Acme Software Company. A year ago he was assigned to work on a project that Acme is doing for the U.S. Department of Defense. The project involves designing a system that will monitor radar signals and launch nuclear missiles in response to these signals.

Carl initially had some reluctance about working on a military project, but he put this out of his mind because the project was technically challenging and he knew that if he didn't work on it, someone else would. Now, however, the project is approaching completion and Carl has some grave reservations about the adequacy of the design. He is doubtful about the system's capacity for making fine distinctions (e.g., distinguishing between a small jet aircraft and a missile). It would be catastrophic, Carl reasons, if the system responded to a nonthreat as a threat (a "false positive").

Carl documents his concerns carefully, including an explanation of design weaknesses and specific modules that could be revised to strengthen software safety against false positive target identification. Carl estimates that the detailed design, implementation, and testing of these changes could be done in approximately six months with the existing staff.

Carl takes his documentation and concerns to his immediate supervisor, the project director; but she dismisses these concerns quickly, mentioning that Acme is already behind schedule on the project and has already exceeded the budget that they had agreed to with the Defense Department. She tells Carl to put his ideas for improving safety into a memo entitled "Future Enhancements," and suggests that this will become part of Acme's bid for an anticipated second phase of development which might start as soon as one year from now.

Carl is convinced that it is a grave error to let the system go as it now is. He is especially concerned that Acme might never get to do the improvements he thinks are necessary because another company might win the bid for the second phase.

Carl feels that he has a moral responsibility to do something, but doesn't know what to do. Should he ask for reassignment to another project? Should he go to executives beyond the project director in Acme's hierarchy and tell them of his concerns? It is difficult to imagine how they will respond. Should he talk to someone in the Defense Department? Should he go to newspaper or television news reporters and "blow the whistle?" If he does any of these things, he is likely to jeopardize his job. Should he do nothing?

Scenario 7.2 Security in a Custom Database

Three years ago Leikessa Jones quit her job as a systems designer and started her own software consulting business. The business has been quite successful and currently it has a contract to design a database management system for the personnel office of a medium-size company that manufactures toys. Leikessa has involved the client in the design process informing the CEO, the Director of Information Technology, and the Director of Personnel about the progress of the system and giving them many opportunities to make decisions about features of the system. It is now time to make decisions about the kind and degree of security to build into the system.

Leikessa has described several options to the client. All of Leikessa's options included several security features, all of which she thinks are necessary in a system that includes sensitive personal information. After reviewing these options, the client has decided to order a system that includes only the most basic security precautions because otherwise the system will cost more than the client expected; in other words, in order to keep the cost of the project low, the client has decided that the "extra" security is not a priority.

Leikessa objects, and explains to the client why, in her professional judgment, the information that will be stored in the system is extremely sensitive. It will include performance evaluations, medical records for filing insurance claims, and salaries. With weak security, it may be possible for enterprising employees to figure out how to get access to this data, not to mention the possibilities for online access from hackers. Leikessa feels strongly that the system should be more secure than the "bare bones" system the client wants her to develop.

Leikessa has tried to explain the risks to her client, but the CEO, Director of Information Technology, and Director of Personnel are all willing to accept little security. Should she refuse to build the system as they request?

Scenario 7.3 Conflict of Interest

Juan Rodriguez makes a living as a private consultant. Small businesses hire him to advise them about their computer needs. Typically, a company asks him to come in, examine the company's operations, evaluate their automation needs, and recommend the kind of hardware and software that they should purchase.

Recently, Juan was hired by a small, private hospital. The hospital was interested in upgrading the hardware and software it uses for patient records and accounting. The hospital had already solicited proposals for upgrading their system. They hired Juan to evaluate the proposals they had received. Juan examined the proposals very carefully. He considered which system would best meet the hospital's needs, which company offered the best services in terms of training of staff and future updates, which offered the best price, and so on. He concluded that Tri-Star Systems was the best alternative for the hospital, and recommended this in his report, explaining his reasons for drawing this conclusion.

What Juan failed to mention (at any time in his dealings with the hospital) was that he is a major stockholder in Tri-Star Systems. Juan placed his stock in Tri-Star into a trust when he started his consulting firm a few years ago; however, the rules of the trust are such that although Juan does *not* have control of the stocks, he *does* have a general knowledge of which stocks are in the trust, and knows that a considerable portion of his trust consists of Tri-Star stock. Juan has always believed that because he does not have control over the buying and selling of the stocks in the trust, he is protected from accusations of conflicts-of-interest.

Was Juan's behavior unethical? Should Juan have disclosed the fact that he had ties to one of the companies that made a proposal? Should he have declined the job once he learned that Tri-Star had made a bid? How much difference does the blind trust make in this scenario?

INTRODUCTION: WHY PROFESSIONAL ETHICS?

The operation and use of IT would not be possible were it not for a huge workforce of computing experts—individuals who use their knowledge and skills to design, develop, maintain, use, and train others to use this technology. A key feature of all information societies is their dependence on individuals with expertise in computing. But what are the responsibilities of such experts? What can or should we expect of them? Should IT professionals be held to (or hold themselves to) a higher standard of behavior because their knowledge gives them so much power?

As fictional Scenarios 7.1, 7.2, and 7.3 demonstrate, IT professionals find themselves in a wide variety of situations in which their behavior can affect the well-being of others. But it is not only in fiction that these kinds of cases arise. The issues of professionalism in computing were dramatically demonstrated in 1987 when the infamous "Therac-25" case came to public attention and again in the late 1990s when the Y2K problem began to come to light.

Therac-25 and Malfunction 54

In 1983, a Canadian company, AECL, released to the market the Therac-25, a radiation therapy machine. The Therac-25 was the latest of a series of Therac machines. This newest machine reused software developed for Therac-6 and Therac-20, and reduced costs by transferring several safety features of previous models from hardware to software.

In the summer of 1985, AECL received word that a patient in Halifax, Nova Scotia had received an overdose of radiation from a Therac-25. AECL notified its Therac-25 users to manually check all radiation settings while they investigated. AECL could not reproduce the problem on the Halifax machine, but they suspected a microswitch problem. They made modifications to all the installed Therac-25 machines, and assured users that they could stop manually checking radiation levels.

In the fall of 1985, there was a second case of radiation overdose with a Therac-25, and early in 1986, a third case. By January of 1987, there were six documented cases of overdoses, and in February 1987, all Therac-25 machines were shut down. Three of the people overdosed died.

Several lawsuits were filed over the deaths and injuries, but all were settled out of court. There was considerable interest in the case, and much has been written about the mistakes made in the design, coding, testing, and certification of Therac-25. Subsequent analysis (Leveson and Turner, 1993) revealed that the design and coding allowed a synchronization problem to occur when an operator made a particular sequence of screen editing changes. This sequence of commands resulted in large, high-powered beams of x-rays to be released into patients even though the operator intended a much lower radiation dose. Earlier versions of the Therac-25 included a mechanical interlock that would have prevented the high dose from being released from the machine in similar circumstances. As well, earlier versions did not include the operator-editing feature.

The Therac-25 case generated a great deal of publicity because many people interpreted it as "software killing people." Clearly, software was a factor in the case, but detailed analysis of the case reveals a more complex set of interacting problems including design, testing, government regulation, medical accident reporting, and safety analysis techniques. (Readers interested in studying the case more closely can visit http://www.computingcases.org/case_materials/therac/therac_case_intro.html.)

Despite the complexities of the Therac-25 case, and almost all other real cases of dangerous malfunctions [http://catless.ncl.ac.uk/risks], it seems clear that computer professionals have responsibilities to the people who are affected by their decisions. And, of course, it is not just others who are affected by the decisions of computer experts; the expert's own personal life and future career may be impacted by the choices he or she makes in situations involving the health, safety, or well-being of others. Poor design and bugs in programs can lead to unreliable and dangerous (even lethal) systems. No matter how many others might be involved in the development of a system, computer professionals surely bear a great deal of responsibility for the systems they create.

The Therac case aside, Scenarios 7.1–7.3 illustrate how the work of IT professionals is enmeshed in social relationships—relationships with clients, employers, employees of clients, and with others who are affected by the computer systems the professional has helped to create. Managing these relationships is an important dimension of the work of computer experts, and it is a dimension that computer professionals ignore at their peril. As the scenarios illustrate, managing these relationships often involves interacting with others who have a severely limited understanding of IT systems and how they work. These relationships often depend on, and affect, the professional's reputation and the trustworthiness of the systems they work on, as well as the reputation of IT professionals and IT in general.

The framework of sociotechnical systems that has been suggested throughout this book goes hand in hand with acknowledging that the work of computer professionals involves social relationships (with clients, employers, and others) and has consequences for people. IT systems are created and function in a social context, and the work of computer professionals can be fully understood only when it is framed in a sociotechnical context.

In this chapter we explore a set of issues that have to do with the nature of computer expertise and the role of computer professionals. We start by sorting out the circumstances of computer experts and examining the foundation of professional ethics. What does it mean to say that an occupation is a "profession"? What is the difference between thinking of an individual as an employee, and thinking of that same person as a professional?

You might think of each of the individuals depicted in the scenarios above as persons who are simply seeking their personal interests and bound by ordinary morality and the laws of their society. Or, you might think of them simply as employees who are expected to do what their employers tell them; they pursue their personal interests but at work that means doing what their bosses tell them. Alternatively, you might think of these individuals, as we have suggested above, as somehow "special" in the sense that they are experts and because of that special expertise, they have special powers and responsibilities. In order to sort this out, it will be helpful to begin with a discussion of the distinction between professions and other occupations and, in parallel, the distinction between being a "mere" employee and being a professional.

THE PARADIGM OF PROFESSIONS

Professions have been studied by sociologists and historians, and there are different theories about why and how certain occupational groups organize themselves, acquire special powers and privileges, and maintain a special kind of authority. Although there are a range of accounts, the most useful for our purposes is to conceptualize the organization of occupations into professions as a social mechanism for managing expertise and deploying it in ways that benefit society. To better understand professions, we have to consider not just the individual members who organize themselves; we have to consider the societies in which professions operate. Societies choose to recognize certain occupational groups as professions because they believe the organization of the group will serve social purposes and achieve social good. Perhaps the best way to conceptualize this arrangement is to think of the occupational group as making a pact with society, a pact that involves promises and commitments in exchange for special powers and protections. The group makes a commitment to practice in ways that are good for (or at least not harmful to) the society. In exchange, the society grants powers and privileges to the group. Often what is granted is: the right to self-regulate, to act as a monopoly with regard to particular kinds of services, access to educational institutions, and the right to do things that nonmembers cannot do such as prescribe drugs (doctors) or use force (police).

This way of thinking about professions is not meant to provide a precise or comprehensive account of how particular professions emerged historically; rather, it is an analytical approach, an admittedly idealized framework for thinking about, and justifying, appropriate norms of behavior. The social contract that professions negotiate with society—even though idealized—is far from simple or straightforward. Indeed, the social contract often evolves over time and may be renegotiated periodically.

In everyday language, the terms "profession" and "professional" are used casually; sometimes "profession" refers to occupational groups that for one reason or another have acquired higher social status and higher salaries. You may, for example, think of corporate executives as professionals. Other times the term is used to refer to a special class of occupations that are highly organized and have a monopoly of control over some domain of activity; for example, only doctors can prescribe drugs or perform surgery. The phrase "strongly differentiated" has been coined to refer to professions that have special privileges of this kind. Lawyers, for example, are allowed to keep whatever their clients tell them confidential; police officers can use force of a kind for which ordinary citizens would be arrested. These are all cases of strongly differentiated professions.

CHARACTERISTICS OF PROFESSIONS

Professions are typically associated with a set of distinct characteristics and are thought to have a special type of relationship with the societies of which they are part. The following are the key characteristics of professions, and they help us understand how professions have a social contract with society.

1. Mastery of an Esoteric Body of Knowledge Professions are occupations in which mastery of an esoteric body of knowledge is essential. Typically, the body of knowledge is abstract and has been systematized such that it can be mastered only through disciplined study—typically higher education. In other words, an individual is unlikely to acquire this body of knowledge simply through practice or hands-on experience. The abstract, systematized body of knowledge is the foundation for practice of the profession. Because the body of knowledge is so important to a profession, a related characteristic of professions is that they often have both researchers and practitioners. The researchers devote themselves to continuous improvement in the esoteric body of knowledge and the practitioners use the knowledge. Examples of this division can be seen in medicine where there are medical research doctors and clinicians, and in engineering where academic engineers develop careers around research whereas practitioners build things.

2. Autonomy Members of strongly differentiated professions typically have a good deal of autonomy in their daily work, as compared to employees who take orders and are closely supervised. Doctors make decisions about treatment for their patients, lawyers decide the best strategy for defending a client, architects decide on the design of a building. This autonomy is justified in part on grounds that the work of the professionals depends on the esoteric body of knowledge. They have to use that knowledge, and being supervised by someone who doesn't have the knowledge counteracts the point of having someone with expertise perform the activity.

As well, professions typically have autonomy collectively, that is, as professional groups. The group—through it's professional organization—is allowed to make decisions about the profession's organization and practice. Typically, professions regulate themselves by setting their own admission standards, educational requirements, and standards of practice. Professions then bar people from entering the profession unless they meet admission standards, and expell professionals whose practice falls substantially below the specified professional standards. This "self-policing" is related to the esoteric knowledge; that is, outsiders should not be regulating the group because outsiders cannot understand what is involved in using the esoteric body of knowledge, for example, curing a disease or providing a skillful defense for a client.

3. Formal Organization Professions generally have a single unifying, formal organization recognized by regional and/or national governments. The profession exercises its collective autonomy through this organization. The organization will typically control admission to the profession, set standards for practice, specify accreditation standards for educational degrees, and in some cases have a say in the criteria for licensing of its members. The formal organization may also have the power to expel individual members from the profession. In the United States, the American Medical Association and the American Bar Association, along with their state organizations, are examples of this type of organization. The Indian Medical Association and the Japanese Federation of Bar Associations are two other prominent examples.

4. Code of Ethics Most of the occupations that are recognized as strongly differentiated professions have a code of ethics (or a code of professional conduct). Although there are many reasons for having a code of ethics, an important factor is that the code makes a public statement committing the profession to standards of behavior that benefit the public. Codes of ethics will be discussed more fully later in this chapter. In brief, a code of ethics sets standards in the field; tells clients, employers, and the public what to expect; and contributes to the creation of a professional culture. In setting expectations, a code of ethics can be understood as a partial specification of the social contract. It is a formal way of stating that the profession is committed to achieving or protecting certain social goods or values. For example, in the case of engineering, the codes of ethics generally make a commitment to protect public safety, and in the case of medicine, the code specifies a commitment to protect human life. Codes of ethics alone may not be powerful, especially because they are often difficult to enforce, but they are an important feature of professions.

5. A Culture of Practice For most of the occupations recognized as professions, a distinctive culture is associated with the practices in that field. The culture arises from the conditions in which individuals work and from the values and purposes the profession recognizes as its reason for being. For example, in the case of medicine the good at which the profession aims is health, and this requires and justifies a number of practices. In the case of auditors, unbiased judgment is critical, and therefore certain practices of keeping a distance from clients become part of the culture. In this way, the culture associated with a profession supports its role in society. The culture of medicine, for example, is one of valuing science but also being compassionate to patients; the culture of engineering emphasizes efficiency and objectivity.

The culture of a profession sometimes comes under attack. This may be because the culture undermines the values that the public hopes the profession will emulate, for example, police over use of force or doctors representing the interests of their HMO employers rather than those of the patient. The satirical view of doctors as arrogant and aloof, lawyers as scheming and dishonest, and engineers as socially inept and myopic are examples of ways in which society recognizes the cultures of professions and exaggerates perceived weaknesses. These "insults" to the professions serve as warnings and social criticisms, but they are also an implicit acknowledgment of the importance of the professions.

These five characteristics make up the paradigm of professions. The paradigm is intertwined with the idea of professions having a social contract with society, a contract that constitutes a system of trust. The occupational group organizes itself and convinces the public that there is *special knowledge* in its domain of activity and only those who have that knowledge should engage in the activity. The group promises (explicitly or implicitly) that it can control membership in such a way that members of the profession will be qualified to engage in the activity. The group makes clear that the culture of practice supports important social goods. In other words, the professional group shows that it can regulate itself in ways that will serve the public good. In order to convince the public to trust the group, the group adopts a *code of ethics* committing itself to certain standards of conduct. If the group succeeds, the public (usually through government regulations) recognizes the *formal organization* of the occupational group, gives it a monopoly of control in its domain, and prohibits nonmembers from engaging in the activity. The monopoly of control gives the group *collective autonomy* and this in turn justifies *individual autonomy* for members who practice the profession.

The paradigm aligns nicely with traditional professions such as medicine, law, and the clergy. However, it would be a mistake to think that all professions unequivocally exhibit each and every characteristic. It would be a mistake, that is, to think that every occupation can easily be classified as a strongly differentiated profession or not. The paradigm is better thought of as an ideal type against which occupations can be compared so as to analyze their features and better understand how they work. Occupations tend to fall somewhere on a continuum, with particular occupations having some or all of the characteristics in various degrees. As we will see in a moment, the field of computing is relatively new, quite complex, and still evolving, and the set of characteristics just described will help us to get a handle on its complexity.

Because we will be using the paradigm of professions and the notion of a social contract, it is important to note that a social contract does not exist forever. The contract may be broken or it may be renegotiated (implicitly or explicitly). Implicit in the idea of contract is the threat that if the profession fails to live up to its part of the bargain (e.g., failing to do a good job of setting standards or controlling admission), then the society will take away the profession's monopoly of control or begin to regulate the domain of activity. On the other hand, a professional group can go to the state and complain that it is not being given the support it has been promised. For example, doctors would justifiably complain if courts began to demand that doctors reveal confidential information about their patients.

SORTING OUT COMPUTING AND ITS STATUS AS A PROFESSION

We can now use the paradigm of professions to examine the field of computing. The point is not to decide whether or not computing is a profession and computer experts professionals, but rather to identify the characteristics of computing as an occupational field and to understand what sort of social contract members of the profession have with society today. This should help us to reflect, as well, on how the field might develop in the future. After this descriptive analysis, we will go further and discuss directions that we think computing *should* take, and how computer professionals can be part of that movement. In what follows, then, we will ask: What is the state of organization and practice in the field of computing? What sort of responsibilities come with (or should come with) being a computer expert? In the future, how are those responsibilities likely to change? How *should* they change?

Delineating the field of computing in relation to the paradigm of professions is challenging because computer experts occupy so many different roles. For example, computer professionals act as programmers, system designers, database managers, software engineers, computer security specialists, researchers, system managers, documentation specialists, and network administrators. Moreover, they hold these positions in a wide variety of contexts: in small and large software and/or hardware companies; in local, state, and federal government and other nonprofit organizations; and in their own private consulting firms. Even when we consider the educational backgrounds of those who work as computing specialists, we find a considerable range of degrees from two-year, four-year, and graduate programs, as well as some successful specialists who have no formal training in computing. At the undergraduate level alone there are degrees in computer engineering, computer science, information sciences, management information systems, library science, Web design, and so on. Moreover, because of the huge demand for computing expertise, many people working in the field do not have college degrees at all and many others have college degrees in fields other than computing. The field of computing—if we can consider it a single field—is relatively new with standards and expectations still being developed.

One of the more professionalized subfields of computing is software engineering. Software engineering will be discussed later in the chapter but for now we will keep our focus on this larger, quite diverse group of individuals who have expertise in computing and are employed in a variety of roles in which they use that expertise. To examine whether or not these individuals can be considered a strongly differentiated group of professionals, we can revisit the five characteristics delineated above.

Mastery of Knowledge

Although the jobs of computer professionals vary a good deal, it would seem that most who work in the field master a fairly abstract and esoteric body of knowledge. This is precisely what differentiates computer experts from users or those who are merely skilled at a particular kind of task or understand only one software system. Nevertheless, some might argue that the knowledge computer experts draw on is not a single (abstract, systematized) body of knowledge; what one needs to know to do a particular job in computing varies a good deal with the job. Thus, an important question is: Is there a core "body of knowledge" that unifies all computer professionals? Computer experts use skill and know-how that they develop from figuring out how to do things with computers. Is this more like a craft than a science? The question is interesting and, of course, there is also the point that this combination of applying principles and using know-how is similar to what engineers do. Hence, it suggests that computer experts may be closer to engineers than scientists, that computing should be classified as a branch of engineering. But, again, it depends on the specific job that the individual is engaged in, and computing encompasses a wide variety of only slightly related kinds of jobs.

Although a college degree is not required for *all* computing jobs, a degree is required for many, and for the requisite degrees, there are now some widely (if not universally) accepted guidelines for these curriculums. For example, the ACM (Association for Computing Machinery) and IEEE (Institute for Electronics and Electrical Engineering) either separately or cooperatively publish curricular guidelines for (among others) four-year degrees in computer science, information systems, software engineering, and computer engineering; and for two-year degrees in information processing, computing technology, and computer support services. The trend toward curricular standardization is a sign that computing is maturing and moving toward a more differentiated status.

One visible sign of this maturing of academic computing disciplines in the United States can be seen in the history of the Computing Sciences Accreditation Board (CSAB), now the single organization in the United States that accredits programs in computer science, information systems, and software engineering. In 1985, CSAB began as a joint project of the ACM and the IEEE Computer Society and was focused on computer science programs only. By 2000, CSAB joined the Accreditation Board for Engineering and Technology (ABET), a larger, older organization that accredits engineering programs in the United States.

In addition to degree requirements, certification is another means by which computer experts acquire "credentials" in an aspect of computing. Many certifications are awarded by corporations, and declare that a person has attained a degree of expertise in a particular application or set of applications. This kind of credential tends to be narrower than two-year, four-year, and graduate degrees. Because certification is often closely tied to a particular company's products, it tends not to contribute to the professionalization of computing.

Another indication of a distinctive body of knowledge underpinning computing is the division in computing between researchers and practitioners. Academic computer scientists at research institutions develop and improve upon the body of knowledge that their students and others will use in practice, in their roles as computer professionals. And, it's not just academic computer scientists doing this work; research laboratories in IT industries develop new approaches to computing.

Formal Organization

No single professional organization encompassing all computing experts exists in the United States or internationally. In no country do all computer experts belong to the same organization, and no single organization controls admission to the field. Instead, there are a variety of professional associations such as the Association of Information Technology Professionals, the Association of Independent Information Professionals, Healthcare Information and Management Systems Society, System Administrator's Guild, and more. The ACM and IEEE-CS (Institute for Electronics and Electrical Engineering Computer Society) are two of the largest and perhaps most influential of these organizations in the United States. Both organizations have— since their origination in the United States—expanded their membership to include those outside the United States.

Although there are no universally accepted formal processes for admission to the field of computing, those who enter the job market with an accredited degree in computer science or computer engineering, or a particular certification, may have an advantage for certain positions. Nevertheless, employers are not required to hire individuals with particular credentials in computer science (as they would in the case of certain medical or auditing positions). Because approval by a professional organization is not commonly required to be employed, professional organizations in computing have only a limited amount of influence over their members. Several organizations include procedures for disciplining members up to expulsion, but these sanctions are rarely invoked.

Autonomy

The picture continues to be complex when it comes to autonomy. Remember that in strongly differentiated professions, members are allowed to do what others cannot; for example, doctors can prescribe drugs and police officers can use force. Computer experts are not legally permitted to do anything that others cannot do, nor are they required to do anything more. A specific position (falling under a specific contract) may require that employees have a particular credential or degree, but there are no general regulations with regard to who can do what in computing. Companies or government agencies can hire whomever they choose to fill jobs involving computing.

While performing work, computer experts have varying degrees of autonomy depending on where they work and what positions they have in an organizational hierarchy. Those who work in private practice, by owning their own companies or consulting firms, have greater autonomy than those who are employed and take orders from supervisors. Similarly, those who have worked their way up the organizational ladder in a corporate or government agency and are now in a supervisory role have greater autonomy than those who are newly hired and lower in the organizational hierarchy. Even in these cases, however, the expert has greater autonomy not by virtue of being a computer professional, but because of the position he or she occupies in the organization.

Something similar must be said about computer experts collectively. Although they have organized themselves into various professional associations, the associations have limited power. They have the power to organize, arrange meetings, promulgate codes of conduct, and speak out, but these are all privileges—the right to association—that any group of individuals has in a democratic society. The control that

ABET has over the accreditation process is, perhaps, the most collective power that any of these organizations have in the United States.

Although their formal organizations do not include the kind of autonomy usually associated with strongly differentiated professions, computer experts have a different kind of autonomy that should be mentioned. Because of their expertise, computer experts have direct and often nearly invisible control over the inner working of computers, networks, telecommunications, and many other systems that rely on computers. In many situations, this "power of code" allows a computer expert to make decisions that are relatively free from outside review. In the limited sense of control over computer code, computer experts do have an important form of autonomy, and this is especially so because they often exercise this power on behalf of others who don't understand and cannot read code. We will return to this form of autonomy later because it correlates to responsibility.

Codes of Ethics

Although there is no single code of ethics binding on all computer professionals, professional organizations have adopted codes of ethics and professional conduct, and many of the elements of these codes are quite similar. On the one hand, codes of ethics are an essential component of professionalization and they are especially important in understanding the contract that a professional group makes with society. On the other hand, although they are extremely important, codes of ethics alone are not the "be all and end all" of professional ethics. That is, an occupation that aspires to be a profession cannot simply adopt a code of ethics and leave it at that. Codes of ethics are part of a strategy for establishing relationships with various constituents, including the public; for articulating shared values; and for setting social expectations. To be effective, codes of ethics must be part of a larger strategy that addresses all of the characteristics of professions: formal organization, a culture of practice, identifying the body of knowledge, and accrediting educational institutions.

Codes of ethics have multiple functions and address different constituents. Perhaps the most important function of a code of ethics is to articulate the collective wisdom of members of the profession. In other words, a code of ethics is a statement of what members of the group have agreed among themselves to be the most important principles to incorporate in practice. The code embodies the values of the profession and often the aspirations or ideals that all members should seek to achieve.

A code of ethics may also be understood to be a statement of agreed-upon rules or standards. Sometimes they aim at providing guidelines for individuals who might find themselves in a tight spot and need help figuring out what to do. Unfortunately, codes of ethics are often not extremely useful for the latter purpose. The circumstances of individual practitioners are quite varied and yet no one will read the code if it is too long and detailed. Thus, codes are generally written so as to capture in a small number of statements the broad principles that apply to many different situations. As such, they have to be quite general and often too general to provide guidance. In the 1992 ACM Code of Ethics, the taskforce developing the Code recognized the tension between generalities and specifics and between ideals and guidelines and they designed a new code that had two parts. The first part of the Code consists of a set of short statements of what every ACM member will do. The second part consists of guidelines that provide much more detail about the meaning of each short statement. The later ACM/IEEE-CS Software Engineering Code has a similar organization, with a short version that is concise and aspirational, and a long version that is more concrete and detailed.

Yet another function of a code of ethics can be to educate and socialize members. If the code is provided to all of those who enter the field, it tells new members what will be expected of them. It informs them of the standards and ideals of the members. In fields like computing, the educational requirements tend to emphasize technical subject matter to the neglect of professionalism. Often, graduates learn about the profession and its practices in their first jobs. If their first job happens to be in a place in which standards are sloppy and unprofessional, the new professional will come to believe that this is the way all computer professionals behave; if the first job is in a place with a highly professional culture and standards, then the new member will believe that is the norm. The point is that what one learns about the profession is somewhat random. If, on the other hand, all individuals entering the field are exposed to a code of ethics, the code provides some control over the socialization of new members. Thus, although exposure to the code is probably not enough, it is a good thing for all members to know about the principles and standards that have been explicated in the code.

Codes are intended not only for members of the profession. They can also be seen as statements to the public about what to expect. Of course, as statements to the public, codes of ethics may be seen as a public relations tool. When people criticize codes of ethics, they sometimes complain that the code merely restates the obvious, endorsing "mom and apple pie." If the *only* reason that a code is written is to make the profession look good, then it could be criticized as demonstrating bad faith with society. However, there is nothing objectionable about encouraging good relations with the public if the code reflects a genuine effort to define and encourage ethical behavior for members. In addition, no matter what the initial motives were for its creation, if a code contains good principles of practice, principles that protect the public, then its self-serving function should not be problematic.

The process of developing and adopting a code of ethics is complex and often highly politicized. Fulfilling all of the functions mentioned above is probably impossible, so achieving some functions must give way to others depending on where a profession is in its development. Nevertheless, the variety of functions that a code can serve is important to recognize in evaluating codes and thinking about how they might be changed.

Most of the codes of ethics for computer experts are available on the Web. They are, as already suggested, remarkably similar in what they identify as the responsibilities of computer professionals.

The Culture of Computing

It is hard to say whether computing has a distinctive professional culture. The culture of a profession has to do with what it implicitly values and takes to be routine.

Because "computer professional" covers so many different types of jobs, it is difficult to generalize cultural aspects. Some would say that the culture is definitely male because relatively few women are majoring or doing graduate work in computing. And, certain aspects of the culture of hacking seem to carry over to computing when computer experts are stereotyped as individuals who are glued to their computers and love nothing more than finding a solution to an intricate programming problem. This caricature works also with the stereotypes of engineers as males who block out their social environment, preferring technical challenges to social interactions.

However, whether or not these stereotypes accurately depict the culture of computing seems arguable. For one thing, being glued to a computer is no longer a nonsocial activity because computers connected to the Internet are now a common vehicle for intense social interactions. As mentioned earlier, computer experts work in such a wide range of jobs and in such a variety of contexts that generalizations seem doomed to fail. The point of mentioning these stereotypes is only to illustrate the idea that there are cultural ideas associated with computing. Indeed, one form of action that computer professionals could collectively undertake would be to change the culture (and ultimately the stereotypes) in the field. In fact, several professional organizations have been taking action to change the gender balance in computing and these efforts are appropriately understood as changes in "the culture of computing."

This examination of the characteristics of computing as a profession indicates that computing has several of the key characteristics associated with professions. It involves mastery of an esoteric body of knowledge and a code of ethics (more accurately, several codes of ethics). On the other hand, computing is not a strongly differentiated profession. That is, computer professionals have no special powers or privileges to do what others are prohibited from doing and no one is prohibited from doing what computer professionals do. The autonomy of computer professionals (individually and collectively) is also limited in the sense that there is little self-regulation. Computer experts have formal organizations, although not a single overarching organization that controls admission and sets standards for all or even most of the individuals practicing in the field. If we think of the differences between professions and nonprofessions on a continuum, computing seems to be somewhere in the middle. It is, for example, much more of a profession than, say, selling cars, waitressing, or working as a bank clerk. On the other hand, the field is not nearly as professionalized as medicine, law, or accounting.

Of course, this account has delineated the field in broad brushstrokes, and there are clear differences between types of computer professionals. For example, there are strict regulations about how a computing expert should develop safety-critical software for airplanes, but there is practically no regulation or oversight about developing software for a Web page. In the next section we will focus on software engineers, who are one subgroup in computing that has been particularly concerned about its professionalism.

SOFTWARE ENGINEERING

Software engineering is the one field of computing that has gone the farthest in developing into a profession; it seems to be solidifying as a distinct professional track. The motivation for this can be understood in the paradigm of professions in that those involved in the process have been concerned about the quality and safety of the software being produced and sold. In seeking a way of controlling this quality, they have targeted the requirements for a special undergraduate degree and licensing.

Although the development of software engineering into a profession seems to be in its early stages, in the United States, the state of Texas has established the licensing of software engineers (in 1998). No other states have followed the Texas lead, but Texas has developed a set of requirements and an exam that candidates must pass in order to receive a license. In the process of developing the system of licensing, the state of Texas recognized that in addition to a set of requirements and an exam, a code of ethics was needed. The state asked for assistance from the ACM and IEEE, and these two organizations created a joint task force to design a code of ethics and professional conduct specifically for software engineering. Even though the ACM subsequently decided not to support efforts in the licensing of software engineers, the code of ethics for software engineers was approved by both the ACM and the IEEE.

In Canada, there has been significant controversy over the use of the word "engineer" in the phrase "software engineer," including a lawsuit by engineering organizations against a university that had a degree in "software engineering." The lawsuit was halted, but at this writing the controversy continues; some software engineering degrees are now approved by engineering organizations, others are not.

In the United Kingdom, engineering and computing organizations worked together to establish "chartered" computer professionals through the British Computer Society (BCS). The Society is promoting international standards for IT professionals. The BCS system and a similar system in Australia do not include a set of exams, although exams are a central part of licensing and certifications elsewhere in the world. In addition to chartering, the BCS and other organizations are cooperating to standardize the skills needed for many computing jobs, including but not limited to software engineering. An example of this is the Skills Framework for the Information Age (SFIA). France and Germany have initiated similar frameworks, and the European Union is also considering adoption of a common framework.

In Japan, the Information-Technology Promotion Agency (IPA) has given a national Information Technology Engineers Examination since 1970. By 2006, Japan was joined by many Asian countries, including India and China, in mutual recognition of the results of many of these exams, including the exams for the fundamentals of engineering, applications system engineering, and software design and development engineering. As the number of computer professionals in Asia continues to grow relative to the number elsewhere in the world, these exams will continue to grow in significance and are likely to define professionalism in computing.

Although software engineers worldwide are engaged in many activities to move themselves toward a more strongly differentiated position, there is still great controversy about these activities and where they might lead. For example, the ACM and IEEE-CS have strong, public differences about licensing software engineers (the ACM opposes it, the IEEE-CS supports it). Even in software engineering, computing specialists are in the early stages of working out their relationship to society as a strongly differentiated group.

PROFESSIONAL RELATIONSHIPS

As already mentioned, computer experts work in a wide variety of contexts and the work that they do varies a good deal with the context and their particular expertise. Whatever the context, the work of computer experts involves relationships with many others including employers, clients, and co-workers. A major component of professional ethics has to do with managing these relationships.

Employer–Employee

When a person accepts a job in an organization, he or she enters into a relationship with an employer, be it an individual business owner or a corporation. Although many conditions of this relationship are made explicit when the employee is hired—tasks to be performed, salary, hours of work—many other conditions may not be mentioned, either because they are assumed or because they cannot be anticipated. The category of assumed conditions may include aspects of the job that are specified by law; for example, employers are not permitted to require that employees do something illegal. As well, there are laws requiring that employers maintain levels of safety in the workplace. Among the assumed conditions are many that an employee may not discover until some time after he or she has been hired. An employee may be: expected to work overtime or on weekends whenever the supervisor requests it, discouraged from speaking out publicly on issues that affect the company, or not allowed to refuse assignments even when the employee deems the project immoral.

The moral foundation of the employer–employee relationship is generally understood to be contractual; the relationship lends itself to being understood in terms of Kant's categorical imperative. Each party exercises his or her autonomy and agrees to the terms of employment; the employee agrees to provide work and the employer agrees to provide compensation. According to the categorical imperative, each individual should be treated with respect and never used merely as a means; thus, neither should take advantage of the other. Among other things, this means that both parties must be honest. For example, the employer should tell the truth about workplace conditions and the employee should be honest about his or her qualifications for the job. If either lies about these matters, they are manipulating the other (using the other merely as a means) to get what they want.

Workplace hazards are a good example of how an employer might exploit an employee. If an employer says nothing about the dangers involved in a job and simply offers a big salary and good benefits, making the job so attractive that it is hard to turn down, then the employer has not treated the job applicant with respect. The job applicant has not been recognized as an end in him- or herself, someone with interests of his or her own and the capacity to decide what risks are worth taking. On the other hand, if the employer accurately explains the work conditions—say there are toxic substances to which employees are exposed and this means an increased risk of cancer—then employees can choose whether they want to take the risk or not. The employee has not, then, been treated "merely" as a means.

For professional ethics, one of the most difficult areas of the employer–employee relationship has to do with what one rightfully owes an employer in the name of loyalty, or what an employer can rightfully expect or demand of an employee. Although loyalty is generally thought to be a good thing, it has both good and bad dimensions. For example, if I have a job in which I am responsible for hiring a new employee, and I choose one of my close friends (out of loyalty to the friend who needs a job), without considering the qualifications and experience of all the other applicants, then I have not treated the other applicants fairly, and I may not have acted in the best interests of my employer. Here loyalty to a friend seems like a good thing, but it works against fairness to others and loyalty to an employer.

Loyalty is a good thing insofar as it allows us to have special relationships (e.g., friendships, family) but the limits of loyalty are often hard to identify. Take a valuable relationship such as that between parent and child. Being a parent means treating your own children in special ways. If I were obligated to use my time and resources to help all children equally (that is, if "my" children had no special claims to my care and attention), then the idea that I was someone's parent would be without meaning. It is the same with friendship. If I treated my friends exactly as I treated all other persons, it would be hard to understand what it means to have a friend. But, how, then, does one balance friendship and family against loyalty to one's employer?

Both the good and bad implications of loyalty come into play in employer–employee relationships. Companies and organizations could not function—at least not well—unless individuals recognized that they owe something special to their employers. For example, hiring individuals who will do what is expected of them, including efforts to coordinate their activities with others and represent the company in the best light, facilitates organizations in accomplishing their objectives. Thus, some kind of loyalty to one's employer seems necessary and even worthy. On the other hand, employees do not owe their employers a blind and limitless loyalty. Employers cannot expect employees to do any and everything they might wish. For example, companies have been known to pressure their employees, in the name of loyalty, to vote in public elections for candidates who the company believes will further the company's interests. Such pressure threatens an employee's right as a citizen to vote as he or she sees fit. Indeed, it threatens democracy. Companies have also been known to expect their employees, again in the name of loyalty, not to buy any products made by a competitor. This also seems to overstep the bounds of legitimate employer expectations.

Trade secrecy is one area where the line may be especially difficult to draw. As we saw in Chapter 5, employers have a legal right to expect their employees to keep trade secrets, but it is often unclear how far employers should go to enforce this. For example, an employer may try to prevent an employee from taking a job at another company for fear that the employee will, intentionally or unintentionally, reveal their secrets to the new employer. In addition to requiring that employees sign agreements promising not to reveal secrets, companies sometimes require employees to agree not to work in the same industry for a certain period of time after they leave the company. Employees often want to move on to another job and their best opportunities are likely to be, if not in the same industry, at least doing the same kind of work. Typically, employees learn a great deal of what might be called "generic" knowledge while working at a company and it is just this knowledge and experience that makes the employee attractive to another company. So, an employer may try to stop a current employee from moving to another company for fear that this will "help the competition" and they may claim that the employee is being disloyal in moving on. Here the employer's legitimate concerns about a trade secret and competition have to be balanced against the right of an employee to work where he or she wants.

Notice that in Scenario 7.1, loyalty might come into play in Carl's consideration and evaluation of his options. Perhaps he has an obligation (of loyalty) to try internal channels to get his concerns addressed before going directly to the client or the media. Indeed, his employer might argue that he has an obligation never to go outside the company with his concerns.

Client–Professional

The client-professional relationship can also be thought of as a contractual relationship and, in fact, in this relationship there is often a formal (written) contract. Each party promises to provide something the other wants. They must agree on what will be done, how long it will take, how much the client will pay, where the work will be done, and so on. The key to understanding client–professional relationships is the disparity in knowledge between the two parties. The client seeks the professional's special knowledge and expertise, but because the client does not possess that knowledge, the client must depend on the professional. "Trust" is the operative term here. The client needs the professional to make, or help make, decisions that may be crucial to the client's business, and must *trust* that the professional will use his or her knowledge in the interests of the client. This is true of doctor–patient, lawyer–client, architect–client, and teacher–student relationships, as well as in relationships between computer professionals and clients.

Different models have been proposed for understanding how this disparity in knowledge should be handled. At one extreme is the agency model. Here the suggestion is that the professional should act as an agent of the client and simply do what the client requests. In this way, the client retains all decision-making authority; the professional may make decisions but they are minor, that is, they may be a matter of implementing a client's decision. If I call a stockbroker, tell her what stocks I want to buy, how many shares, and what price, and she executes the transaction without offering an opinion on the wisdom of the trade, then she is acting as my agent.

Some client–professional relationships are like this; however, in many cases, were this model to be followed, the client would not benefit from the expertise of the professional. Often the professional has knowledge beyond implementation, knowledge that is relevant to the client's decision. It would seem that clients often go to professionals for help in making key decisions, not just in implementing them. Thus, the agency model doesn't accurately capture what is important about client–professional relationships.

At the opposite extreme is the paternalistic model in which the professional's knowledge plays a dominant role. Here the client transfers all decision-making authority to the professional and the professional is expected to make decisions in the best interests of the client. This model clearly recognizes the special expertise of the professional, so much so that the client has little "say." Doctor–patient relationships used to be of this kind. A person would go to a doctor, report his or her symptoms, and the rest was up to the doctor, who would decide what was needed in the way of treatment. Patients were not expected to have much of a say; they simply did (or didn't do) what the doctor said. This arrangement was justified by the doctor's superior knowledge and authority. The problem with the paternalistic model of client–professional relationships is that it expects the client to turn over all autonomy to the professional and cease to be a decision maker. The client must place him- or herself at the complete mercy of the professional.

The third model of client–professional relationships takes the best of both of the models just discussed. The "fiduciary" model gives both parties (client and professional) a role in decision making. The client and professional exchange information with a focus on the client's needs and the ultimate decisions are the result of the exchange. "Fiduciary" implies trust. In this model, both parties must trust one another. The client must trust the professional to use his or her expert knowledge and to think in terms of the interest of the client. The professional must also trust that the client will give the professional relevant information, listen to what the professional says, and ultimately share in the decision making. In other words, the client retains decision-making authority but makes decisions based on information provided by the professional and has access to the professional for finergrained information.

To illustrate the differences between these three models consider, again, the doctor–patient relationship and which of these models captures the norms appropriate to that relationship. In the agency model, the patient goes to the doctor and tells the doctor both what the problem is and what should be done. The doctor implements the decision of the patient. At the other extreme, in the paternalistic model, the patient goes to the doctor, tells the doctor her symptoms and then the doctor prescribes the appropriate treatment or tells the patient what regime to follow. Neither of these models seems appropriate. In the first, the patient doesn't fully benefit from the doctor's knowledge. More accurately, the knowledge of the doctor is presumed to be relevant only after diagnosis and analysis; the doctor simply implements treatment. In the second model, the doctor's knowledge is recognized as relevant to the diagnosis and treatment, but the decision about treatment is seen as purely medical and the patient's values and preferences are not seen as relevant. Here the patient suspends judgment, putting him- or herself fully at the mercy of the doctor. The fiduciary model recognizes that the decision about treatment is complex; it involves medical and nonmedical elements. The "best treatment" for the patient involves a combination of medical factors and the patient's particular circumstances, values, and preferences. Hence, decisions about treatment should involve an exchange of information between the doctor and patient and this means shared responsibility, all aimed at the good of the patient.

The analysis of doctor–patient relationships transfers easily to client–computer professional relationships. Computer professionals should not act simply as agents of their clients nor act paternalistically, leaving their clients out of the decision-making process. As we saw above, the former means that the client doesn't fully benefit from the computer professional's knowledge and the latter means that the client has no say in the computer system they get. Computer professionals should aim at fiduciary relationships with their clients. When designing software systems, for example, computer professionals should give their clients the opportunity to make decisions about features of the system, tradeoffs that may have to be made, and so on.

To be sure, establishing a fiduciary relationship is not always easy, as can be seen in Scenario 7.2. Leikessa Jones seems to be working on the assumption of this sort of relationship with her client because she has informed her client of the possibilities and made a recommendation. The problem now is that she doesn't think her client is making the right decision. The decision facing Leikessa has to do with these alternative models of client–professional relationships. If the fiduciary model captures the ideal relationship, then Leikessa ought to go back to her client and try to explain why she thinks the system shouldn't be built with less security. She should listen carefully to the client, explain her concerns clearly, and see whether they can agree upon a strategy. By contrast, the agency model recommends that she need not try to convince her client; she should simply do what the client wants. She should recognize that the client has a view of the situation that includes many factors that she herself may not understand. On the other hand, in the paternalistic model, she should simply build the system with the security she thinks appropriate and not give the client any opportunity to decide the level of security.

In the Juan Rodriguez scenario, we see a computer professional doing something that threatens to undermine the trust that is so important to client–professional relationships. Juan has allowed himself to enter into a conflict-of-interest situation. His client—the hospital—expects him to exercise professional judgment on its behalf, that is, on behalf of the hospital. Although Juan may think he will be able to evaluate the proposals made by each software company objectively, he has an interest in one of those companies that could affect his judgment. If representatives of the hospital find out about this, they might well conclude that Juan has not acted in "good faith" on behalf of the hospital. Even if Juan recommends that the hospital buy software from another company (not Tri-Star), there is the possibility that his judgment has been distorted by his "bending over backwards" to treat the other companies fairly. In that case, the hospital would not have gotten the best system either. Thus, whichever proposal he recommends, his judgment can be called into question.

Other Stakeholders–Professional

When professionals exercise their skill and act in their professional roles, their activities may affect others who are neither employers nor clients. For example, computer experts may design a computer system that is used in a dangerous manufacturing process, putting workers—as well as people living in the neighborhood around the plant in which the system is used—at risk. Or, as in Scenario 7.2, a computer professional may design a database management system for a company, and the security of the system will have implications for those whose personal information is in the database. People who are affected by computer systems in this way are often neglected in the process of system development and operation, so it is important to identify these relationships and keep them in mind.

Sometimes the interests of these stakeholders are protected through legislation that affects the work of computer experts. For example, laws setting safety standards or requiring disclosure are made in order to protect the public interest. But the law does not and cannot possibly anticipate all the effects of the work of professionals, especially computer professionals. Because of their special knowledge, computer experts are often in the best position to see what effects their work will have or to evaluate the risks involved. Again using Leikessa in Scenario 7.2, she, having designed the system, is likely to understand the security risks of the system better than anyone else. Similarly, when it comes to computer systems used in air traffic control, nuclear power plants, or radiation treatment, the computer professionals involved are in the best position—because of their expertise and familiarity with the system—to understand the risks to those other than their clients (as well as to their clients).

The relationship between computer professionals and people affected by their work may seem distant and obscure. A programmer working on a module for a large system may not even know exactly how the module is being used in the larger system; the programmer may not know who will buy or use the system. Furthermore, it is often difficult to accurately predict how any system will ultimately affect people. This doesn't mean that computer professionals have no responsibilities to the people affected. Rather, it means that computer professionals must have a different understanding of their responsibilities to these stakeholders, different, that is, from professionals (such as physicians and lawyers) who may have more direct contact with the people affected by their work.

The paradigm of professions is helpful here in conceptualizing the responsibilities of computer professionals because it specifies that society grants the members of a profession (or the profession as a whole) the right to practice their profession *in exchange for* their promise to practice the profession in ways that serve society, or at least in ways that do no harm to society. This means that professionals cannot focus exclusively on their clients and entirely neglect all the other stakeholders who will be affected by what they do for a client. Professionals receive the right to practice and to other forms of societal support (e.g., legal protection, access to educational systems) in exchange for taking on the burden of responsibility for managing themselves so as to protect the public. If a profession were not committed to public good, it would be foolish for society to allow its members to practice.

Professional–Professional

Many professionals (and most professional codes of ethics) claim that members have obligations to other members of their profession. For example, professionals are often reluctant to criticize each other publicly and they often help each other in getting jobs or testifying at hearings when one of them is being sued. However, whether or not such behavior is justified is controversial.

Our earlier discussion of loyalty is relevant here. Suppose that you are a computer professional employed in a company making air traffic control software. Suppose further that one of your co-workers is an alcoholic and, as a result, not doing a competent job in testing the software. You know about the alcoholism because you have known the co-worker for a long time and know that he periodically gets the alcoholism under control and goes to AA meetings. Your sense is that at the moment, the co-worker does not have it under control. You want to keep the problem a secret so as not to jeopardize the co-worker's job and reputation, but if you keep it a secret, the software may be released without adequate testing. What do you owe your co-professional? What do you owe your employer? What do you owe the public, especially those who will be affected by shoddy air traffic control software?

Balancing obligations to multiple parties isn't easy and it would seem that sometimes trade-offs have to be made. Every professional has an interest in the reputation of the profession as a whole because it affects how individual members are perceived and treated. Hence, the computer professional's self-interest, as well as the interest of the profession, might support doing something about the co-worker. On the other hand, there are times when the very same concerns will point to protecting the co-worker. For example, in the case above it might be argued that the professional has a responsibility to help his co-worker precisely because the co-worker's behavior will affect the reputation of the profession.

One way to think about what professionals owe to one another is to think of what they owe each other in the way of adherence to certain standards of conduct. This is different from thinking only of what they might do to help and protect one another in the short term. Rules about being honest, avoiding conflicts of interest, and giving credit where credit is due can be understood to be obligations of one member of a profession to other members.

Conflicting Responsibilities

The complexity of managing responsibilities to employers, clients, co-professionals, and other stakeholders should not be underestimated. The contexts in which computer professionals work are often not structured so as to make it easy to keep these responsibilities in harmony. Issues of professional ethics often arise from conflicts between responsibilities to these different stakeholders.

Possibly the most common—at least, the most publicized—conflict is that between responsibilities to an employer and responsibility to the public. Such a conflict is illustrated in Scenario 7.1. Typically, the employed professional is working on a project and has serious reservations about the safety or reliability of the product. For the good of those who will be affected by the project and because of the integrity of the project, the professional believes the project should not go forward yet. On the other hand, the employer (or supervisor) believes that it is in the interest of the company for the project to go forward. The professional has to decide whether to keep quiet or do something that will "rock the boat."

Acts of whistle-blowing arise out of precisely this sort of situation. Whistle-blowers opt against loyalty to their employer in favor of protecting society. Whistle-blowing is, perhaps, the most dramatic form of the problem. Other issues that arise for computer professionals are more subtle aspects of this same tension—between loyalty to employer and social responsibility or professional responsibility. Should I work on military projects or other projects that I believe are likely to have bad effects? What am

I to do when I know that a certain kind of system can never be built safely or securely enough, but I need the money or my company needs the contract? What do I do when a client is willing to settle for much less safety or security than is appropriate?

A LEGAL PERSPECTIVE ON PROFESSIONALISM IN COMPUTING

As discussed earlier, law and ethics are not identical, but they are certainly interrelated. Professional ethics is intertwined with law and in this section we turn our attention to several areas of overlap. Although interesting global initiatives are being undertaken, our primary focus is on legal developments in the United States.

Licensing

Licensing is a legal means of regulating who can engage in certain activities. As previously discussed, in the United States, Texas is the only state that licenses software engineers. Few licenses have been issued; at this writing, the Texas Board of Professional Engineers lists 64 licensed software engineers. Computer experts who have a private practice advertised as "software engineering" are, in Texas, required to have the license. However, the vast majority of individuals working on software do so as employees, not as independent practitioners; they are not required to have a license.

Why have no other states followed the Texas lead? Although it is difficult to say, the following factors seem to come into play. First, establishing and maintaining licensing regulations is expensive, and if only a few practitioners obtain licenses, then the cost–benefit trade-off hardly justifies setting up a system. Second, the Texas regulations are controversial. They rely on older, well-established standards and tests designed for the more traditional engineering disciplines. Many computer experts believe computing to be quite different from the traditional engineering disciplines and, therefore, find the standards and tests irrelevant. The licensing test is a multiple-choice exam and some question whether any standardized test of knowledge can adequately measure the skills and temperament necessary to be an effective software engineer.

Furthermore, the breadth of activities undertaken by computer experts makes it difficult to determine with any certainty a well-defined "body of knowledge" for software engineering or any other computing specialty. (The IEEE Computer Society has identified a body of knowledge for software engineering [http://www.swebok. org/], but it remains controversial.) Without consensus on this body of knowledge, it is difficult to foresee agreement on academic accreditation, appropriate exams, or other necessary regulations for effective licensing. As long as employers and the public (through its legislators) are content to pay people *without* a license to work with computers, then there is little motivation for computer experts to seek out a license.

Thus, at the moment there seems to be a "standoff." Until a professional organization has the power to grant computer experts a credential that determines what kind of job they can hold, the organization does not have the "leverage" it needs to enforce standards of practice and ethics. At the same time, until the organization demonstrates its willingness to protect the public from unethical and incompetent practitioners, public authorities have no motivation to give any sort of monopoly or credentialing power to a professional organization. In the United States and elsewhere, this problem, as well as deep issues about the unique, intellectual core of computing, is at the heart of current struggles over licensing.

Selling Software

The law comes into play when it comes to the buying and selling of computer software and hardware, although the law isn't always clear and decisive. Indeed, the laws in this area continue to change and significant change is likely to occur in the United States and elsewhere. We will briefly describe this legal environment, starting with a distinction between selling a product and providing a service. These two activities are treated differently in the law; that is, different sets of law apply.

In the early days of computing, there was a good deal of discussion about whether software was a product or service and especially about who was responsible for what when computer experts provided software to users and something went wrong. Any number of issues arose: the software purchased was filled with bugs, it failed and caused damage to the buyer's business, the software didn't do what the buyer expected, it didn't work with the buyer's hardware, and so on. Of course, part of the problem was that buyers didn't know much about what they were buying. Because programmers were designing systems and writing code for a wide range of activities that had never been automated before, no one—computer experts or their clients and customers—fully understood the consequences of implementing these systems.

When things went wrong, those who were affected—clients and customers—turned to the law, but initially, at least, it was unclear how the law applied to these situations. A big part of the uncertainty had to do with whether or when product law applied or the law regulating provision of services. This uncertainty has now largely been resolved by treating purchases of packages as buying a product (the packages are sold as ready-made systems and can be customized by the user only in specified ways) *and* treating the hiring of an expert to design a customized system as purchasing a service. In the latter case, the computer expert provides services that involve creating a whole new system entirely for the client's use. However, it is not quite that simple because when you purchase software packages, you don't exactly buy the software, you purchase a license to use it and the license restricts what you can do with the software. In other words, you purchase a product but the product is a license to use rather than a physical object.

A significant effort began in the early 1990s to write guidelines for U.S. laws about commercial transactions involving software. The Uniform Computer Information Transactions Act (UCITA) is a package of model laws that were initially developed by a joint committee of the National Conference of Commissioners on Uniform State Laws (NCCUSL) and the American Law Institute (ALI). Because of several serious criticisms of UCITA, the ALI withdrew its support of UCITA. NCCUSL passed UCITA on its own, and two states (Maryland and Virginia) adopted UCITA provisions as state law. However, there was a great deal of opposition to UCITA, and no state has passed UCITA since Maryland and Virginia, although some aspects of UCITA have been incorporated in U.S. federal law.

At this writing, the ALI is working on a new effort to suggest legal principles in this area. Entitled "Principles of the Law of Software Contracts," the project started in 2004 and has produced initial drafts. In 2007, the ALI website predicted that the "project is likely to last several more years before completion." [http://www.ali.org/index.cfm?fuseaction=projects.proj_ip&projectid=9]. For more details about the ALI effort, see [http://www.kaner.com/pdfs/Law%20of%20Software%20Contracting.pdf]. Because the state of U.S. law is in such flux, a more general approach may be helpful here.

Selling–Buying and the Categorical Imperative

Perhaps the best place to start is with the categorical imperative as it applies to the relationship between buyer and seller in a market transaction. As explained before, the categorical imperative entreats us never to treat a person *merely* as a means but always as an end in him- or herself. At first glance, this may seem to suggest that selling is immoral; the seller seems to be using the buyer as a means to his or her end, that is, making money. This especially seems so when we consider that sellers must charge more for a product than what it cost them to produce or acquire because they have to make a profit to stay in business. On the other hand, sellers will be quick to point out that they aren't simply using buyers; they are providing the buyer with something the buyer needs or wants.

Remember that the categorical imperative doesn't prohibit using others as means to our ends; rather, it entreats us never to treat a person *merely* as a means. The "merely" means that we are constrained in *how* we use others. We must always recognize the other as an end—a being with needs, desires, plans, and the ability to make his or her own decisions. There is, then, nothing wrong with selling something to people if they are informed about what they are buying and are freely choosing to buy it. This means that the seller must be honest with the buyer about what he or she is selling and refrain from using coercion. If a salesperson gets a customer to buy something by deceiving the customer about what he or she is getting, or if the salesperson pressures and manipulates a customer into buying something the customer doesn't really want, then the salesperson is using the customer *merely* as a means to the salesperson's ends.

In short, there is nothing inherently wrong with selling software as long as the buyer is freely choosing and accurately informed about what he or she is buying. The seller has a duty to be honest about the product and not to coerce or manipulate the buyer. (Duties also fall to the buyer; for example, to pay the amount promised, but we will not discuss these here.) Although this sounds simple enough, honesty and coercion are both complex notions. Yes, a software salesperson shouldn't lie to customers, but how much is the salesperson required to tell? It would be ridiculous to expect sellers (vendors) to tell literally everything about the software they are selling. Most customers don't want to hear this and many could not understand it. Similarly, avoiding coercion might seem obvious; it would be wrong (and wouldn't make the seller very successful in the long run) to hold a gun to a customer's head and compel the person to buy the software. On the other hand and at the opposite extreme, although it wouldn't be immoral, complete passivity on the part of sellers won't work either. Advertising and telling customers about the features of a product are helpful to customers. Trial periods during which customers can try out products and return them for a full refund is a practice that respects the customer's capacity to make an informed and independent choice. In between these extremes are many possibilities for providing relevant information to potential buyers and offering enticements without crossing the line into exploitative practices.

The selling–buying relationship is at its core a contractual relationship. In a simple transaction, the seller provides a product and the buyer pays. However, when it comes to software, and especially when it comes to the provision of services, a wide range of conditions might have to be negotiated in a formal contract. Who will install the software? How long will it take before the system is up and running? If the system fails, who will be liable? When these aspects of the purchasing transaction are specified in a contract, then the buyer can sue the seller for breach of contract (e.g., if a software system cannot effectively perform one of the functions specified in the contract).

Although a contract seems a good way to clarify all the terms of a buying and selling arrangement, disputes can still arise. As mentioned before, in the early days of computing, buyers were often ignorant about computers and software. Even though a contract was drawn up, buyers didn't know exactly what to specify in the contract. This happens less frequently today because buyers are more computer savvy and companies often hire consultants or lawyers to develop the specifications in the contract. Nevertheless, contractual issues involving software can and do end up in court. These disputes are worked out by appealing to a complex body of *case law* dealing with various disputes that have arisen in the buying and selling of all kinds of things, not just software.

Torts

In addition to the contract, the buying and selling of software may be covered by a category of law referred to as *torts*. Torts deal with any wrongful act other than a breach of contract for which a civil action may be brought. Just how this body of law applies to software depends on whether software is understood to be a product or a service. This is especially important because if software is a product, strict liability may be imposed, and if software is a service, the question of negligence may arise. This takes us back to where this chapter began, to professional ethics and professional standards. Negligence is a fundamental failure in professional responsibility.

Negligence

In general, negligence can be understood to be a *failure* to do something that a reasonable and prudent person would have done. In common law, it is assumed that individuals who engage in certain activities owe a duty of care; negligence is a failure to fulfill that duty. If, for example, a security guard were knocked unconscious by a burglar, the guard would not be blameworthy for the robbery that took place while he or she was unconscious. However, if the guard had been drunk while on duty, making it easier for the burglar to break in and knock him or her out, then the guard would be considered to have been negligent in performance of his or her duties.

Negligence presumes a standard of behavior that can reasonably be expected of an individual engaged in a particular activity. Negligence is often used to describe the blameworthy behavior of members of professional groups. This is so because members of professional groups are understood to have role-responsibilities (duties), and members who fail to adequately perform one of those duties are considered derelict. Thus, software engineers, for example, have a responsibility to design software that doesn't crash under routine conditions of use. If a software engineer designs a database management system that repeatedly fails whenever files are merged or the database is sorted by an essential category, then the designer might be found to be negligent. The designer has failed to do what any competent database designer would have known to do.

When role-responsibilities are clear, it is easy to determine whether an individual has been negligent or not. The case of the security guard is simple because being drunk while on duty is unambiguously contrary to the guard's role-responsibility. On the other hand, when role-responsibilities are unclear or continuously changing, negligence is much harder to determine. In the field of computing, negligence is complex and contentious because knowledge, technology, and techniques frequently change. For example, a software engineer might be considered negligent when he or she delivers customized software that has been tested to a standard that was adequate five years ago, but is deficient by current standards. This raises the complex and difficult question of how up to date a software engineer must be to be considered competent, or— the flip side—how far behind a software engineer can fall before he or she should be considered not just out of date, but incompetent and negligent.

To prosecute computer professionals for negligence, prevailing standards in the field must be identifiable such that a plaintiff or prosecutor can show that the accused professional failed to do what any competent and responsible professional would have done. Generally, other professionals are in the best position to articulate those standards and distinguish between reasonable behavior and blatant incompetence. So typically, in court cases involving professionals accused of negligence, members of the professional group will be called in to testify about standards in the field. As just explained, standards in the field of computing are continuously changing.

Of course standards in other fields change as well. The parallels between standards for reliable software, automobile safety, and adequate health care are interesting. In all three, it is often the case that the experts know how to do things above and beyond the standard, but this knowledge is not put into use because of its cost or risk. In other words, experts are not considered derelict when they opt *not* to do everything possible to make the software reliable, the automobile safer, or the treatment more extensive. In all three cases, trade-offs can be made between the reliability, safety, or adequacy of treatment *and* the risks, costs, and other factors. Automobile designers can do many things to make automobiles much safer than they are, but the additional measures of safety will increase the cost of the car, alter the style, decrease fuel economy, and so on. Similarly, doctors are often aware of treatments that might improve the condition of a patient but they don't prescribe these treatments because they are considered unnecessary by insurance companies or too experimental by experts in the field.

Standards in software design are like this insofar as they balance a variety of factors with reliability. What counts as adequate testing of customized software is, for example, a function of what is technically feasible, what is reasonable to expect, what the costs will be of achieving a higher level of reliability, and so on. This means that it is often not a small matter to determine when a software engineer has been negligent.

A FINAL LOOK AT THE STATE OF THE PROFESSION

We began this chapter by considering how computing fits the paradigm of professions and then went on to examine the relationships that computer experts have with others and the legal environment in which computer experts typically work. Because computing is still a relatively new field, these three dimensions of the work of computer experts provide the backdrop for thinking about the future of the profession.

Guns-for-Hire or Professionals

In order to get at the future of computing as a profession, it may be helpful to push a distinction that overstates the situation, but helps to illustrate the stakes in developing computing in a particular direction. A distinction can be made between professionals and guns-for-hire. One might argue that the epitome of a nonprofessional is a gun-for-hire. A gun-for-hire is someone who puts his or her expertise up for sale to the highest bidder and is willing to use that expertise to do anything anyone wants, as long as it is legal (or unlikely to result in prosecution) and pays well. The gun-for-hire sees his or her expertise as a means and leaves it to others to decide what ends will be pursued. In other words, a gun-for-hire doesn't care what he or she builds or makes happen. In our analysis of client–professional relationships, we identified the agency model as the model of client–professional relationships in which the professional acts simply as an agent of the client doing whatever the client wants. "Guns-for-hire" is another characterization of that kind of relationship.

To be fair, some professionals argue that it is not their place to decide the ends; they argue that clients and customers should decide their ends and if society considers something dangerous or threatening, society ought to make it illegal. They claim that as long as a gun-for-hire does nothing illegal, there is nothing wrong. Sometimes they even claim that it is wrong for an expert to impose his or her personal values on the rest of the world. A gun-for-hire stays neutral and serves the interests of others. This stance is coherent, but is at odds with the traditional view of a professional with special privileges and, therefore, special responsibilities.

Remember that in the paradigm of professions, an occupational group demonstrates to the public that because of the nature of an activity, not just anyone should be allowed to engage in it. Society, the group claims, will be better off if there is some control over those who engage in the activity, and experts are in the best position to determine this. In this way, the creation of professions can be seen as a means of protecting certain activities from the pressures of the marketplace. For example, when doctors professionalized, the intention was to distinguish themselves from "charlatans" and "quacks," those who claimed they could heal patients but had no scientific understanding of how the human body worked, had not been trained appropriately, and had not taken an oath. Once the field of medicine became professionalized, patients could go to any doctor and if the doctor had an MD degree, the patient could be assured that the person had a level of training and a commitment to adhere to practices approved by the American Medical Association. In other words, patients are guaranteed a level of competence. So, although medical practice is not out of the marketplace (doctors make money by providing medical care), not just anyone can "put out a shingle" and claim they are a doctor.

By contrast, computing specialists who act as guns-for-hire are individuals who can just "put out a shingle" and if they get a job or find a client, there is no legal prohibition against them doing any type of work. Individuals who declare themselves computer experts are, of course, required to obey the law (as all of us are), but that is all. Given that the law frequently lags well behind science and technology and how little the general population understands about computers, having computer experts as guns-for-hire means that clients and customers, as well as employers, are quite vulnerable to charlatan computer experts.

In IT-configured societies the marketplace exerts pressure for quickly and cheaply produced software. As explained earlier, those who buy software and other computing products and services are not in the best position to determine whether these are safe and reliable. Thus, from the perspective of the public, it would seem that a field of computing consisting of guns-for-hire is far from ideal. Indeed, a stronger profession of computing and a stronger sense of professionalism among those with computer expertise would seem to be in the interest of both the profession and the public.

Currently, computer experts are often caught in the middle ground between being professionals and simply being employees. They often find themselves in situations in which they are caught between the pressures from above to get things done quickly and at low cost, whereas their expertise tells them to take more time to test or improve upon what has been done. As an employee, the expert should do what the supervisor requests, yet as a professional, he or she may know that better design, more careful development, and continued testing should be done before the product or system is released. Computer experts are evaluated by double standards: by the criteria of computer science—standards of quality, efficiency, elegance, and creativity—and by the criteria of the marketplace—getting things done quickly with as little cost as possible and in a way that makes them marketable.

Efficacy, Public Trust, and the Social Contract

We noted earlier that computer experts do not seem to have any special powers and privileges; they are not allowed to do, or are prohibited from doing, anything different from ordinary individuals or citizens. We need now to revisit this idea because there is one important sense in which individuals with expertise in computing have power, and this power provides a strong basis for professionalization. Computer experts have a form of *efficacy* in virtue of both their expertise and their professional roles. "Efficacy" refers to the ability and capacity to affect the world; efficacy can come not just from privileges granted by the law but from one's knowledge and one's role in an organization. When a software engineer designs a system or a database manager sets the security levels of a patient records database, they are using their knowledge and the powers associated with their role to make decisions that affect others. Often this kind of efficacy is exercised as individual contributions to a larger enterprise. A computer professional makes a contribution, say, to the development of a computer system, and this contribution works together with the contributions of others to create a system that does something.

So, computer experts have efficacy because of both their special knowledge and their roles in organizations. This efficacy forms the foundation for responsibility. We can return to the social contract idea. Given the efficacy of computer experts and the dependence of the public on the work of computer experts, it seems critical that computer experts take responsibility for safe and reliable computing.

The same point can be put in terms of the consequences of public mistrust. If computing experts don't act so as to garner and maintain public trust in computing, the field and its potential to bring great benefit to the world will not be realized. The biggest threat here seems to be in the reliability of IT systems. When software is bug-ridden and routinely fails, or if disasters occur because systems fail, then the public will lose trust in computing systems and in the computer professionals who developed those systems. Thus, it would seem that both the public and computer experts have an interest in aspiring to at least some of the features of professions.

Conclusion

Early in this chapter we described the paradigm of professions. The list of characteristics specified there could serve as a set of steps that an occupation has to take to become a profession—identify and develop the field's distinctive body of knowledge, seek autonomy for members based on specialized knowledge and for the group as a whole, create a professional organization, and make sure the field has a positive culture and public image. Often the first step taken by an occupational group moving in this direction is to adopt a code of ethics. This step has already been taken in computing. However, as suggested earlier, it would be a mistake to think a code of ethics is a magic bullet to solve all the problems of professional integrity. Perhaps the most overlooked step in the process is attending to the culture of the profession.

Computer experts collectively and proactively can shape the culture of computing. This means engaging in a variety of activities that inculcate values and attitudes in those who are studying to be experts and in those who already practice. This shaping could include cooperation worldwide in creating widely accepted standards about what skilled computer professionals should know, and the skills they should possess. An essential component of this should be knowledge and skills in computer ethics and sociotechnical analysis. Making such a perspective widely accepted among computing experts is, of course, a daunting task. It would, indeed, constitute a sea change in computing. Nevertheless, the change is essential; computer professionals who conceptualize their work as building, maintaining, and using sociotechnical systems will no longer see their work as simply building devices. They will be more able to see what they are doing as intimately connected to people and social practices. In short, they will have a clearer view of the nature of computing, and this will make them more effective at computing, more professional at their work, and more fulfilled human beings.

Study Questions

1. What is the professional ethics issue central to the Therac-25 case? Explain.
2. Explain the pact that professions could be said to have with the society in which they operate.
3. What five characteristics are usually associated with professions? Explain each.
4. Use the five characteristics of professions to describe the state of computing. Which characteristics does computing have? Which characteristics does it lack? Contrast the subfields of software engineering and Web page design with respect to the five characteristics.
5. What functions can a professional code of ethics serve?
6. How is software engineering more like a profession than other fields within computing?
7. How does the categorical imperative apply to the employer–employee relationship? How does it constrain employers in treating employees?
8. Are there limits to the loyalty an employee owes to an employer? Explain and illustrate.
9. How do the agency, paternalistic, and fiduciary models of client–professional relationships deal with the disparity of knowledge between the client and professional? What is wrong, if anything, with each of these models?
10. Blowing the whistle on one's employer might be thought of as a manifestation of conflicting responsibilities in the role of computer professional. Explain.
11. How does the categorical imperative apply to the buying and selling of software?
12. What is negligence? How is it determined?
13. What is the difference between a "gun-for-hire" and a professional?
14. Take one of the scenarios at the beginning of this chapter and use material introduced in the chapter to analyze the situation of the computer professional in the scenario.

WEBSITES

American Law Institute
http://www.ali.org/index.cfm?fuseaction=projects
.proj_ip&projectid=9
http://www.kaner.com/pdfs/Law%20of%20
Software%20Contracting.pdf

John Perry Barlow
http://w2.eff.org/Misc/Publications/John_Perry_
Barlow/HTML/complete_acm_columns.html

CCTV in the U.K.
http://www.guardian.co.uk/uk/2008/may/06/
ukcrime1

CDT's Privacy Policies
http://www.cdt.org/privacy/guide/basic/topten.html

Center for Democracy and Technology
http://www.cdt.org

Center for Digital Democracy
http://www.democraticmedia.org

CNN
http://edition.cnn.com/2004/LAW/01/13/killers
.online.ap/index.html

Dangerous Malfunctions
http://catless.ncl.ac.uk/risks

Electronic Frontier Foundation
http://www.eff.org

Electronic Privacy Information Center
www.epic.org

EPIC on Facebook
http://epic.org/privacy/facebook/default.html

Facebook Images
http://news.bbc.co.uk/2/hi/technology/7196803.stm

Facebook's Beacon
http://blog.facebook.com/blog.php?post=
7584397130

Fair Information Practices
http://www.cdt.org/privacy/guide/basic/generic
.html

Federal Bureau of Investigation
http://www.fbi.gov/pressrel/pressrel07/
botroast112907.htm

Federal Trade Commission
http://www.ftc.gov

Goodwin Proctor IP Advisor
http://www.goodwinprocter.com/~/media/
3CFC3F710F8E4A02A92F1C7AB5FC75F1.ashx

Google's market share
http://marketshare.hitslink.com/report.aspx?qprid=4

IEEE Computer Society
http://www.swebok.org/

Internet Crime Complaint Center
http://www.fbi.gov/majcases/fraud/
internetschemes.htm

W. Kennard, Spreading the Broadband Revolution
http://www.nytimes.com/2006/10/21/opinion/
21kennard.html?_r=2&oref=slogin&oref=slogin

L. Lessig, 21st Century Reaganomics
http://lessig.org/blog/2006/10/
21st_century_reaganomics_helpi.html

Lidl Case
http://www.spiegel.de/international/germany/
0,1518,545114,00.html
http://www.spiegel.de/international/business/
0,1518,druck-543485,00.html
http://www.businessweek.com/print/globalbiz/
content/mar2008/gb20080326_558865.htm

Phishing
http://en.wikipedia.org/wiki/Phishing accessed
January 7, 2008

Privacy International
http://www.privacyinternational.org

privacy.org
http://www.privacy.org

Project Gutenberg
http://www.gutenberg.org/wiki/Main_Page

Software Patents
http://www.codinghorror.com/blog/archives/
000902.html

Therac-25 Case
http://www.computingcases.org/case_materials/
therac/therac_case_intro.html

U.S. National Library of Medicine
http://www.nlm.nih.gov/medlineplus/

U.S. Patriot Act
http://www.guardian.co.uk/world/2007/mar/09/usa
http://www.cdt.org/security/usapatriot/031027cdt
.shtml

Wikipedia on RFID
http://en.wikipedia.org/wiki/RFID

REFERENCES

Aharonian, Gregory. 1993. "Setting the Record Straight on Patents." *Communications of the ACM* 36:17–18.

Anonymous. 2008. "Two More German Chains Caught Spying on Employees." *Der Spiegel Online,* April 3. http://www.spiegel.de/international/germany/0,1518,545114,00.html (Accessed May 9, 2008).

—. 2008. "Discount Chain Accused of Spying on Others." *Der Spiegel Online,* March 26. http://www.spiegel.de/international/business/0,1518,druck-543485,00.html (Accessed May 9, 2008).

Barlow, John Perry. 1991. "Electronic Frontier: Coming into the Country." *Communications of the ACM* 34(3):19–21.

Bentham, Jeremy. 1995 (1787). "Panopticon." *Jeremy Bentham: The Panopticon Writings.* Edited by Miran Bozovic. London: Verso.

Cocking, Dean, and Steve Matthews. 2001. "Unreal Friends." *Ethics and Information Technology* 2(4):223–231.

Danna, Anthony, and Oscar H. Gandy. 2002. "All That Glitters Is Not Gold: Digging beneath the Surface of Data Mining." *Journal of Business Ethics* 40(4):373–386.

Dibbell, Julian. 1993. "Rape in Cyberspace or How an Evil Clown, a Haitian Trickster Spirit, Two Wizards, and a Cast of Dozens Turned a Database into a Society." *Village Voice,* December 21, 36–42.

Fairbanks, Eve. 2008. "Wiki Woman." *The New Republic,* April 9, p. 5.

Floridi, Luciano. 1999. "Information Ethics: On the Philosophical Foundation of Computer Ethics." *Ethics and Information Technology* 1(1):37–56.

Fried, Charles. 1968. "Privacy: A Moral Analysis." *Yale Law Journal* 77(1):475–493.

—. 1978. *Right and Wrong.* Cambridge, MA: Harvard University Press.

Goldsmith, Jack L., and Tim Wu. 2006. *Who Controls the Internet? Illusions of a Borderless World.* New York: Oxford University Press.

Goodwin Proctor IP Advisor. 2006. "Getting a Handle on the Software Patent Explosion." January 24. http://www.goodwinprocter.com/%7E/media/3CFC3F710F8E4A02A92F1C7AB5FC75F1.ashx (Accessed November 4, 2008).

Hobbes, Thomas. 1950. *Leviathan.* New York: Dutton.

Hoofnagle, Chris Jay. 2005. *Privacy Self Regulation: A Decade of Disappointment.* Electronic Privacy Information Center, May 4. http://epic.org/reports/decadedisappoint.html.

Hughes, Thomas P. 1994. "Technological Momentum." *Does Technology Drive History?: The Dilemma of Technological Determinism.* Edited by Merritt Roe Smith, pp. 101–113. Cambridge, MA: MIT Press.

Introna, Lucas D. "Towards a Post-Human Intra-Actional Account of Sociotechnical Agency," Unpublished Manuscript.

Kennard, William E. 2006. "Spreading the Broadband Revolution." *The New York Times,* October 21, p. A13.

Lessig, Lawrence. 1999. *Code: And Other Laws of Cyberspace.* New York: Basic Books.

Leveson, Nancy G., and Clark S. Turner. 1993. "An Investigation of the Therac-25 Accidents." *Computer* 26(7):18–41.

Mill, John Stuart. 1859. *On Liberty*. London: J. W. Parker and son.

Miller, J. I. 2004. "Don't Be Evil: Gmail's Relevant Text Advertisements Violate Google's Own Motto and Your E-Mail Privacy Rights." *Hofstra Law Review* 33:1607–1641.

Moor, James H. 1985. "What Is Computer Ethics?" *Metaphilosophy* 16(4):266–275.

Nissenbaum, Helen. 1995. "Should I Copy My Neighbor's Software?" *Computer Ethics and Social Values*. Edited by Deborah G. Johnson and Helen Nissenbaum, pp. 201–13. Englewood Cliffs, NJ: Prentice Hall.

—. 2004. "Privacy as Contextual Integrity." *Washington Law Review* 79(1):119–58.

Nunziato, Dawn C. 2005. "The Death of the Public Forum in Cyberspace." *Berkeley Technology Law Journal* 20:1115–1171.

Orwell, George. 1949. *1984*. New York: Harcourt, Brace & World.

Rachels, James. 1975. "Why Privacy Is Important." *Philosophy and Public Affairs* 4(4):323–33.

Rawls, John. 1971. *A Theory of Justice*. Cambridge, MA: Belknap Press of Harvard University Press.

Regan, Priscilla M. 1995. *Legislating Privacy: Technology, Social Values, and Public Policy*. Chapel Hill: University of North Carolina Press.

Reiman, Jeffrey H. 1995. "Driving to the Panopticon: A Philosophical Exploration of the Risks to Privacy Posed by the Highway Technology of the Future." *Santa Clara Computer and High Technology Law Journal* 11:27–44.

Royce, John. 2003. "Trust or Trussed? Has Turnitin.Com Got It All Wrapped Up?" *Teacher Librarian* 30(4).

Spafford, Eugene H. 1992. "Are Computer Hacker Break-Ins Ethical?" *The Journal of Systems and Software* 17(1):41–47.

Stallman, Richard. 1995. "Why Software Should Be Free." *Computer Ethics and Social Values*. Edited by Deborah G. Johnson and Helen Nissenbaum, pp. 190–99. Englewood Cliffs, NJ: Prentice Hall.

Stewart, Alison, and Rachel Martin. 2008. "Obama, Clinton Wiki-Warfare." The Bryant Park Project. National Public Radio. April 3.

U.S. Department of Health Education and Welfare, Secretary's Advisory Committee on Automated Personal Data Systems. 1973. "Records, Computers, and the Rights of Citizens." DHEW Publication No. (OS) 73–94.

Vargas, Jose Antonio. 2007. "On Wikipedia, Debating 2008 Hopefuls' Every Fact." *The Washington Post*, September 17, p. A1.

Walderman, Anselm. 2008. "Lidl Accused of Spying on Workers." *Businessweek*, March 26. *http://www.businessweek.com/print/globalbiz/content/mar2008/gb20080326_558865.htm* (Accessed May 9, 2008).

Watson, Tracie, and Elisabeth Piro. 2007. "Bloggers Beware: A Cautionary Tale of Blogging and the Doctrine of at-Will Employment." *Hofstra Labor and Employment Law Journal* 24(2):333.

Whitbeck, Caroline. 1998. *Ethics in Engineering Practice and Research*. Cambridge, U.K.: Cambridge University Press.

White, Lynn Townsend, and American Council of Learned Societies. 1962. "Medieval Technology and Social Change," p. 194. London: Oxford University Press.

Winner, Langdon. 1986 (1980). "Do Artifacts Have Politics?" *The Whale and the Reactor: A Search for Limits in an Age of High Technology*, pp. 19–39. Chicago: University of Chicago Press.

Wolfendale, Jessica. 2007. "My Avatar, My Self: Virtual Harm and Attachment." *Ethics and Information Technology* 9(2):111–119.

Zamyatin, Yevgeni. 1972 (1920). *We*. New York: Harmonsworth, Penguin Books.

INDEX